The C  e

David,

I've enjoyed our brief conversations and look forward to many more in the future. I hope you enjoy the book.

Colin

The CMDB Imperative

How to Realize the Dream and Avoid the Nightmares

Glenn O'Donnell
Carlos Casanova

PRENTICE
HALL

Upper Saddle River, NJ • Boston • Indianapolis • San Francisco
New York • Toronto • Montreal • London • Munich • Paris • Madrid
Cape Town • Sydney • Tokyo • Singapore • Mexico City

Many of the designations used by manufacturers and sellers to distinguish their products are claimed as trademarks. Where those designations appear in this book, and the publisher was aware of a trademark claim, the designations have been printed with initial capital letters or in all capitals.

The authors and publisher have taken care in the preparation of this book, but make no expressed or implied warranty of any kind and assume no responsibility for errors or omissions. No liability is assumed for incidental or consequential damages in connection with or arising out of the use of the information or programs contained herein.

The publisher offers excellent discounts on this book when ordered in quantity for bulk purchases or special sales, which may include electronic versions and/or custom covers and content particular to your business, training goals, marketing focus, and branding interests. For more information, please contact:

U.S. Corporate and Government Sales
(800) 382-3419
corpsales@pearsontechgroup.com

For sales outside the United States, please contact:

International Sales
international@pearson.com

Visit us on the Web: informit.com/ph

Library of Congress Cataloging-in-Publication Data:

O'Donnell, Glenn.

The CMDB imperative : how to realize the dream and avoid the nightmares / Glenn O'Donnell, Carlos Casanova.

p. cm.
ISBN 978-0-13-700837-7
1. Configuration management. 2. Management information systems. 3. Information technology–Management. I. Casanova, Carlos. II. Title.
QA76.76.C69O36 2009
004.068'8–dc22

2008050499

Pearson Education, Inc.
Rights and Contracts Department
501 Boylston Street, Suite 900
Boston, MA 02116
Fax (617) 671-3447

ISBN-13: 978-0-13-700837-7
ISBN-10: 0-13-700837-6
Text printed in the United States on recycled paper at R.R. Donnelley in Crawfordsville, Indiana.
First printing February 2009

Associate Publisher Greg Wiegand	**Project Editor** Jovana San Nicolas-Shirley	**Publishing Coordinator** Cindy Teeters
Acquisitions Editor Katherine Bull	**Copy Editor** Water Crest Publishing, Inc.	**Cover Designer** Alan Clements
Development Editor Ginny Bess Munroe	**Senior Indexer** Cheryl Lenser	**Compositor** Nonie Ratcliff
Managing Editor Kristy Hart	**Proofreader** Geneil Breeze	

To my beautiful, brilliant, and delightful wife, who has tolerated me for 25 years and especially over the past several months of long hours writing this book.
−Glenn O'Donnell

To my beautiful wife and best friend, Raquel, and our two amazing children, Julian and Katherine, all of whom are the driving forces in everything I do. Thank you for enduring my crankiness over the months while I spent every spare moment in my office writing.
−Carlos Casanova

Contents

Foreword

The ever-increasing complexity of the technology stack and the business demand on IT is obvious not only to every CIO and IT employee, but also to every businessperson. Emerging technologies, including virtualization and cloud computing, combined with absolute dependence on technology, have made it critical that IT understand the business services. IT must also understand the technology components, business processes, business service levels, and their relationships. This knowledge makes certain that IT can act dynamically to guarantee that business services are delivered appropriately. To understand these relationships, many corporations have turned to the Configuration Management Database (CMDB) or Configuration Management System (CMS) to reduce service unavailability, understand business impact, and ensure that IT and the business can communicate effectively.

I am a little surprised and perplexed that IT has taken so long to adopt standards and best practices, such as ITIL, and to investigate and roll out CMDBs. The manufacturing industry has taught us the importance of the Bill of Materials, which enables the production of repeatable products with consistent quality at a predictable price. A colleague recently reminded me that IT professionals previously had many of the relationships between IT components and linkages in their heads or documented in a manual. That used to work just fine because individuals in IT were the interface with the customer or business process. All this has radically changed and continues to do so. The advent of technologies, such as virtualization and cloud computing, combined with outsourced components and the dramatic increase in the rate of change demanded by the business, dramatically adds to the complexity of the computing environment that has led to frequently missed expectations and diminished confidence in IT.

Another barrier to the implementation of the CMDB has been the definition of the benefits. The CMDB itself is simply a repository of relationships that has minimal value. The true value is in understanding how these relationships impact IT and business services. These relationships range from service outages, whether planned (such as a change) or unplanned (such as a hardware failure), to how future changes impact IT services and business performance. With the changing delivery environment where multiple suppliers and IT organizations are leveraging current and emerging technologies, the value of a CMDB is becoming clear.

A constant barrier to the successful implementation of the CMDB has been the continued lack of detailed prescriptive implementation information. In ITIL v3, we experience the evolution of the CMDB to the CMS, which provides more granular guidance, but is still not a detailed and efficient guide for implementation.

In this book, Glenn O'Donnell and Carlos Casanova provide the prescriptive guidance needed to assist you on your journey, from concept to making implementation choices to constructing infrastructure models to managing the IT environment to drive business value. The unique authoring combination of a leading industry analyst and a visionary practitioner provide you with a vision for the future growth of the CMS and the practical steps by which you can realize that vision. With tightening budgets, it is ever more critical that you carefully align the practicality of your efforts with the ultimate design you want to achieve. I wish you well in your CMDB journey, and I can think of no finer place to start than the next page.

—Robert E. Stroud
Vice President Service Management, CA, Inc.
International Vice President, ISACA
Treasurer, itSMF International

Prologue

This discussion comes from many years of experience in this field, watching companies start and stop their initiatives for a variety of reasons, most of which had some merit but almost all of which were simply postponing the inevitable. Some have survived punitive outsourcing by fighting against such punitive measures. How much longer they can prevail depends upon their continued vigilance. We hope this book helps all companies succeed by giving them a guide to this vigilance.

As authors of this book, we began to form our vision together, discussing the concepts of federation, leveraging of the DMTF CIM models, and usage patterns in 2003 and 2004. We won't reveal who first suggested it, but one day during one of our usual exchanges, we decided to write this book. We both heard the same questions and concerns about the CMDB and always found ourselves giving the same responses. It was clear that a comprehensive and authoritative guide was needed and that no books existed to offer the pragmatic view. The timing of ITIL v3 and the CMDB Federation Working Group appearing on the scene told us that this was the right time to do it. In hindsight, we now think we were right even more than we did then. We hope you agree.

We are excited that aspects of our vision are starting to become a reality, but are also very disappointed that more companies didn't move faster to address systemic foundational problems within their organizations. We have seen, and in some cases been directly impacted by, the failure of companies to address some of these systemic issues. Our mission is to help prevent such nightmares. The CMDB (or more accurately, the CMS) holds great promise as one of the greatest forces toward the dream of disciplined IT Service Management. We trust that *The CMDB Imperative* will help you to realize this dream and avoid the nightmares.

Acknowledgments

We wish to express our deep gratitude to Rob Stroud, one of the leading voices in the IT Service Management and Governance arena. Under a very tight deadline, Rob graciously offered his deep insight in the form of an eloquent foreword for the book. Rob is a Vice President at CA and is a board member of the USA chapter, of the International organization of the IT Service Management Forum (itSMF), and also of ISACA (formerly known as the Information Systems Audit and Control Association). His leadership in these global communities is stellar, and we are honored to have him distinguish the book with his foreword!

We also thank another shining star of the IT service management community, Sharon Taylor, Chief Architect of ITIL v3 and President of Aspect Group, for her support through the development of this book.

We would like to thank our reviewers Evelyn Hubbert, Vivek Jain, Bonita Moyer, Craig Norgard, and Marv Waschke, who spent countless hours reading over every chapter to help us refine the book. Our work has benefited immeasurably from their input and insight. We also thank Brian Lett, who under a very tight deadline proofread the entire manuscript and provided us with edits that helped raise this book to a superior level of quality. The success of this book is as much a reflection of their knowledge and commitment as it is of all the people who have helped us throughout the years to form our opinions of ITIL and the CMDB/CMS that we wrote in this book.

Special thanks are due to our development editor, Ginny Bess Munroe, and our acquisitions editor, Katherine Bull, at Pearson Education, Inc. for helping us navigate the amazing journey of writing and publishing a book. It is a journey that one must experience to appreciate, especially if you fast-track it. With this being our inaugural venture as book authors, we learned so much about the process from these two ladies. It has been eye-opening, at times maddening, but in the end, it was an enjoyable and rewarding endeavor. We would be remiss if we didn't also thank Bernard Goodwin from Prentice Hall for accepting our original submission and keeping it alive for several months until it was picked up by Katherine.

Winston Bumpus, president of the Distributed Management Task Force (DMTF), and Marv Waschke and Mark Johnson of the CMDB Federation

Working Group (CMDBf) were very helpful to us as we tried to accurately express the often-confusing world of object modeling standards. This is deep techie material that we know, but these guys are the creators! We thank their brilliant minds and their generous hearts.

Although we tried hard to refrain from mentioning vendors throughout the body of *The CMDB Imperative*, we must acknowledge the contributions the vendor community has made to our philosophy and to the market in general. Love them or hate them, their contributions are undeniable. To this end, we thank them, and we list them in alphabetical order to avoid any impression of favoritism: ASG, Axios Systems, BMC Software, CA, Compuware, EMC, Fujitsu, HP, IBM, Managed Objects (recently acquired by Novell), Microsoft, N(i)2, Oracle, SAP, Service Now, Tideway Systems, and Tripwire. There are many more in the CMDB/CMS market, of course, but these are among those who have influenced us and this book the most.

It is right to thank each other, since this book probably would not have ever materialized if one didn't prod the other to make it happen and to keep it on track. We first met several years ago and continued to debate the market issues and technology trends through today. It was during one of these "energized" sessions of violent agreement in late 2006 that we first came up with the idea to write the book. Finally, in late 2007, we started the wheels in motion. The creative process has worked unusually well, maybe because all of our preceding discussion brought us both to a converged view of the world. Our synchronized thinking as we wrote the book was uncanny in its similarity. Each of us has a huge amount of respect for the other's experience and wisdom (and now the tenacity to persevere!). We think we made a great team during this process.

In the many years I have been in the technology business, thousands of people have shaped my ever-changing philosophy. One of the greatest privileges of my life has been my remarkable exposure to remarkable people, both in vast quantities. It is impossible to even scratch the surface of this venerable community of influencers, yet I will make a respectful attempt to point out some of the more notable figures.

When I started way back in early 1980, I had no aspiration for IT. I was a naïve young semiconductor engineer. Bob Kershaw, Jack Grant, and Howard Moscovitz at Bell Labs recognized some potential in this young geek to take on the VAX minicomputer system administration. As they say, the rest is history! That first VAX was the seed for what became a now 29-year career in

IT. Blame these three gentlemen for taking a chance, and thereby inflicting me upon the world of IT! I thank them for the freedom and guidance to launch an exciting new career path.

One of the first people I met on the job in 1980 was Brian Gray. Brian was an early colleague and mentor, and to this very day, he is one of my closest confidants and one of the best friends a guy could want. More than just my Chinese buffet lunch buddy, he is an intellectual buddy with whom I can always vet ideas, no matter how ridiculous they may be.

The CMDB/CMS phase of my life began in the late 1990s, when my colleagues Martin Koot and Ken Kapes came to me with word of this new movement called ITIL that was sweeping across Europe. Martin lives in the Netherlands, which was, and still is, a hotbed for ITIL. I actually built my first CMDB in 1986, and had been in the trenches of IT operations for years, but ITIL was a revelation that there was indeed some common sense that guided the world around us. I became a believer. Thanks Martin and Kenny. Thanks also to Kurt Kanaskie, who enlightened me to the finer points of object modeling and the wide world of XML-based standards.

My perspective evolved over the next several years. When I was at EMC, I got even deeper into the CMDB phenomenon and, together with Carlos, decided then to write this book. I have to thank Brian Lett, Darren Tonnessen (my brother Darren), Darren Orzechowski (my other brother Darren), Srikanth Gopalaswami, Dan Lanzi, Bob Quillin, Naresh Parshotam, Schmuel Kliger, Patricia Florissi, Dave Reiner, Wayne Heffner, Peter Eck, Peter Charland, and Peter Anger (the three Peters) at EMC for their roles in grooming the CMDB/CMS philosophy I brought to this book. There were so many great thinkers there. I apologize for inevitably missing some of them here.

I joined Forrester Research after starting the book. I must say, this is a wonderful place to work. I especially thank my managers, Rob Whitely and Simon Yates, for supporting my book ambition. Their support was critical to making this happen. Recruiter Charles Telep adeptly shepherded the additional hassles that a midstream book author brings to the hiring process. Evelyn Hubbert, Jean-Pierre Garbani, Peter O'Neill, and Thomas Mendel cast the Forrester CMDB position prior to my arrival. This body of work has been helpful to me both before I joined the firm, and since. It is a huge honor to now be a member of this venerable team.

On a personal note, I first give thanks to my parents, Francis and Joanne O'Donnell. They are the foremost artisans who instilled the most fundamental principles within me during those formative years. They sacrificed a lot to give me and my siblings the emotional and intellectual tools to face the struggle we call life. We had humble beginnings in our small town, but we did have an abundance of love. I will always appreciate my roots and the values I picked up in these nascent years. I hope Mom and Dad are proud of what I've been able to accomplish and of their pivotal role in making this all happen.

Last, but certainly not least, I thank my beloved wife. Nobody sacrificed more during the many months of this book's preparation, nor has anyone else given me more support, love, and guidance through the quarter century that we've been married. All others, collectively, cannot even come close to the influential force she has been to me. She is truly the most phenomenal human being I know, beautiful, brilliant, fun, successful in her own right, and generous of spirit. My proudest achievement in life is that she actually agreed to spend the rest of her life with me. I try to be a humble man, but she is the only thing about which I truly gloat. Thank you, baby!

—Glenn O'Donnell

I have grown into the person I am today because of the many people I have encountered in life and worked with over the years. The most influential person, of course, is my wife, who is my balance in life and keeps me from being too serious and always ensures that we have fun. My opportunities were made possible by a choice my parents, Frank and Alda, made in the late 1960s to give up their comfortable life on the beautiful island of Sao Miguel in the Azores to bring me as an infant and my brother as a young boy to the United States. They had one reason for this, and it was not for their own benefit but for ours. They knew that by picking up and leaving, they would be giving us opportunities in life that we might otherwise never have—opportunities that have materialized into two successful professionals and now, an author as well. My brother has been very influential throughout my professional career. He provides me with a business perspective that I can add to my technologist background in order to see the "Big Picture." This perspective is what has enabled me to adapt my skills and apply them in the numerous industries I have worked in over the 18 plus years of my career.

From very early on, I have always loved to create and build, sometimes out of necessity, since many of those things I was trying build were in one piece before I pulled them apart to figure out how they worked. My education in the electrical engineering field provided for me a problem-solving skill that I not only have never lost, but have applied to every challenge I have encountered both personally and professionally. I have been graced with the opportunity of a diverse career that spans electronics design, military contracting, software architecture, management consulting, business process modeling, account management, entrepreneurial startups, and technology architectures. To all of those over the years, starting with my professors who demanded excellence, I thank you because I would never have accomplished what I have without you.

Most recently and more closely associated with the topic of this book, I was privileged to become friends with a co-worker named Craig Norgard. He has been, and I hope will continue to be, a friend and is very influential in my vision of the CMS. He is someone who can cite chapter and verse from the ITIL books like no one else I have ever met and will never let you veer off the ITIL path. We have spent more hours than I can remember over the last four years together discussing ITIL, and I could never have arrived at my current level of understanding about ITIL and the CMDB/CMS without those discussions with him. I'd also like to acknowledge Troy DuMoulin, who, especially in my first years of researching Configuration Management and the CMDB, was an invaluable resource. With the inclusion of Glenn, I have three individuals around me who have been my ITIL trinity and without whom I could have never formed my vision of the CMS.

I leave you with the following.... It is hard sometimes to accept change, but when you look inward at yourself, ask: "Am I really happy? Am I really doing what I want in life? Is this how I want to spend my life? Am I contributing to a greater good?" Do you like the answers you receive? We should be excited about and look forward to creating something new every day. If you're doing what you enjoy, it isn't considered work—it's creation. Is there anything more satisfying than knowing that you have created something that others will benefit from? Remember that the pleasures you experience today are the creations of others that came before you. If the creation of this book benefits you in even the slightest way, then I am content I have done my part today.

—Carlos Casanova

About the Authors

Glenn O'Donnell is a Senior Analyst with Forrester Research, a top technology industry research and advisory firm. He is a trusted adviser to IT organizations worldwide, serving Infrastructure and Operations professionals. He is the Forrester analyst covering CMDB, configuration and change management, and IT automation and is a major contributor to Forrester's growing ITIL and ITSM coverage. He was previously a Principal Product Marketing Manager with EMC's Resource Management Software Group, responsible for marketing and strategy development for the EMC application-oriented software offerings and EMC's overall IT service management strategy. Prior to EMC, he was a Program Director at META Group, also as a top IT Operations analyst. A prolific speaker and author, Mr. O'Donnell is a world-renowned authority on management systems, IT Service Management, IT Operations, and automation technologies and holds an ITIL certification. Since 1980, he has proven to be an innovator and thought leader in various technology development, operations, and architecture roles at Western Electric, Bell Labs, AT&T, and Lucent Technologies.

Carlos Casanova is the President and Founder of K2 Solutions Group, Inc. K2 Solutions Group, Inc., offers professional services, training, and technology products that support the delivery of CMDB/CMS, and ITIL initiatives. Prior to this, he was a Sr. Enterprise Architect with MetLife, Inc., where he was the visionary and manager for the first CMDB deployment and subsequently helped design its second-generation, enterprise-wide ITSM platform. He has been a speaker at major ITIL conferences on Configuration Management and CMDB, has several ITIL certifications, and is well known and respected by ITIL leaders. Mr. Casanova's career spans electronic hardware design, military contracting, software architecture, management consulting, business process modeling, account management, entrepreneurial startups, and technology architectures. In addition, his professional experience in IT Risk Management, Business Continuity, and IT Security has provided him with a broad foundation and perspective that enables him to maintain a constant client/end-user focus with integrity and objective reasoning at the core of all his designs.

CHAPTER 1

The Need for Process Discipline

By most measures, the information revolution can be declared a roaring success, despite the fact that this revolution has only begun. It is now undeniable for almost all businesses that IT is the engine of execution for a wide array of business functions. Companies that have altered their industries can attribute much of that success to a highly effective use of information technology to streamline their business processes. To this end, some of the heroes should be those who conceive, deploy, and manipulate these technologies. We should honor those who set out on this venture long ago with little more than a belief and internal fortitude; however, in only a few cases have these individuals been honored.

Our profession is unfortunately more often plagued by a reputation for poor quality and sloppy execution. The IT profession faces a serious crisis, one that is largely self-inflicted. A maturity gap emerges that threatens to destroy many IT organizations while rewarding the few that can execute well (see Figure 1.1). Natural selection is playing out here, so it is imperative to adapt to survive.

Gone are the heady days of the technology bubble, where value, both literally and figuratively, was measured in how much technology was deployed and how much talent was employed to manage this technology. Many companies lost huge sums of money through this *irrational* exuberance,[1] but the

---

1. The term *irrational exuberance* became synonymous with the greed of the technology bubble. It was popularized after being uttered by then U.S. Federal Reserve Bank Chairman Alan Greenspan in a speech to The American Enterprise Institute for Public Policy Research in Washington, D.C., on December 5, 1996. The full text of the speech is at http://www.federalreserve.gov/BoardDocs/speeches/1996/19961205.htm.

bursting of the bubble is actually a positive development in the evolution of business-focused technology. The reason it's positive is because it finally forced company leaders to be more pragmatic about technology investments and the skills needed to extract genuine value from this technology.

A Credibility Crisis for IT

Many business leaders have made the transition to this more pragmatic vision of technology, but IT professionals seem mired in behaviors fueled by the bubble craze. We speak admirably about providing technology to enable the business, yet actual behavior suggests mediocre attention to true business service and more of the same myopic technology focus of the bubble days. Business leaders certainly see this dynamic at work...and they are not pleased. Their frustration with IT is growing, and those of us in IT must mobilize to quell this frustration. If we do not, the implications on the IT organization are bleak.

We now find ourselves at a critical juncture in shaping the future of the IT organization. Sloppy and unreliable applications and infrastructure operations encourage business leaders to seek alternatives. In a growing number of instances, the result is *punitive outsourcing*. Left with no option to successfully transform the in-house IT organization, they turn to professional outsourcing firms to rein in IT complexity. We should not view them as being cruel with such moves. They are fiscally responsible to business stakeholders to remain competitive. When your competitors are operating IT at 4% of revenue while you pay 6%, drastic action is needed to ensure the future viability of the entire enterprise. In short, IT needs to build up its credibility with business leaders. This will lessen their need to institute punitive outsourcing and in turn reward those leaders who set out on the journey with their beliefs and internal fortitude.

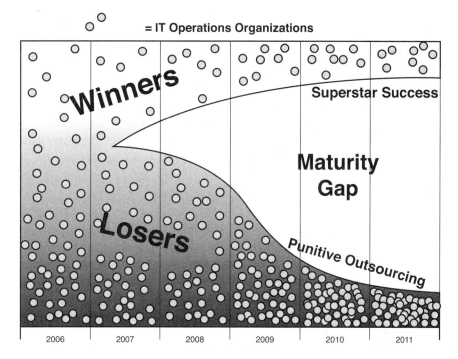

FIGURE 1.1   The IT maturity gap

How IT Can Redeem Itself

The solution to this dilemma is to instill and nurture a culture of discipline across the entire IT organization. This sounds easy, but such a cultural transformation is a painful proposition for many, and unfortunately, the odds of transition to a high-performance organization are discouraging. Behavioral change is difficult for individuals, but it is downright excruciating for large groups.[2] Despite these odds, the imperative is clear: Try or die! We must do all we can to avoid the unsavory consequences of the status quo.

The sort of discipline needed is similar to the field of engineering. Although we label many IT professionals with engineering titles, few actually *engineer* anything meaningful to the business or have the skills to do so. IT is more accurately defined as local excellence and global mediocrity. This is a testament to the deep subject matter expertise exhibited but a deserved criticism of the *system engineering*, where the many parts must function as a more complex entity. Engineering implies a broad and deep application of knowledge to build a complex system for a purpose. Great examples are found in airplanes, skyscrapers, and bridges. If Boeing or Airbus instead followed common IT practices instead of sound system engineering principles, air travel would be as risky as a game of Russian Roulette.

Thankfully, true engineers consider a dizzying variety of failure modes and plan for these in their overall system designs. The system is not just one narrow aspect of the design; it is the entire process that results in an engineered end product. For Boeing, it is a 777-passenger jet—not the control system, the engines, the skeleton, or any other part, but all of these working together in harmony as a full aircraft at an acceptable and competitive cost. The end result is high quality and reliability, attributes that can easily represent the difference between life and death.

IT services to the business are complex machines, similar in many ways to a Boeing 777. The complexity in IT is exploding. With the advent of each new technology, such as server virtualization and service-oriented architecture (SOA), complexity jumps another order of magnitude. The old methods of building overly complex, one-of-a-kind systems with no definitive and measurable business value or ROI metric are unsustainable. Complexity will destroy the enterprise if not managed properly. Those in IT need to think more like real engineers and engineer IT like Boeing engineers a 777. The secret is

---

2. Here are some studies that capture people's resistance to organizational change:
   - *Resetting the Clock: The Dynamics of Organizational Change and Failure*, Terry L. Amburgey, William P. Barnett, and Dawn Kelly, *Administrative Science Quarterly*, Vol. 38, 1993.
   - *Challenging "Resistance to Change,"* Eric B. Dent and Susan Galloway Goldberg, The George Washington University, *The Journal of Applied Behavioral Science*, Vol. 35, No. 1, 25–41 (1999). http://jab.sagepub.com/cgi/content/abstract/35/1/25.
   - *Rethinking Resistance and Recognizing Ambivalence: A Multidimensional View of Attitudes toward an Organizational Change*, Sandy Kristin Piderit, *The Academy of Management Review*, Vol. 25, No. 4 (Oct. 2000), pp. 783–794.

discipline. The result is superior quality. Rather than view this discipline imperative in fear and become a victim of change, view it as an opportunity— an opportunity to *drive* change.

The Power of Process

Many changes can be implemented to drive organizational discipline, but full coverage of these changes is ambitious enough to justify another book. Instead, we focus on the rapid growth of IT service management process best practices, such as ITIL,[3] or what we often refer to more comprehensively as IT Service Management (ITSM).

We believe this is a good point to elaborate a bit on IT processes. Many feel processes and procedures are similar. They both share a sense of structured execution, but a *procedure* is merely a series of tasks, whereas a *process* is far richer in its oversight and governance, its feedback mechanisms for improvement, and its flexibility to adapt to changing conditions. A process is also heavily integrated with other processes, so they all work together in a unified operation (for example, the linkage between configuration and change management).

Process execution can be manual or automated. Most start as heavily manual processes and then migrate slowly to more automation, but the difference to the process itself is just a matter of execution speed. Processes also should account for both normal operation (for example, change approvals in change management) and emergencies (for example, logging all changes in change management regardless of how they were implemented). Urgent situations are no excuse to bypass the process, but by the same token, processes must not be so overloaded with bureaucracy that they impede progress.

ITIL defines many processes to outline the discipline for running the IT operation. ITIL originally stood for "IT Infrastructure Library," but the ITIL community has strayed from this myopic yet vague definition. Despite its name, ITIL is applicable far beyond infrastructure. ITIL v3 actually covers well beyond the "IT" part of ITIL, a welcome development indeed! It represents a

---

3. ITIL® is a Registered Trademark and a Registered Community Trademark of the Office of Government Commerce, and is registered in the U.S. Patent and Trademark Office. It is an abbreviation for the *IT Infrastructure Library*, a collection of IT operational best practices developed by an agency of the British government (now called Office of Government Commerce, or OGC) in the late 1980s and enriched over the years by a global coalition of IT professionals. To learn more, visit the official OGC ITIL web site at http://www.itil.co.uk/. The IT Service Management Forum (itSMF) also provides a wealth of information. Their web site is http://www.itsmf.org.

foundation on which to logically build your process refinement, but it also has flaws (to be fair, ITIL v3 addresses many of these flaws quite well). ITIL should be pursued with this pragmatic perspective in mind. Use the process framework definitions as a starting point and implement them in the optimum manner for your particular technology and business environments. Avoid ITIL fanaticism, and in its place, embrace ITIL for what it is, the foundation for process discipline. You need to fully understand and truly digest what it means to your organization rather than just focus on the literal words you read.

This is precisely why we prefer to identify the industry movement as ITSM. ITSM uses ITIL as its foundation, but it is a broader coverage of IT operational excellence. There is no formal set of publications for ITSM like there is with ITIL. We like to view ITSM as a philosophy strongly rooted in ITIL. Like any philosophy, everyone will interpret it a bit differently; however, by tying it to the rigor of ITIL as a basis, this philosophy will fuel the operational machinery toward a culture of engineering discipline.

The discipline of ITSM is warmly embraced by senior executives. The socialized philosophy of trustworthy services pervades the IT organization and it becomes contagious. The business leaders and others in the company catch the spirit of discipline and the entire enterprise benefits. Great companies are great because their people are great. Great people perform with efficiency and discipline; the kind of discipline you get from tight adherence to a proven ITSM philosophy. This is the power of process!

A Brief Review of Configuration in the ITIL Processes

The ITIL process definitions are numerous and in the midst of a major transition from version 2 to version 3 (see Figure 1.2). Within all this information lies the core ITIL processes. At this point in ITIL's evolution, it is prudent for us to mention the ITIL v2 processes, but the emerging adoption of ITIL v3 is instituting some changes to these processes. The core processes are changing little, but the reorganization of the ITIL books means some of them are shifting their placement in the overall ITIL framework. For those of you who trained in ITIL v2 and truly understood its intention, the transition to v3 will not be much of a transition at all. It will be largely a name change and additional expansion of service lifecycle and business integration. If you didn't train in ITIL v2, or if you did but took it as the black and white of the words in the books rather than fully absorbing its meaning and intention, the shift to ITIL v3 provides a notion of continuous improvement and fluid interconnectivity that v2 did not. ITIL v3 centers on the service lifecycle structure, not the individual processes, with a purpose of service value and not process quantity. ITIL v2 was not able to convey these principles clearly, whereas v3 has tried.

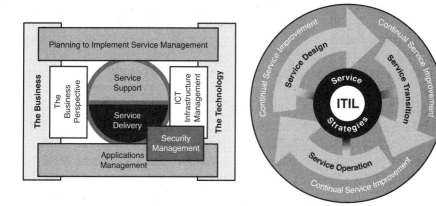

FIGURE 1.2   ITIL v2 (left) and ITIL v3 (right)

Regardless of the ITIL version, however, configuration information is the core of all process execution, driving all decisions. For now, assume configuration information to be the organized data that defines the IT and business environment. It is this information, after all, that is the source of knowledge upon which we base every action we take. Each process uses this configuration information as one of its inputs (see Figure 1.3). Later in the book, we expand on a broader definition of configuration information and practical methods where the Configuration Management Database (CMDB) will specifically benefit real-life use cases.

ITIL, even in v2, defines several high-level applications of the processes; however, almost all the attention has been placed on the ITIL foundation: the service support and (to a slightly lesser extent) the service delivery processes. The processes within each are listed in Figure 1.4, along with their common names of the *blue book* and *red book* processes (guess the colors of the books' covers!).

When IT operations seek process refinement, the Service Support processes tend to receive the most attention. There is good reason for this, as these are the most fundamental of all operational functions. Specifically, Configuration and Change Management form the center of the operational universe because these two govern the integrity of the information we use and hope to embody in the CMDB.

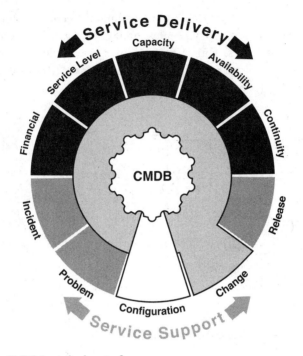

FIGURE 1.3   CMDB is at the heart of process.

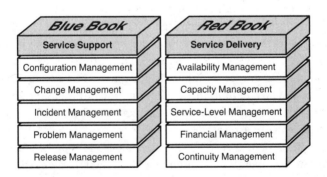

FIGURE 1.4   Core ITIL v2 processes

ITIL v3 adds a lot of wonderful new content beyond the operational aspects of IT. It embraces and articulates a lifecycle approach to business services that has previously been lacking. We are excited about v3 because it is the first true guide for *engineering* business services. It applies far beyond IT operations, although these are the people who have been the ITIL v2 advocates and adopters, and they continue to be the major force in ITIL v3. Those who are in operations need to champion v3 principles and practices across the entire organization. Happily, most CIOs are ITIL v3 believers who are committed to supporting the cause.

Configuration and Change Management

We cover Configuration Management extensively in this book, but we also expand a lot on the partnership between Configuration and Change Management as they form the central core of everything we do. In fact, the process definitions are changing to reflect this fact. Configuration and Change Management are threaded throughout every other process. Every function requires accurate configuration data because it is what drives every decision we make. Each decision then results in an action that mandates a change. If you're not changing anything, what good is the decision?

Changes come in various forms: some that have high impact, some that are not even noticeable, and all colors of the spectrum in between. The process determines how much rigor is needed for each level—tight rigor with full change advisory board approval for major changes, and complete automation for the simplest, most routine, low-risk changes. In every case, however, the change is logged and reflected in the CMDB.

The final step of any change execution should be verification that the change was executed as requested. This involves an inquiry of the changed element and then comparison with the CMDB. If they match, the change is successful. If not, there is a flaw in the change management system that must be rectified.

Incident and Problem Management

Incident and Problem Management are the most commonly executed processes in IT. Everyone performs the basic functions, although many identify them as something else (for example, fault management, firefighting, panic, and chaos). The primary purpose of the IT organization is to keep the technology running.

This is the simple view of Incident and Problem Management. They address the efficient management of troublesome situations. The general state of enlightenment with these two processes is rather low. Most are in a chaotic state, but ITIL's meteoric growth is changing this. Of all the benefits of ITSM, better Incident and Problem Management are often the most immediate and tangible, especially at the beginning of process refinement.

One of the main reasons for the chaos is the lack of good information to drive decisions. The decisions in Incident and Problem Management fall into the following categories:

Root Cause Analysis (RCA)

- When something goes wrong, you need to urgently restore the disrupted service and then find the root cause to prevent recurrence.

- RCA is difficult in complex environments, and this complexity is only getting worse (see Figure 1.5). Here we see how complexity has outpaced the ability to manage the IT environment. At a point in the late 1990s, the explosive expansion of distributed systems, exacerbated by web-based applications and e-commerce, drove technology to a point where even the best and brightest people could no longer comprehend the details of business services.

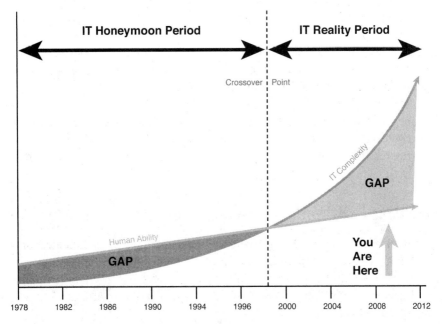

FIGURE 1.5   The challenge of managing complexity

- The gaps represent the ability to first stay ahead of the innovations, and then it illustrates how we are falling behind. The gap is growing, so improved processes and automation of those processes are needed.

- Nowhere is this need for a new approach to complexity more obvious than in Incident and Problem Management. Complexity has considerably changed how we execute on both processes. Note that the processes themselves have not changed, but the challenges have. Where we once had to deal with relatively simple issues with infrastructure, we now have shifted our attention to application-level services. Everything is much more complex here, so when something breaks, the effort required to isolate the cause is extraordinary. It's no longer as simple as locating a dead router or server.

- The only way to combat this complexity is through the assistance of automation. Automated RCA requires fine configuration detail to feed configuration settings, relationships, and behaviors to the analysis tools. RCA tools are evolving rapidly, and they all are betting their futures on the CMDB as their source of information.

- To be fair, any tool that performs RCA already does use a form of CMDB. In almost all cases, however, these CMDBs are too narrow or inflexible. Each of these CMDBs can contribute to the greater notion of a federated CMDB or CMS (Configuration Management System), as described in ITIL v3, which we cover later in the book in Chapter 4, "The Federated CMS Architecture."

- The future of automated RCA will revolve around tight integration with a standards-based CMDB. The true magic will be embedded within the analysis engine, but that engine will be useless without the CMDB. These tools will focus primarily on the applications and tie in the various infrastructure elements as needed.

- With such RCA, you can demonstrate incredible improvements in Incident and Problem Management process execution. Not surprisingly, these improvements also enhance the other processes and contribute greatly to overall operational excellence.

- Some may remember the days prior to the complexity crossover point as "the good old days of IT," but those who do are merely living in an unrealistic cocoon. The reality that IT must operate as a business unto itself is now upon us. The "good old days" are yet to come for those who can thrive in a complex atmosphere.

Prioritization

- Incidents and problems will always be part of the IT landscape, although the goal is certainly to minimize them. As we attempt to process them through the workflow, we will inevitably be faced with multiple situations simultaneously. When this happens, we need to prioritize their resolution.

- The CMDB helps here because it offers a unified view of infrastructure, applications, services, users, business units, and many other dimensions of the environment. If all of these dimensions are properly linked with their actual relationships, we will have a map that we can navigate to identify which incidents and problems exhibit the highest priority and, thus, are addressed first (see Figure 1.6).

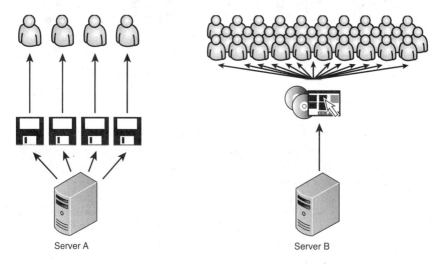

Server A   Server B

FIGURE 1.6   Business impact of two servers

- Figure 1.6 provides a good example of what the impact of two servers failing might be. Server A is a file server in product development and Server B supports the main order entry system. Mapping to the services, we naturally conclude that Server B should get top priority. The CMDB provides the information required to make this decision.

- What if we complicated this scenario a bit? What if Server B was part of a redundant server farm? Figure 1.7 demonstrates how the failure of this server alone does not necessarily warrant panic. In this example, because of the redundancy in the server farm, it is conceivable that service is still available, albeit at a possibly degraded level, but it is not completely unavailable just because one server failed. The

CMDB provides the insight to understand the true impact of an infra-structure failure in a business perspective. By properly analyzing the server failure and its impact on the order entry system, we determine that the system shows no signs of trouble. The redundant infrastructure performed exactly as designed! In this case, Server B must still be restored, but its priority is far lower.

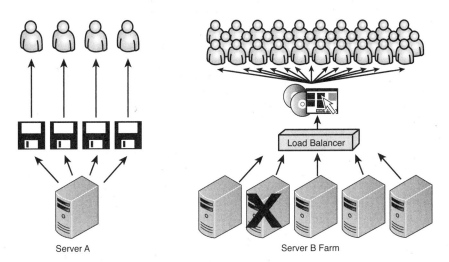

Server A   Server B Farm

FIGURE 1.7   The impact of redundancy

Dispatching

- If you are reading this, you are most likely an IT professional who can understand this next point all too well. Just try to recall the many incidents in which you were responsible to resolve an incident, only to find that you were the wrong person. Incident and problem dis-patching has long been a severe handicap in most IT organizations, resulting in the dreaded finger pointing.

- If the automated RCA highlights the root cause, it is quite simple to dispatch the right person to resolve it. Why call in the Linux adminis-trator when the root cause is a WAN link?

- Proper dispatching helps you exonerate yourself, too! We would rather not promote such defensive behaviors, but this book is about the real world, and in this world an immense amount of energy and money is spent on exoneration and vindication. "I want to prove it's not me!" is a common refrain. Instead of pointing fingers in all directions, we can point all fingers in the right direction. You can indeed prove it's not you when it truly is not, and if it is you, you need not be defensive. You will know what to do about it, and everyone will proceed.

Incident and Problem Management are two of the most important of all ITIL processes because of their central role in overall operations and their relative maturity. This, combined with the plethora of tools available for the basic process execution, position them as ideal proof points for early gains in the ITIL deployment. These gains can help justify additional investment by senior management and can have direct impact on increasing customer satisfaction by delivering better and more reliable service.

The Service Desk

We haven't touched on the Service Desk yet for a reason. Contrary to the opinions of a (thankfully) diminishing number of ITIL purists, Service Desk is *not* a process. It is, however, the single most important organizational entity in the ITIL pursuit. It is where ITIL tends to have its roots in the organization because the individuals in the Service Desk area recognized long ago that they needed good processes and solid information to do their jobs well.

The Service Desk largely embodies and performs the Incident Management process. Until now, we've focused on automation, and you certainly must automate everything possible, but the human element is the lifeblood of any business, IT included. When customers have troubles, questions, or concerns, they contact the Service Desk.

Before ITIL, CMDB, and general automation, the Service Desk was the brunt of many jokes (the helpless desk). To the end users (your customers), the "help" desk was little help at all. They did a decent job of taking the information from the customer and logging it, but then launched a frustrating search for the right responder. This usually was done in a terribly inefficient and ineffective manner by calling people on the phone until they miraculously found the right person. Even the response staff tried to shirk these calls because they often found them annoying and misdirected. These were the dark days of service management when our profession was just starting to get complex enough to mandate some process, yet the processes and their adoptions were extremely poor.

The Service Desk is significantly better today. They finally have some automation in place, with commercial trouble-ticket tracking software that enforces logging and incident workflow. Self-service and Knowledge Management products for routine requests, like forgotten passwords and "How do I...?" questions, are maturing nicely. More incidents can be resolved on the spot by Service Desk agents, which helps filter the mundane tasks away from your brightest subject matter experts. When you call, they increasingly know who you are and a lot of detail about your technology and business situation. They know more about existing problems (known errors in ITIL-speak) and their resolution status, so they are better prepared to tame the frustration building within the customer. In short, there is much better "service" in the Service Desk. At the heart of all of this is CMDB technology. Its power, flexibility, comprehension, automation, and integration vary widely, but these CMDB elements are great starting points. In fact, it should be no surprise that the major Service Desk vendors have been launching the most aggressive CMDB campaigns.

We should follow the lessons learned in the Service Desk and build upon them to further develop the automation mechanisms and even to further enhance the human interface of the Service Desk. If you are looking for someone to help drive CMDB evolution in your organization, ask the Service Desk people. They will have some good ideas.

Release Management

Release Management can be viewed as a superset of Change Management, with a lot more workflow and evaluation technology involved. Releases are delivered based on several criteria, such as urgency, quiet periods, existing versions, dependencies with other elements, compliance implications, other scheduled RFCs, and platform dependencies.

As you push out new releases, you need to know a lot, such as business cycles/impact, downstream implications, conflicting changes, or changes that were executed since you submitted your request for a change on the same infrastructure items you intend to modify. Chances are, you know very little of what you need, so the Release Management process tends to be wrought with a lot of risk. The CMDB can supply the information you need. The tools used in the process, including those cerebral tools we all possess, then take this information to make the decisions. With enough information, the risk is minimized to an acceptable level. Risk will never be eliminated, but we need to make it reasonable. The right information allows us to do just that.

Service Delivery Processes

Although not as tightly connected as the service support processes, all the service delivery processes also require accurate configuration information to be effective. In fact, almost all of the detail that defines the parameters of each of these processes is ideally embodied within the CMDB.

Financial Management remains one of the least mature ITIL processes because of the sheer difficulty in collecting the appropriate information. Once this information is in the CMDB, the process can mature rapidly, but the initial population is an impediment for at least a few years. Standard interfaces to financial details and sufficient detail to apportion costs according to the process must evolve. Also, ITIL v3 has some new information that changes the discussion a bit around Financial Management.

Either way, like any process, the only way to make them work well is to supply them with the right information. We've become enamored with the "garbage in, garbage out" motto in IT. Nowhere is this more obvious than the CMDB and its impact on all processes.

The Configuration Management Process

The purpose of this book is not to regurgitate the full details of the Configuration Management process as described in ITIL v2. This is partly because there are better sources for that, and in ITIL v3, it is described as more of an enabler than anything else, which is what ITIL v2 attempted to describe but with little success. ITIL v2 described Configuration Management as a discrete process, and we must overcome that notion to appreciate the more robust definition in what ITIL v3 now calls Service Asset and Configuration Management (SACM). We must, however, still provide an overview of the activities that occur in what ITIL v2 called the Configuration Management process to frame the basis for the book.

At the time of publication of this book, you could encounter an IT environment that had ITIL v3 available for almost two years. The significance of this is that ITIL v3 essentially eliminates Configuration Management as a process and redefines and expands the infamous CMDB as a Configuration Management System (CMS). In order "to manage large and complex IT services and infrastructures, Service Asset and Configuration Management requires the use of a supporting system known as the Configuration Management System (CMS)... At the data level, the CMS may take data from several physical CMDBs, which together constitute a federated CMDB."[4]

---

4. Office of Government Commerce (OGC). 2007. *Service Transition, ITIL Version 3.* Ogdensburg: Renouf Publishing Co. Ltd.

This is a tremendous step forward for everyone on the ITIL journey; it takes away the hyper-focused energies that most companies have used to design a singular database to capture the Configuration Item (CI) data and thus increases the likelihood of successful ITIL implementation.

What we must not forget, however, is that the activities originally defined in ITIL v2 have not gone away. The tasks and activities must still be performed, but they are typically performed as an aspect of the other complementary processes, such as Change and Release Management. It is important to remember that the main Configuration Management functional activities encompassing Identification, Control, Accounting, and Verification/Audit must still be performed if we expect the data shared across ITIL processes to be accurate and reliable. In the following sections, we walk through each of these functional areas at a high level, so it becomes clear that whether under the former Configuration Management process or as an activity in a different process supporting the CMS, the task/activity needs to be executed by someone or some technology regardless of its associated process.

Identification

Identification is one of the most difficult aspects of Configuration Management. This is simply because there is no holy grail available when starting out to determine what your Configuration Items (CIs) should be.[5] The elements that should be included, and their individual configuration settings, are often a deep mystery. This gets to one of the key driving forces for automation of the CMDB: *"I don't know what I don't know, but I **must** know what I don't know!"*

Many view the CMDB as a panacea to solve this dilemma, but one must first carefully understand the process linkages, the technology components to execute the process, and most importantly, the appropriate level of detail for business purposes. You must find the "Goldilocks" level: not too much, not too little, but just right. This is far from easy, but it is a critical consideration for any CMDB architecture. In Chapter 2, "What Is a CMDB?," we offer more tips and advice to finding this balance of data richness.

Do not underestimate the issues associated with organizational composition. In most situations, there will be a logical chain of command under a

---

5. A CI is an elementary object in the configuration information set. We describe CIs more thoroughly in Chapter 2. For now, consider CIs to be objects like servers, network elements, people, applications, and so on. The actual CI definition is much broader, but this is a good starting point.

single CIO. In some very large companies, there might be several IT organizations, each with its own CIO and its own IT staff. Even in these more complex scenarios, however, common operations are recommended. This includes the CMDB. The federated CMDB introduced in Chapter 2 allows for the distribution of responsibility while maintaining some central structure to the whole CMDB. This allows for more effective decisions, process execution, and automation across all units of the business.

Two forces make identification difficult. First, every organization has its own unique cultural, organizational, and technical dynamics. This complicates several issues, including the fact that automation tools cannot easily account for these idiosyncrasies. Second, few organizations have gone through the full cycle of establishing a complete ITIL program, including additional iterations of enhancement and maturing. Each organization needs to evaluate why it is adopting ITIL and then establish the CI level of depth and scope that is cost effective for the organization to place under Change and Configuration Control. The difficulty in identifying the CIs comes from several factors such as cost, organizational structure, regulatory compliance requirements, perspectives on CIs, and sheer lack of understanding.

Cost is probably the easiest to understand because it is the most straightforward. For every CI you place under control, you incur some downstream cost associated with the Control, Accounting, and Verification and Audit aspects of making it a CI. If you are fortunate enough to have technology in place to help execute the other functional activities of Configuration Management, you might be able to identify more IT elements as CIs; if you don't, you will need to staff up certain departments to address the additional workload that they'll be required to perform. Automation can help in many ways, but it cannot fulfill all the needs. We still need humans...at least for now!

Organizational structure is the most difficult challenge to overcome because you will be fighting established habits and potentially exposing flaws and maybe even deep-rooted cover-ups in how the organization is managed. As is the case with most business problems, organizational politics is always the most stubborn (and possibly dangerous!) of all elements. Consider the example of a department that has for years delivered equipment counts related to applications or lines of business, which in turn are used as the basis for chargeback to a line of business. Think about the resistance you will encounter from that department when you come along and potentially expose the fact that they never really had a good mechanism for delivering the equipment counts. In fact, they blended all the counts and distributed them out proportionally based on relative business size instead of actual usage.

Regulatory compliance requirements are generally straightforward in the identification space, although often are more difficult to execute. Under most audit findings, you are told explicitly which objects need to be audited or controlled and the rigor around those controls. New automation based upon the CMDB is now emerging to radically alter this facet of configuration management.

Perspective on a CI is a rather new concept that we're introducing that could help organizations visually present the CI hierarchy and relationships to a variety of departments in the terms with which they are most comfortable, while not corrupting the underlying CMS/CMDB model. These perspectives can be thought of in terms of a *role-based* view of a CI. For example, when assigning a ticket, the Service Desk needs a higher-level, less-technical structural tier to define the CI associated to that ticket. On the contrary, the network engineer would very likely seek out a more granular technical tier structure. Once implemented in this fashion, the user interface system determines the logged-in user and the role they are performing, select the appropriate tier structure library, and then compose the CI view accordingly. The first difficulty in implementing this (besides the fact that most tools do not offer this capability) is in controlling how many of these "perspectives" you can create and maintain, and then getting the organization to accept the reality that different departments could use the same term but be referring to a slightly different structural object (that is, server vs. virtual server instance).

Another aspect that makes this concept difficult to implement is that there will undoubtedly be reports and metrics that are distributed by different departments that, on the surface, appear to contradict each other. An agreement must be reached across the organization that, although they might have different visual representations based on the day-to-day role they execute, they must generate reports and metrics using the reporting role, *not* their daily operations role. If this is not agreed to, you will most likely create more confusion across the organization and ultimately lose all credibility.

Finally, we arrive at an area of difficulty that should be the easiest to overcome, but because of human nature is the most difficult: lack of understanding. There is so much ITIL/ITSM literature and training available that there is no reason for lack of understanding or uninformed decision making. Most companies embarking on this journey train their employees but not the managers or leaders. Those untrained managers and leaders will make overarching decisions, often without fully comprehending the situation and discounting the input of those trained employees. If you get nothing else out of this book, just remember this one thing: *Trust your trained employees whom you pay for their experience and decision-making ability.* You invest in them daily, and they generally look out for the best interest of the entire organization. If you can't bring yourself to trust them, the organization is at risk. Hold your employees accountable for their decisions, but do not make uninformed decisions after spending money on training them.

Control

Although closely tied with the Change Management control elements, the purpose of the Configuration Management Control activity is to ensure that the CI data reflects the authorized changes around its attributes or relationships. It also ensures that any new CI is recorded properly in the CMDB/CMS and that its status is changed as it travels through its natural lifecycle through your IT environment. It is important to remember that any of these changes must be associated with an approved Request for Change (RFC) in order for it to be an authorized change. Also important to note is that it could come in the form of a pre-approved standard change from a technology implementation. The detection and then automatic reconciliation of a CI record to an approved RFC for a change detected in the environment can then also be implemented using technology solutions. This increases efficiencies while not losing the audit trail and change history for a CI.

Accounting

Accounting is essentially the reporting mechanism surrounding the CIs. As with all other process areas, a certain level of metrics and key performance indicators needs to be established and results distributed. The identification, design, generation, and distribution of reports is a critical element in the success of the CMS in that it is the vehicle by which you will be able to measure your progress and gain the backing by the consumers of the data.

Verification and Auditing

This area is probably the least understood and most commonly misinterpreted. ITIL v3 does a great job of helping to dispel the misconceptions that many people had with ITIL v2 in that verification and auditing must be a manually performed activity. All that anyone needs to understand about this activity is that the data can be verified and audited by either a person or technology, with the sole factor being that the results can be demonstrated as being accurate and not tampered with. There are many affordable technological solutions that can be of great assistance with this area that really would benefit organizations in time to market, scope of deployment, depth of CIs, and speed to ticket closure.

Why the Term "CMDB" Must Go Away—and It Is...Slowly!

We must be clear about one important detail regarding the CMDB phenomenon. Enlightened ITIL practitioners hate the term "CMDB." We hate it because it connotes an incorrect perception about how the CMDB should be built and used. Of course, this begs the question of why we chose to write a book about something we hate. We love the concept—we just hate the name. The concept is profound and is central to any IT organization striving for operational discipline. Every IT organization needs a CMDB, and most have probably built several in the past under different names, but there is enormous confusion around the concept and much of this confusion stems from the name itself. We wrote a "CMDB Book" to help clarify this confusion and in future editions, hope to reference CMDB only in a historical context.

A major problem with the "CMDB" term is that it implies the CMDB is a single monolithic beast wherein all configuration details are collected and maintained. From a logical or philosophical perspective, this is correct, but the CMDB is not a DB in the traditional sense of a database. As we describe in detail, the CMDB is far more complex and far more flexible than a monolithic database. We must accept that the CMDB is a view into a federation of distributed data elements that in many cases must remain distributed. Therefore, this new notion of a CMDB should be identified by another name.

With the publication of ITIL v3, the industry is finally starting to abandon the CMDB term. Now called the Configuration Management System, the new term may not be perfect, but it is far superior to CMDB. At a minimum, it suggests a systems approach to configuration information. This is notable because, as we will present, a systems approach, with the federated elements, is the only approach that will work in the long run.

Very few organizations are ready or willing to scrap *all* of their existing systems and data repositories to create a monolithic CMDB, so ask yourself: "Was it ever a realistic expectation that this single DB could ever come to fruition?" The problems are that naming conventions are traditionally weak, and additional costs would be incurred because each source is wrapped in its own departmental/team processes that would also need to be re-engineered.

Even we authors sometimes fall into the trap of identifying this Configuration Management System as a CMDB because the industry will move slowly to migrate away from the term. It is so deeply embedded in our vernacular that behavioral inertia impedes the mental transition, probably for a few years. Going forward, when one of us writes or speaks about a "CMDB," we are actually referring to the federated model we present in this book. Until the industry migrates to the right threshold of adoption, some people might not resonate with a *Configuration Management System*, but almost everyone will perk up when the topic is CMDB.

Frequently Asked Questions

Question: Alignment between IT and the business is good in our organization. Why do I need to worry about the credibility crisis or the threat of punitive outsourcing?

Answer: If the business side of the partnership agrees with that assessment, congratulations! You are among an elite class of IT organizations. If you are unsure of the business side's true assessment of the relationship, maybe "good" is an overstatement. Ask. The first step in any relationship is communication. Have both sides talk and jointly understand the relationship. Even the best can improve, so it's always wise to do this regardless of the strength of the partnership.

Question: The characterization of local excellence and global mediocrity is offensive. Our organization is widely regarded as superior at planning, process, and execution. Why do you make this accusation?

Answer: Again, if you are able to effectively produce good results across all IT domains at a level that is satisfying—or even exceeding—business expectations, then you deserve accolades for a job well done. Yes, there are others like you, but not many. Most IT organizations are great within their domains (also known as silos), but struggle to bring it all together in a systems engineering manner.

Question: Isn't ITIL just another management fad that will not catch on?

Answer: ITIL is here to stay, and it has proven to work in countless situations. Many ITIL implementations are young and have yet to demonstrate the full benefits, but even these organizations show progress as they reduce wasted effort and improve service relia-bility. If you want the truth, talk to people who actually make ITIL work. The IT Service Management Forum (itSMF) is a great place to start. The structure of the itSMF includes local interest groups that meet regularly, and they always welcome new members and even non-members.

Question: The tools I use in my environment already have the information about the infrastructure items they are being used to manage. Why is the CMDB any better than what I have now?

Answer: Nearly every management tool collects some amount of data needed to perform its task, but it is specialized data and usually isolated. The CMDB is general purpose data that can be sliced, diced, rearranged, and assembled in many different ways. Your existing data might indeed have a place in the evolution of the CMDB. We will explain as you progress through the book.

Question: We already have an asset database as part of our help desk imple-mentation, and it seems to capture the data we need. Therefore, why would we need a CMDB?

Answer: An asset database is not a CMDB. The CMDB extends well beyond the common asset database by reflecting the huge number of rela-tionships and dependencies. An asset database also relies on too much manual population and maintenance. Too much manual effort is unacceptable in a world that is exploding in complexity. We cover these issues and their solutions throughout the book.

Question: The criticism of the term "CMDB" seems harsh. It is, in fact, a database, and why would the ITIL founders make such a grievous mistake like that?

Answer: It could be a matter of semantics, as a purist interpretation of *database* might be correct in the context of a CMDB. Our concern, and that of a growing body of experts in the industry, is the impli-cation that the CMDB is just a typical relational database (that is, the ubiquitous SQL database). As we cover extensively in subse-quent chapters, the CMDB requires many distribution, modeling, and federation capabilities not found in the typical RDBMS. RDBMS systems will, however, play a role in many of the feder-ated management data repositories.

Summary

Most of us in the IT field are technologists, but we need to accept that our IT world is changing. It is changing in ways that we can no longer just program our way out of. We can no longer tell our business partners to just believe us because we are the *technology experts*. We must adapt to the service- and process-oriented world that is upon us. This world makes many in IT uncomfortable because they are not sure they can make this shift in mindset. For these individuals and departments, their credibility will be lost with no chance of redemption because of resisting the changes, and their fate will likely end with punitive outsourcing.

The IT environments have become far too complex to be managed efficiently with the loose processes or lack of processes that most IT organization currently have in place. An almost apathetic mentality to the impact of these weak or nonexistent processes on business has forced business leaders to question decisions like never before. They question decisions because IT has lost some credibility over the years and because they are being pressured to reduce operating costs. We need to step up to the challenge posed by our business leaders and demonstrate that we are capable of instituting process rigor to help them meet their objectives. IT needs to become an active partner with the business leaders. It must demonstrate a capability for not only supporting business and financial objectives, but also advancing those goals with innovative ways of leveraging technology while still maintaining process discipline.

CHAPTER 2

What Is a CMDB?

Rarely can an IT operations or management tool discussion occur today without someone inevitably bringing the conversation around to the Configuration Management Database (CMDB). It is a term that is intimately intertwined with the IT Infrastructure Library (ITIL) and any other IT operations concept. In fact, the whole notion of operational excellence is a panacea without a robust CMDB serving as its foundation.

When you think about it, every function performed in IT requires accurate information to drive decisions. Indeed, this relationship between information and decisions spans far beyond IT. With no information, decisions are based on mere guesswork. It is no wonder that these decisions are so frequently erroneous. To make informed decisions, you need to gather the necessary information first. This information is most effective if it is available from a known, trusted source. That trusted source is, in theory, the CMDB, and this is the ultimate goal of the CMDB.

Information is the key to all decisions, and information is constructed from building blocks of raw data. This data is encapsulated in the CMDB. To derive information from the data, one must have an application in mind. These applications of the CMDB are covered in Chapter 9, "Leveraging the CMS," but first, we must define the CMDB and how it is evolving into something we call the CMS. In Chapter 3, "Planning for the CMS," we walk you through all the different steps you need to take to transition from the CMDB to the CMS. The definition of the CMDB is not as straightforward as you might think and certainly not what many prevailing definitions would suggest. This chapter discusses the true definition of a CMDB.

The Birth of the CMDB

As long as there have been complex IT systems (since the 1950s and 1960s), there has been a need for some form of CMDB. Early implementations were likely paper and pencil (or even stored in some person's brain!) because life was so much simpler then. Few called them CMDBs, but this is precisely what they were.

The CMDB term did not come into use until after the 1989 arrival of ITIL. Indeed, the advent of ITIL was necessitated because of the hyperbolic expansion of complexity. IT systems were no longer isolated, simple machines. They had grown to encompass multiple computers across networks and distributed software components. The only way to keep track of the complex nature of these systems was through technology. This technology came in the form of a CMDB, or what most people called an *asset database*.

More notably, these complex systems had become inextricably bound to business execution. Prior to the 1990s, computers were either isolated, well-defined islands that ran the back office of the business or they were intellectual tools. By the late 1990s, it became clear that the state of IT had a direct impact on the state of the business, and the state of IT was not good. The 1990s saw the rise of distributed computing as the central nervous system of the business, and a mechanism was needed to bring discipline to the operation of this wily beast.

Along came ITIL. Although it grew across Europe in the late 1990s, its worldwide appeal finally exploded on the scene in 2004 when North American adoptions reached critical mass. The chart in Figure 2.1 shows how ITIL hit its inflection point in 2004, followed by the latent impact on membership in the U.S. branch of the IT Service Management Forum (itSMF),[1] the international organization dedicated to the development and promotion of ITIL and IT service management.

Because CMDB is threaded throughout the ITIL literature, the CMDB phenomenon has grown along with ITIL, albeit more slowly than the general adoption of ITIL. This relationship also consolidated the function around common terminology, so CMDB is now the prevailing term for the trusted data source.

---

1. The growth figures for itSMF membership were taken from a presentation by David Cannon, president of itSMF USA. Mr. Cannon presented these growth figures at the April 10, 2008, meeting of the National Capitol local interest group serving the Washington, D.C., area.

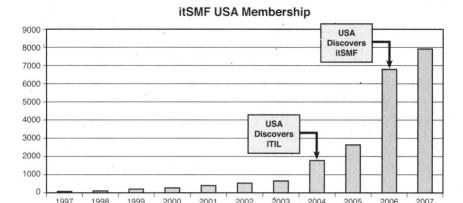

FIGURE 2.1   ITIL growth

The Configuration Management process in ITIL was inspired by the early work by the U.S. Department of Defense and by the newer Software Configuration Management (SCM) process used in software engineering. Because of this heritage, you will notice many similarities across the two process models. Among these are the concept of a Configuration Item (CI) and a CMDB. In SCM, a type of CMDB is called the Definitive Software Library (DSL). It is not a full CMDB in the context of modern ITIL taxonomy, but it is a good first step toward true CMDB. As you will see in Chapter 4, "The Federated CMS Architecture," the DSL has been preserved to play a role in a broader federated CMDB, employing multiple CMDBs in what is now called a Configuration Management System (CMS) in the language of ITIL v3.

Configuration Items

Each element in the IT environment is an individual entity requiring accurate capture of its attributes. The representations of these entities in the CMDB are *Configuration Items* (CIs). A CI is a software model that contains the attributes of the represented entity. In databases, this is described in the schema. Each entity consists of several attributes of specific data types (for example, string and integer). Each instance of the entity is its own CI (for example, 200 identical servers equals 200 CIs, all with the same schema, but as independent instances with some unique attribute settings). A CI can be physical–that is, real and tangible (for example, hardware and software code)–or it can be logical abstractions of these (for example, business processes and distributed applications).

If we examine 300 Windows servers and 20 Cisco routers, this subset of the overall environment represents at least 320 CIs. We say "at least 320" because it is possible, indeed likely, that each device is built from other devices. For example, each Cisco router may consist of a chassis and multiple cards within the chassis. It is possible to treat the entire router as one CI, but it makes more sense to also break down the CIs to more granular levels. We explain why later in the book, but the short reason is that it enables more flexible abstraction models to be constructed and manipulated.

The concept of a CI must be extensible. Some believe a CI is the most atomic level only, but a CI is also a more complex assembly of lower-level CIs. In the server example, a physical server has special attributes. A virtual server also has special attributes unique to that virtual instance, even though it is resident on the physical server. This relationship between the two means they will share certain attributes, but also contain other attributes unique to each perspective.

Applications, business services, and customer organizations are also CIs (see Figure 2.2) at even higher levels of the CI hierarchy. Similar relationships link these various layers to reflect reality. To accurately capture and maintain the atomic details as well as the relationships, the CMS and the CMDBs are built upon traditional relational databases and object-oriented models, as well as a myriad of other formats that include text files, Simple Network Management Protocol Management Information Bases (SNMP MIBs), and software Application Programming Interfaces (APIs). The object-oriented technologies are especially important in the continued development of Configuration Management information. We cover these technologies in more detail in Chapter 4.

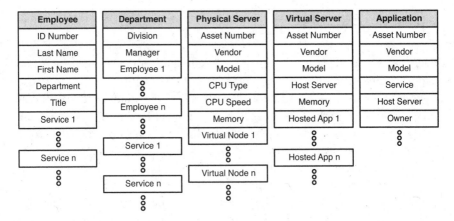

Employee	Department	Physical Server	Virtual Server	Application
ID Number	Division	Asset Number	Asset Number	Asset Number
Last Name	Manager	Vendor	Vendor	Vendor
First Name	Employee 1	Model	Model	Model
Department	⁝	CPU Type	Host Server	Service
Title	Employee n	CPU Speed	Memory	Host Server
Service 1	⁝	Memory	Hosted App 1	Owner
⁝	Service 1	Virtual Node 1	⁝	⁝
Service n	⁝	⁝	Hosted App n	
⁝	Service n	Virtual Node n	⁝	
	⁝	⁝		

FIGURE 2.2   Example Configuration Items

Each CI has several attributes associated with it. Some are compound abstractions that refer to a number of other CIs (the Department CI consists of several Employee CIs). By simply viewing the CIs as individual items, it is difficult to envision how these various CIs interact to form something more useful. We need to link the correct objects and attributes by creating the appropriate relationships, as shown in Figure 2.3 by the dark black lines.

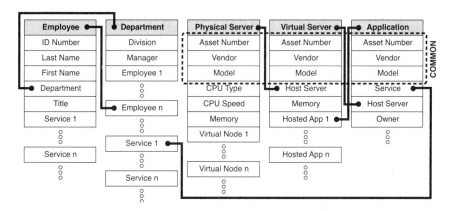

FIGURE 2.3   Relationships among the CIs

Here the CIs are linked to expand on the appropriate attributes, and it becomes easier to navigate the map of CIs to each other and to their impact upon the overall service. The links can be established in many ways, such as relational database table references and Java class pointers. When we talk relationships in the CMDB, the links are best implemented with XML. We explain these relationship links in more detail in Chapter 4 and Chapter 6, "Integration—There's No Way Around It!"

In this example, you can also see how there is common data across some CIs. Good database administrators try to normalize the data to eliminate the possibility of data overlap. With distributed objects, the normalization is a bit more difficult. In this particular case, it is possible that these specific attributes might be linked in from an Asset Management database as yet another CI.

You will see many references to relationships in this book—maybe so many that you will find the repetition annoying. We relentlessly preach about relationships for a reason. They are indeed the glue that binds everything together to result in information that is more meaningful. Without adequately capturing relationships, the CMDB crumbles into a worthless disarray.

A CI can be a small morsel of data or it can be a complex, multilayered composite of other CIs and other composites, or it can be any level in between. This flexibility is essential to a smooth Configuration Management process. Do not limit your perspective of a CI to just the infrastructure devices. Such a myopic perspective makes the system of CMDBs inflexible, fragile, and even more complex than the object-based model. This is one aspect of the discipline (or lack thereof) noted in Chapter 1, "The Need for Process Discipline." The future of the operation can be placed in jeopardy if these deleterious factors exist.

CI Candidates

Many elements of the IT and business environment qualify as CIs as we describe in Chapter 5, "CMS Deployment Strategy." Ideally, every identifiable unit of importance can be captured in the CMDB, but realistically, you will be driven by your business service needs and bound by priorities, staffing, and technology capabilities. Exactly which CIs you incorporate and in which order will be determined by each of these factors. Existing technologies offer plenty of information that can help. In Chapter 4, we cover how this data is leveraged. Configuration items fall into many domains, which are discussed in the following sections and in yet more detail in Chapter 5.

Infrastructure CIs

When people think of a CMDB, they usually limit their perspective to the infrastructure elements (servers, routers, storage, and so on). This is a myopic view, but the rationale behind this mode of thinking is understandable. Throughout much of the history of IT, what is now called the CMDB was known by various other terms, the most common being an asset database. This infrastructure-centric view persists today, even though the CMDB contains far more than infrastructure elements.

Such a database was used to maintain a record of the individual hardware assets owned by the enterprise. Advanced organizations expanded the asset database to include software also. An asset database represents a limited subset of a CMDB, but an important one. It is often the initial phase of a CMDB journey because of this historical view (and the fact that much of the data has already been collected).

Infrastructure is most closely associated with the hardware devices in the environment. For each device, many attributes are identified, collected, and maintained. Figure 2.4 shows a few common attributes of a CI representing a server.

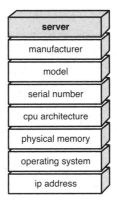

FIGURE 2.4 A few server CI attributes

Even in this simple server CI, you can see some attributes that raise additional questions. Attributes such as manufacturer and model are straightforward, but what about CPU architecture and operating system? CPU architecture could be Intel x86, s/390, or SPARC, and each opens up its own unique twist on the basic server definition. The operating system could be Windows Server 2003, Red Hat Enterprise Linux 5, VMware ESX 3.5, or even something like OpenVMS 7.2-1. Each of these attributes requires more detail, detail that may be unique to Windows, but totally irrelevant to Linux, for example.

Where such extensions are needed, object-oriented (OO) technologies can link the relevant extended attributes. This raises some interesting debates about precisely what constitutes infrastructure. Traditional examples of infrastructure are network devices (such as hubs and switches), servers, storage (including disk drives and SAN hardware), and mainframes. This is what we typically consider to be hardware.

As we continue to embed more sophisticated intelligence into the hardware, the line between infrastructure and applications becomes blurred. Virtually every single piece of today's hardware is a complex mixture of genuine hardware (for example, silicon, steel, and plastic) and software (for example, operating system, BIOS, microcode, and embedded web server). For the sake of the CMDB discussion, we consider infrastructure to be the self-contained package of hardware and its embedded software. Infrastructure is hardware *and* software.

Software infrastructure differs from applications, as we describe in the next section. This is sometimes called system software, but software infrastructure extends beyond traditional system software (such as Linux and VMware) and into those elements that support applications (such as Tibco and JBoss). Although they are software, we recommend that infrastructure should include these software elements as well as traditional hardware. Infrastructure is no longer limited to those tangible hardware components that require electrons. The basic intelligence that manipulates those electrons also counts as infrastructure.

The structural and behavioral aspects of certain attributes will morph over time. Virtual servers are a good example. Whereas a server once supported a single operating system, it can now support many.[2] The operating system attribute must now be abstracted to link to multiple possible virtual operating system instances (virtual machines [VM]) on a particular physical server. To complicate matters even more, that relationship between physical to virtual server can now be highly dynamic (for example, VMware's VMotion software easily shuffles a VM from one physical server to another).

Your CMDB plans, architecture, technology, and operations must be flexible enough to address these frequently shifting requirements. This is a major reason why object-oriented technologies are becoming more popular for the CMDB. An OO approach enables you to adapt data structures to changing demands. IT systems are irreversibly becoming more dynamic. The so-called *cloud computing*[3] that is gaining popularity marks an acceleration of dynamic systems, not a plateau.

Application CIs

Applications are the software elements that are directly touched and felt by end users. Examples include Microsoft Exchange, Siebel, and a custom shipment-tracking system. Products like SAP, Microsoft Internet Explorer,

---

2. Mainframes and some minicomputers have long supported virtual machines, but the concept's popularity has exploded in the distributed server market, thanks mainly to VMware.

3. Cloud computing is a new concept receiving the usual hyperbolic media attention as this book is being written. Its advocates tout it as the next form of delivering IT to the business. The most notable characteristic of *the cloud* is outsourced infrastructure and application services, sometimes including the entire IT operations organization. Cloud computing has some merits, but it is too early to declare it a success or failure. Wikipedia's page on cloud computing is even somewhat vague and not yet fortified by the usual verifiable references and citations (http://en.wikipedia.org/wiki/Cloud_computing).

and Adobe Flash Player can also be seen as applications, but here we are getting more into the domain of software infrastructure, as we just pointed out in the section on infrastructure CIs. What you deem an application and what is software infrastructure is up to you, but you should be consistent within the context of the CMDB.

As you build out your application-level models, you will find that many applications are abstractions built upon other applications. The gray line between applications and software infrastructure is where these situations will occur. Some applications that are used by some end users (such as a database front-end) may become software infrastructure for another, more complex application (for example, a shipping application built on top of SAP and using this database).

The value of clarifying the demarcation between applications and software infrastructure comes when using the CMDB for more sophisticated purposes. We cover these purposes in more detail in Chapter 9, but we present a simple example here—one that is deeply desired, but also extremely difficult to achieve.

Consider the exercise of identifying the root cause of an application performance anomaly. The application consists of many software and hardware components, so the first thing we need to do is understand the structure of the application's relationships to these elements (see Figure 2.5). The hierarchy of the relationship map will be multiple tiers for the typical modern business application.

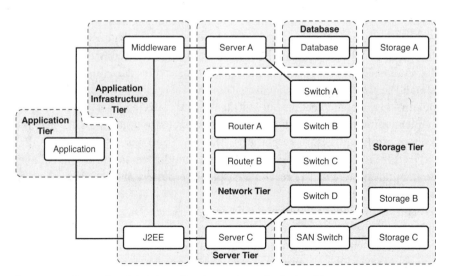

FIGURE 2.5   Example of tiered application structural relationships

To determine the root cause, this structure is navigated, and each component's impact on the overall application behavior is assessed. This assessment first capitalizes on the relationships that bind the various components together, as they form the paths followed in the navigation. They give us visibility to potential cause-effect mappings and significantly narrow the field of possibilities.

The performance, availability, and configuration state of each of these components can then be analyzed. The mapping significantly reduces the set of possible root causes by including only those elements that truly matter to the application in question. By narrowing the scope, you can then attack the problem more effectively.

Of course, it would be wonderful if you could automate this analysis to the very end, but this remains a dream for now. This is where the difficulty arises with application analysis, but such is the topic for another book.

In Chapter 9, we offer more guidance on how the CMDB/CMS works in conjunction with the Change Management process. In that chapter, we also show how changes can point to many of the root causes of a myriad of problems, including the elusive application performance problem. It all begins with having accurate configuration data or—as we like to call it—the truth. You must also not forget that there is a Continual Service Improvement component to ITIL v3; some of which we describe in Chapter 8, "Continual Improvement for the CMS."

Known Error CIs

There is a condition in Incident and Problem Management called a *known error*. A known error is an incident or problem whose diagnosis is complete, but whose final resolution is either delayed or implemented with a temporary fix. As incidents arise with the known error as a root cause, operations staff should be able to quickly identify the known errors and take appropriate action. Actions include proper notification of affected users and possibly implementing work-around solutions. As the operation gains experience, the known errors are tied to resolutions. This forms a cause-effect linkage that accelerates resolution. The error is detected, and the resolution is immediately found and presented. The responders therefore have a map to guide them to speedy service restoration.

One of the more important management aspects of known errors is the need to capture them and maintain them throughout their lifecycles, including through end-of-life. To enable this, a known errors database is maintained. Many of the common Service Desk products now include some form of known errors database. Service Desk staff developed a need for this database for the purposes we mention here, as they are the front lines of the IT organization. Vendors of Service Desk automation software responded to this need with full inclusion of a known errors database or supplying it as an optional module.

Naturally, the known errors database represents yet another family of CIs for the CMDB. The value of this class of CIs helps streamline many of the daily functions such as incident analysis and long-term pattern analysis for Problem Management, capacity planning, and continuous improvement.

The known errors are related to infrastructure, application, and other classes of CIs. These relationships need to be captured and mapped, as the known errors are attributes of these "host" CIs. The known error attributes are subject to change, and there can be multiple known errors for a single host CI, which could be dependent, for example, on their particular environment, configuration, or architecture, so the object model must support such a zero-to-many set of similar relationship attributes.

Business Process CIs

If applications are abstractions of infrastructure, the next step above applications is the business service level. Like applications, there can be multiple layers of business services (for example, a web-based product ordering service is a component of the broader supply chain automation service). At the highest level of this structure are the business processes. Chapter 5 and Chapter 7, "The Future of the CMS," have figures that demonstrate this notion of business services sitting atop the remaining IT structure.

Business process modeling is a functional domain unto itself within the IT community. It is one of the tightest integration points between IT and the business and is increasingly owned and controlled by the business side rather than the IT side. Unfortunately, the CMDB and CMS vendors do not yet offer complete solutions that automate the discovery of the services without significant human intervention. The current state is still very much silo oriented, but it is changing.

You should work with the business community and the Enterprise Architecture organization to incorporate business process information into the CMDB/CMS. Stay up to date with the standards being developed by the Business Modeling and Integration Domain Task Force so you will be prepared to input your work more easily into the vendor tools when those tools do come along. All parties will benefit. Newer developments are making this much easier now because standard object modeling and integration technologies are gaining acceptance.

Standards have been under development for over a decade. Standards took a positive turn in 2005 when the Business Process Modeling Initiative (BPMI) merged with the Object Management Group (OMG) to form the Business

Modeling and Integration Domain Task Force (BMI).[4] BMI and OMG are responsible for some standards, OASIS for others, and the W3C for still others.[5] The flexibility offered by XML allows for many derivatives to be developed. That's the good part of XML-based standards. The downside is that it allows for many derivatives to be developed. You can easily become overwhelmed by the plethora of standards available.

As you pursue the CMDB, your role in the selection of these specific standards will be limited. You should leave the painful selection to those in the Enterprise Architecture team (who have this responsibility anyway), but we highly recommend you collaborate with that team to help determine the optimum path to linking the business process standards with your CMDB. Chapter 4 provides the basis for your discussions about a federated structure with the architecture groups.

Much discussion is taking place about Business Service Management (BSM), the higher-level aspects of IT that produce and manage technology in the eyes of the business, not so much in the eyes of technologists. The business processes and the business services that feed them are the linkage between core IT (infrastructure and applications) and actual business value. The relationships between and within these tiers enable us to determine business impact of a server failure, for example. Without these relationships, assessing the business impact is mere guesswork—and very often wrong. Accurately understanding business impact via the CMDB and its use cases is absolutely essential if you want to position the IT organization as a valued business partner. Just as it is in all other functions of IT, the CMDB is a fundamental supporting pillar of BSM.

Business processes are an often-overlooked element of the CMDB because of the aforementioned misconception that the CMDB is all about infrastructure. The omission of business processes further exacerbates the "us and them" division between IT and business. Inclusion of business processes ensures more business relevance to the CMDB and enables use cases to have

---

4. The Business Modeling and Integration Domain Task Force web site (http://bmi.omg.org/) contains many details about the group's standards efforts.

5. Standards are a veritable alphabet soup that confuses actual progress. The BMI initiative owns BPMN (Business Process Modeling Notation), OASIS (Organization for the Advancement of Structured Information Standards) owns BPEL (Business Process Execution Language), and W3C (World Wide Web Consortium) owns WS-CDL (Web Services Choreography Description Language). There are still others in this ever-growing family of standards. Collectively, they are all part of the greater Service-Oriented Architecture (SOA) movement to componentized business processes and the software used to automate business processes.

more value to business service management efforts. The result will help change the language from "us and them" to just "us" in a unified journey toward business execution excellence.

Human CIs

Human beings are the most important elements of any business. IT services are no different. You and your colleagues, your end users, your reporting structure (in both directions), vendors, partners, and many, many others all contribute to your technology and business services. How each of these people fits into the overall picture is a requirement of any good CMDB. "People" are identified, tracked, used, and managed according to each individual's contributions and responsibilities. Here are just a few attributes of people that are useful:

- **Identity.** Each person needs a unique identity, sometimes called a digital identity. This identity is a complex data structure far beyond the person's name. Among the many attributes tied to the human CI is a unique key, a means to identify that John Smith is the John Smith you think he is.

  Software tools used to manage IT services are notoriously disjointed with respect to identities. Each usually has its own identities, requiring tedious replication of data across tools, data that nearly always falls out of sync. Common identity management technologies are finally showing promise to unify identities across tools, but the various tool vendors must support them. Happily, there is increasing momentum to support common mechanisms like Active Directory and Kerberos.

- **Authorization.** After identity is established, the next step is to assign authority to take certain actions. These authorizations can be for specific software or built into managed infrastructure. Here also, the multitude of mechanisms and individual points of management greatly complicates this situation.

  The identity and authorization must be intertwined. Companies are using identity management products that work in conjunction with other products using AAA protocols[6] and related technologies to

---

6. AAA stands for authentication, authorization, and accounting, a generalization for the interrelated technologies for maintaining secure systems. See the Wikipedia page, http://en.wikipedia.org/wiki/AAA_protocol, for more information on AAA.

understand, manage, and enforce access controls, control privileges, and other authorization policies.

When a management software function is executed, it must ensure that the action is allowed (for example, "Can I change the OSPF parameters on this router?" or "Can she view the schema of the HR database?"). Proprietary and isolated mechanisms can support these actions, but managing the dizzying array of identity-authorization mappings without automation technologies is intractable.

Here lies the solution to this dilemma and one that is already starting to take root in IT organizations. Configuration and Change Management (CCM) products highlight a good example that is bringing some sanity to the tedious and error-prone tasks of manual configuration change execution. The tool manages a common AAA mechanism for all covered elements and then the tool itself is executing the changes. The disparate access controls are managed centrally in this common tool.

Logically, each CCM tool has a strong CMDB at its heart, so the tool can sufficiently understand the configuration of what it is acting upon and various policies regarding these actions. The result is a common platform for normalizing task execution that is faster and more trustworthy, but there are yet other benefits to the CMDB effort.

CCM tools include a CMDB, so they are valuable as elements of an overall CMDB architecture. By virtue of their basic function, they almost always do their own discovery of their covered domain and usually more effectively than other discovery tools in their domain (there are many). This means the data is highly accurate. As you build out your wider CMS, these tools are effective CMDBs for their individual domains.

- **Roles.** Individuals are the soldiers in the service management war, but these individuals can be classified to guide common tasks across a related team of individuals. You have many of these teams, and members can belong to multiple teams. The teams may not even be formal; they just have common goals, so we'll call them roles instead.

  By assigning authorizations to roles, the tools that drive actions can be simplified. Instead of managing authorizations for each individual, you can just manage them for roles. The system then cross-checks roles with people who are assigned to those roles.

Roles institute an additional layer of structure into the human CIs, but the additional layer is well worth the minimal overhead because of the operational simplicity we just mentioned. As with the known errors CIs and many others, the model requires flexibility to support many roles per person. Here the relationship will be at least one role, but probably more.

The human CIs are certainly included in the bigger CMDB structure (CMS, to be more precise). You need not and indeed should not create this CMDB from scratch. Leverage what already exists, a data source full of excellent data on your people. It's called the HR database, and it is most often embedded within software tools used for HR functions, such as Peoplesoft.

In Figure 2.3, we showed a CI called Employee. The populated Employee CIs and their attributes can all be extracted from the HR database, requiring little additional embellishment for CMDB purposes. You won't need a lot of the detail existing in the HR databases (they won't give it to you anyway, nor should they!), although basic identity information (for example, employee number, name, department number, title, reporting structure, and roles—if they exist there) will be very handy and more available.

Document CIs

Finally, we present another class of CI that is often overlooked, despite repeated references in the formal ITIL positions on the CMDB and CMS. That class is documentation. Together with known errors and other sources, they embody what some call *Knowledge Management*. We view this as a valid categorization.

Documents are different data types than those normally maintained in a CMDB or relational database. They are files, such as PDF, Excel, MS-Word, and so on. The document CI has as a core attribute, the path name or (preferably) the URL that points to the document file. The host CI (infrastructure, application, and so on) then points to the document CI as appropriate.

If you need to see the installation instructions for a Dell PowerEdge™ M600 server, the attribute for the installation guide in the document CI can be set to the specific PDF document on Dell's web site, or you can have your own internal copy (likely a better idea). The UML diagram for the Order to Cash business process can be a PDF link included as an attribute in the business process CI for Order to Cash.

How Much Data Does a CI Need?

Raw CIs (the actual devices, software elements, and other real-world entities, not the data stores) contain far more data than you will need in the CMDB. You must trim this overwhelming data set but still maintain visibility into enough to be meaningful and useful.

Consider the example of an SNMP MIB[7] for a small branch office router. This device tracks thousands of individual attributes in its internal memory! Try performing an SNMP Walk operation on one, and you will see firsthand the massive set of data that can be gathered. Clearly, you don't need all of this. Trying to manage such a voluminous data set would be unwieldy, even for a few devices.

Where then do you draw the line to delineate what is tracked and what is not? A good starting point to this answer lies in the DMTF's CIM standard.[8] CIM is an impressive body of work, developed by many brilliant people over several years. It is an elegant and comprehensive object model that is finally getting some traction after a slow start. We go into more detail on the DMTF and the CIM specification in Chapter 6.

The final determination of the CI data's richness lies in the use cases for the data. Some use cases (for example, fault analysis) require very little detail. Some such as data center automation need much deeper detail. You will struggle to reach the appropriate level of detail on your own, so this is why we recommend starting with CIM. Part of the brilliance of CIM is the work they've already put into assessing the right level of detail.

A Brief Explanation of CMDB Federation

Federation, described in much greater detail in Chapter 4, is a new approach to maintain accurate configuration information about the IT environment,

---

7. The Simple Network Management Protocol (SNMP) was originally defined in the IETF document RFC 1067 (http://www.ietf.org/rfc/rfc1067.txt?number=1067) in August 1988. It uses a Management Information Base (MIB) structure to define the attributes represented in a networked device. It has been expanded to be applicable to servers, applications, and many other configuration items, but it continues to be seen as largely related to the network.

8. The Distributed Management Task Force (DMTF) produced and maintains the definition of common data specifications called the Common Information Model (CIM). The first version of CIM was released in 1996, so it has benefited from years of refinement. XML, UML, and MOF files for CIM Version 2.18.1 are available at http://www.dmtf.org/standards/cim/cim_schema_v2181.

although the concepts behind federation date back to the 1980s. CMDB federation was proposed soon after the CMDB first gained traction on the coattails of ITIL, but formal federated CMDB acceptance has been elusive until recently. The new breakthrough is a definition for integrating data sources called the CMDB Federation standard. The name is not the most clever title, but its publication marks an important step toward a successful CMS. Developed by an ad hoc group of vendors called the CMDB Federation Working Group (CMDBf), the specification has now been handed off to the DMTF for further development. We explain the concepts and some details of the CMDBf specification in Chapter 6.

The federated model enables more flexibility than a monolithic database model. The standalone model was originally the accepted model and assumes all data is collected in a single database. This is impractical for a CMDB, as it is easily corrupted by synchronization issues with data that is usually geographically diverse and rapidly changing. The monolithic model places a heavy burden on the database, its related infrastructure, and the related administrators. Sheer resource utilization forces lengthy update intervals, which hamper timely updates to the database. Data quickly becomes stale in such a scenario, and stale data is more harmful than no data at all.

Federation enables a "divide and conquer" approach to the CMDB architecture, distributing the load and leveraging the optimum tools for each technology domain and locale. By using the best tool for a specific domain, the CMDB contents are better tailored to a domain's unique needs and can be updated more frequently. Both result in higher accuracy.

To overcome CI differences and still capture the relevant data for the CMDB, the CI definition extends beyond a simple single-table database structure. Relational databases can be used to organize and capture these CIs in a more complete form across multiple linked tables, although the interchange and federation of data is best addressed by object-oriented technologies such as object repositories and XML. If a relational database is used for the remote linking, federating the data is much more cumbersome. Many will dispute this assertion, but the explosive success of XML is evidence enough that it is the superior mechanism for linking and exchanging remote data. This fact does not diminish any RDBMS for what it does best. The RDBMS is indeed integral to the many pockets of the CMDB. It just doesn't work well for the complex linking of the distributed and seemingly disparate data sources. For this, XML works best in partnership with the databases.

In federation, the data is spread across multiple CMDBs, more accurately referred to as Management Data Repositories (MDR), illustrated with the simplified example in Figure 2.6. There is no single CMDB. Instead, the aggregate "CMDB" is an abstraction built upon the contents of the MDRs, and metadata models dictate the assembly of relevant MDR data based upon needs. The MDRs may reside in different systems and data storage formats. Federation is at the heart of what ITIL v3 now refers to as the Configuration Management System (CMS).

If the CIs from Figure 2.3 are reflected in a federated structure, you would see something similar to Figure 2.6. Here, the MDRs are aligned with domains as we advise in the CI candidate descriptions.

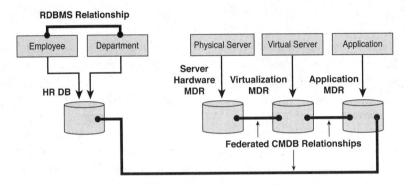

FIGURE 2.6   CMS relationships across MDRs

Note how the HR database is represented as one of the MDRs. Two of the CI categories are embodied within the same database, with a relationship inherent inside the database. This relationship is a branch of the federation structure, even though it appears to be isolated. This illusion of isolation results from viewing federation too myopically.

The HR database is maintained separately from most other MDRs, but its inclusion emphasizes a growing practice in the whole CMDB arena, that of the *foreign CMDB*. A foreign CMDB is an element (an MDR, if you will) that is not under direct control of the IT organization or those responsible for the CMDB architecture, design, and operation. It is a data source rich in information that can be used, but it is available only in a "read-only" mode. There is nothing wrong with this. In fact, it is indicative of the future, as third parties will assume more responsibility for certain domains and therefore the MDRs and CMDBs of those domains. Your overall CMDB needs this data, so proper integration and federation are needed beyond just the HR database.

CIs as the CMDB "DNA"

We can propose a simple analogy to highlight the power of CI reuse and federation from the CMDB. Our example is DNA, the basic building block of all organic life forms (at least those on Earth!) and how the basic genetic elements are abstracted to eventually form complex organisms.

Every living organism is built from the same four building blocks. Geneticists call these nucleotides and represent them by their letters: A (adenine), T (thymine), C (cytosine), and G (guanine). The reason each plant or animal is different is because these nucleotides are assembled differently. Arrange them one way, you get a Bengal tiger; arrange them another way, and you get Tiger Woods.

If we consider the genetic CMDB to contain only four CIs, being the four nucleotides, we can turn this raw data into extremely sophisticated organisms using abstraction models known as codons, genes, chromosomes, and organisms. Everything uses the exact same CIs. The secret to each unique finished organism lies in the abstractions.

Abstractions are themselves CIs with their own special attributes, so we need a CMDB mechanism to store and retrieve them. It is best to store the abstractions in separate CMDBs from the one containing the four nucleotides. This is where federation brings value to the overall CMDB structure. As we explain later and in Chapter 4, the federated model allows flexible references to the CMDB data to produce actionable information. In this case, the abstractions point to the nucleotide CMDB to obtain the correct low-level details, and all of this is assembled in a usable form based on the structure defined in the codon, gene, chromosome, and organism CMDBs.

Figure 2.7 depicts the genetic hierarchy followed as we navigate from the top-level organism all the way down to the nucleotides. Obviously, genetics is a far more complex field than is shown in this example, but it does illustrate how the various abstractions interact and relate. Note how each abstraction layer uses its own CMDB to hold the models that define the structure of the abstraction and the references to the layers below. An organism model defines the right mix of chromosomes, each chromosome model defines the right mix of genes, each gene model defines the right mix of what geneticists call codons, and each of the 64 codon combinations is built from a unique structure of nucleotides. If there was a need to further deconstruct the nucleotides, one could break down each nucleotide to its molecules, atoms, and subatomic particles through the use of additional abstraction layers.

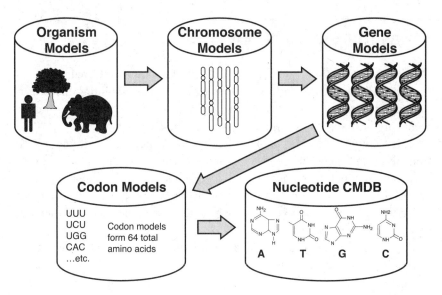

FIGURE 2.7   Genetics example of federated CIs

It would be wasteful to replicate copies of data from each lower level of this structure. By the time we get to the chromosome level, the number of nucleotide combinations is astronomical. The use of abstraction tiers greatly simplifies this situation. For example, the chromosome level only needs to reference models of individual gene strands, not the entire structure of each. The raw data remains accurate and up to date, and we have the flexibility of creating new abstractions merely by rearranging the most practical model. Everything below that model remains unchanged.

Every good CMDB follows a similar pattern of hierarchical references as the models and data are navigated for a particular use case. The idea is similar to database normalization, where the goal is to optimize flexible data construction with a minimum of data replication and maximum performance. Object federation in a CMDB structure differs from database normalization in that it can link a wider variety of data sources in many physical places (if needed). Object models can also contain behavioral information such as rules. Good object models go far beyond mere structural information.

Data from the level below is not duplicated in each model. This would cause severe data overload and synchronization issues, especially at the higher levels. Each abstraction merely references the appropriate elements of the layer below. For example, there is no need to define the molecular structure of every codon when simply referring to the A, T, C, and G nucleotides and their assemblies are sufficient. A behavioral aspect of the genetic CMDB that can be encoded in the model further simplifies the nucleotide references. Because the only possible nucleotide combinations in the genetic code can be A to T and C to G, there are not four possibilities, but only two (an A-T pair and a C-G pair—or a one and a zero, if you wish).

It is ironic that life forms can be deconstructed down to the same binary code used in computer science! This is one reason we chose the genetic example. Clearly the genetic code is hideously complex, but building the layered models greatly simplifies the navigation of the system and optimizes performance, data reuse, and reliability. IT services are no different. If a federated model can allow us to tackle something as convoluted as the genome, IT services should be much easier. Nobody can credibly state that a federated CMDB is easy, but we often overcomplicate an already complex mission by our failure to leverage best practices and novel solutions. CMDB federation is such a novel solution, and ITIL (or similar process models) can offer the best practices.

Reconciliation

In the existing world of CMDB, reconciliation is considered to be a necessity and indeed it is...today. *Reconciliation* is the synchronization of two or more matching database segments to ensure consistency across them. Data stores that should be identical copies are compared. If any differences exist, the reconciliation engine attempts to correct this inconsistency. Most existing CMDBs are isolated, and integration involves a periodic upload or download of bulk data. It is not federation. In this "unfederated" model, data synchronization decays over time. The copies drift apart and become inaccurate. Reconciliation attempts to sync the CMDBs, usually in a brute-force manner that scans all CMDBs and makes corrections as the reconciliation engine finds discrepancies.

Reconciliation is driven by policies that determine who "wins" when a conflict arises. Some may be by majority vote (for example, three of the four CMDBs agree, so the fourth is forced into agreement), some by pre-establishing the winner (for example, the network CMDB is the trusted source for the network), and others can get more complicated. Full reconciliation can be automated to correct the discrepancy, or it can merely inform a CMDB manager to take action to reconcile. Initial phases will be the latter, but those that are trustworthy or become annoyingly repetitive can be automated.

Figure 2.8 shows a simplified example of three CMDB instances where reconciliation is needed. This VMware virtual server is identical across all instances except for the middle one's physical host. This is a bit like that *Sesame Street* game "one of these things is not like the other."

Europa	
mfgr	VMware
model	ESX
version	2.5.5
host	Saturn
memory	4 GB

Europa	
mfgr	VMware
model	ESX
version	2.5.5
host	Jupiter
memory	4 GB

Europa	
mfgr	VMware
model	ESX
version	2.5.5
host	Saturn
memory	4 GB

FIGURE 2.8   Three CMDBs needing reconciliation

The reconciliation engine scans these three and recognizes this discrepancy. It can either notify someone of the issue or it can correct it to match the other two. If automated action is taken, you must be absolutely certain that the results will be as desired. In this situation, one might think that the "majority vote" rule would apply, but that middle instance might be the trusted source extracted directly from VMware. Because it reflects the truth, it has precedence over the other two, and they, not the middle one, must be corrected. As systems become more dynamic (for example, virtualization), situations like this will become more common. By the way, Europa is the sixth moon of Jupiter, so of course the middle instance is right!

No matter how you view reconciliation, all agree that it is difficult to get it right and even harder to get it properly automated. From firsthand experience, we can tell you that there will be many weeks and months spent tweaking your reconciliation rules to try and automate the reconciliation process. The ideal CMS would eliminate reconciliation because it is too painful (our VMware example is only the tip of the iceberg). As the CMDB gets ever closer to the CMS ideal, we will approach the ideal of eliminating the need for reconciliation. When we finally achieve that ideal is a great mystery, but don't expect to totally shed reconciliation before 2012.

A properly federated CMS will significantly minimize the need for reconciliation because the very nature of federation (as you will see in Chapter 4.) implies that data is always captured and managed only once. There is no need to reconcile CI details because there should never be duplicate copies! The only attributes that are duplicated—and therefore need reconciliation—are those representing the matching criteria for referencing the relevant data. As in RDBMS development, these are the indices (the matching attributes) to point to the right federated data. Even these attributes will eventually graduate beyond a need for reconciliation as better XML-based remote-linking technologies emerge. Technologies that enable an idealized view of federation are only now beginning to appear. Over the next several years, vendors and end users alike will chip away at the pockets of duplicate data. Someday we will tackle that final step, but be patient and diligent. If there was ever a real-life situation where "slow and steady wins the race" in IT, it is in the pursuit of a true CMS.

The CMS Arrives

In June 2007, the UK Office of Government Commerce (OGC)–the official ITIL caretakers–released ITIL version 3 (ITIL v3). In this book, we do not expand on the many improvements in ITIL v3, but the most significant change to configuration data is the emergence of the CMS.

A CMS is a vast improvement over a simple CMDB for many reasons. A few of the more prominent benefits of CMS are the following:

- CMS implies distributed data in line with, but beyond, the historical notion of a CMDB. The CMS is inherently federated, whereas the CMDB required a dramatic new twist. As you will see, the new concept of a federated CMDB is really a CMS.

- ITIL v3 more clearly articulates practical applications for configuration data and endorses references to and from the broader CMS, rather than direct integration to a CMDB. The distinction between federation and integration is important, and we describe this difference in detail in Chapter 4.

- The genesis of the CMS marks the beginning of the end of the CMDB term. CMDB is a misleading term, but its ubiquity will make it persistent for years. Still, it is much more fruitful to shift many of the CMDB discussions to CMS instead. Even in the CMS description in the ITIL v3 literature, the CMDB term remains, but it is redefined into what is essentially an MDR. We believe that the CMDB Federation Working Group's concept of the MDR will prevail in the long run and that "CMDB" eventually will fade away from the vernacular.

- CMS is richer in its inclusion of applications and services. Prior notions of the CMDB were vague and fragmented beyond simple infrastructure characteristics. Because the CMS is inherently object-oriented, it can make use of behavioral information to make the structural information more accurate and more useful.

- Relationships are at the heart of the CMS. CMDB was often viewed as just a repository of attributes. Linking and federating these attributes were usually limited by technology solutions that were in fact designed according to these misguided, restrictive attribute-centric requirements. CMS is a force to break this cycle by mandating the relationships necessary to make raw data meaningful.

Throughout the remainder of this book, we use the MDR, CMDB, and CMS terms. As much as we dislike the CMDB term, it remains relevant for now. A CMDB in the newer order represents a specialized repository, usually targeted at a specific technology domain. We prefer to call this an MDR, and we will usually do that. Note that the two are nearly interchangeable in the new order of the CMS. It is also important to sometimes refer to CMDB in its historical context. To properly convey the meaning and value of the CMS, we must address, and in many cases overturn, common CMDB perceptions.

Populating the CMS

The CMS is only useful if it is accurate. In fact, the most dangerous situation with a CMS is when the data is wrong, which is why the concept of federation, as described in Chapter 4, is so critical to your design. Decisions are based on the CMS, and when the data is wrong, the decisions are wrong. Instead of the CMS being an enabler for improvement, it can actually cause further deterioration when the data is suspect. CMS population, therefore, is among the most important of all facets of Configuration Management. How you populate your CMS and keep it accurate will directly affect the success or failure of the CMS and—as we pointed out in Chapter 1—the entire IT operation itself.

The CMS is populated in two ways: manually and automatically. The majority of CMDB population so far has been manual. This is one main reason most CMDB initiatives have suffered or failed altogether. Manual population is risky because it is too difficult to maintain its accuracy. By the time population is finished, the contents are already partially obsolete.

To optimize CMDB accuracy, you want to automate as much of the population as possible. We call this *automated discovery*, or *auto-discovery*. For our purposes, we refer to *discovery* as the automated population mechanism.

Discovery is a wonderful innovation for the CMDB, but alas, many CMDB elements cannot be discovered. Therefore, you will inevitably have a mix of both population modes. The following figures show how this mix works.

Figure 2.9 is a simple diagram showing a collection of CIs in a CMS. It is merely illustrative of the point, not an actual CMS.

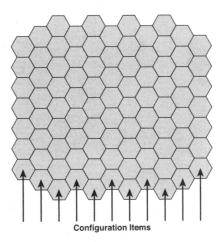

Configuration Items

FIGURE 2.9   CIs in a CMS

You need to identify what can be discovered and what must be manually populated. By segmenting the CMS in this way, you can set forth with your plans to build automation technologies and operational tasks to build and maintain the CMS. Figure 2.10 shows how the CMS is divided between the two. Discovery usually gives you the core elements, whereas manual methods are used to supplement this core.

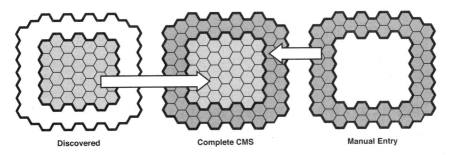

Discovered   **Complete CMS**   **Manual Entry**

FIGURE 2.10   Two modes of populating the CMS

Both modes can be further broken down into the relevant CMS domains, which are most effectively aligned with the MDRs. Figure 2.11 shows this additional breakdown. Note how many domains will have both discovered and manual components.

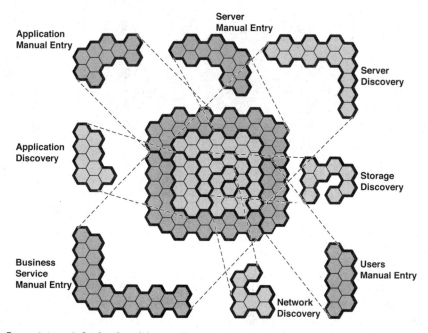

FIGURE 2.11   A further breakdown of CMS population

Domains like the network lend themselves well to discovery because the common instrumentation (for example, SNMP) is pervasive and full of useful data. Others, such as business services, are more heavily manual because of a lack of instrumentation. As we explained earlier, even these domains are improving for discovery. As new technologies emerge to enable discovery, you should capitalize on them to continue building more accuracy into the CMS.

CMS as an Integration Mechanism

Data integration is a longstanding problem with software systems, especially with management software. Proprietary management tool interfaces have long ruled this market. They created a nice development partner ecosystem for the major vendors, but the practice makes it difficult to plug tool A into tool B to attain more comprehensive value from the union of the two. In defense of the major vendors, they appeared on the scene at a time when proprietary integration was the only option. Once established, these interfaces took on a life of their own and are now so deeply entrenched, they are nearly impossible to replace. That said, however, it is time to change. The integration pain has become so severe that progress toward unified service management is being hampered.

Software tools are gravitating toward functions that act as either data providers (such as discovery) or data consumers (such as analysis tools). These classifications establish the major points of integration, where one must integrate with the other. Some tools act as both providers and consumers (for example, the server agent), consuming data for one purpose (localized analysis on the server, for instance) and providing data for another (in this example, presenting the server's data for analysis in a broader context). Either way, integration can be a quagmire.

Figure 2.12 is a picture of a simple integration challenge. As you can see, many integration points are required, each with its own data model and its own access and exchange protocols. As the number of tools increases, the integration challenge grows exponentially. Clearly, this is not sustainable in a large environment.

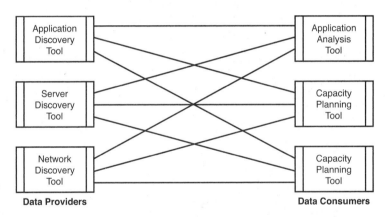

FIGURE 2.12   Proprietary tool integration

The DMTF's CIM and other standards promised to address this situation long ago. Until recently, the standards were held back. Either vendors were unwilling to support the standards effectively or technology limitations prevented a vendor from "shoehorning" a standard into its antiquated technology. New technologies based on true object models and object integration are finally now gaining enough of a groundswell to move the industry toward acceptance of standards-based integration.

Data and messages are the basis of tool integration, with much of the emphasis being on the data. Standards for message exchange are already accepted practice (for example, SNMP trap or CIM Event), although more work is needed. The data side of integration is the gap, and that gap is filled very nicely by a CMS.

As the CMDB gains popularity, vendors and users alike are recognizing its potential to simplify the integration problem. The very nature of the CMS is grounded in common data formats and interchange specifications, so it seems to be suitable for tool integration. Indeed it is. You will see many more possibilities emerge over the next few years to act in this capacity. Most of the innovations will not even be so explicit, but if two tools are using a common CMS, there is no need to explicitly send a piece of data from one tool to another. The data is already in the right place. Figure 2.13 indicates how the CMS simplifies the integration problem of Figure 2.12.

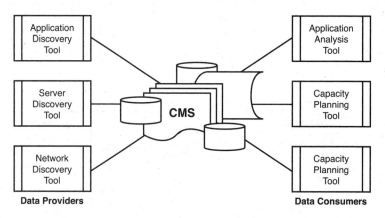

FIGURE 2.13   CMDB as a common tool integration point

Frequently Asked Questions

Question: What are the Citizen CMDB and Core CMDB? You do not mention these here, but many others do.

Answer: The Citizen and Core CMDBs are relics of the monolithic model of the CMDB. The premise is that the core CMDB is the "master" CMDB that holds the unified expanse of all data. The Citizen CMDB "feeds" data into the Core. It implies, in most cases, a two-tier hierarchy. We already mentioned that a true CMS will be multiple levels, built upon a chain of Management Data Repositories and liberal use of relationships. You can view the Citizen as the

MDR at the lower level of a link in the chain and the Core as the higher level of that same link. As you traverse the chain, Cores become Citizens at the next higher link, and the inverse is true as you move lower. It is admittedly rather confusing, but we explain this more suitable structural chain in Chapter 4.

Question: Why did the early asset databases fail to deliver the promise of the CMDB?

Answer: There are two major reasons, among others. First, the asset databases did not generally contain relationships rich enough to support the navigation of dependencies between assets and the services they support. Second, the data itself was difficult to populate and therefore inaccurate. As we mentioned in this chapter, inaccurate data is not just useless—it is harmful!

Question: The CMDB appears to be very similar to a data warehouse. Can we use a data warehouse as a CMDB?

Answer: Technically, the CMDB is similar in many philosophical ways to a data warehouse. Where they differ is in the actual delivery of the technology and how the whole system of data is used within an ITIL-based organization. As a CMS with federation, the parts (the MDRs) are linked differently than a data warehouse, and the tools that produce and consume the data are aligning with the CMS direction. It is certainly conceivable—and indeed expected—that data warehouses will play some role in the CMS, just as traditional relational databases will. The overall system that brings all of these parts together is the CMS.

Question: I would love to include my applications in my CMDB, but it is too difficult. How can I do this?

Answer: The majority of CMDB efforts are now aimed at infrastructure. Applications are indeed more difficult because of the lack of instrumentation to tell us the real structure of the applications. New discovery tools are now available to help. We explore how these tools work in Chapter 4.

Question: How can you advocate extending the CMDB to such high-level concepts as business processes, documents, and the human element when we are still struggling with the basic infrastructure? Isn't this an overly aggressive "boil the ocean" approach that is bound to fail?

Answer: A "big bang" attempt at a CMDB/CMS is almost guaranteed to fail. Like any other ambitious journey, you make progress one step at a time. We do advocate building the higher layers of abstraction, but infrastructure is a necessary foundation that supports these higher layers. Get the lower levels to a reasonable state of maturity before moving "up the stack," and your journey will be easier. A growing number of organizations are now in a position to make this move, as their infrastructure layer is in a more capable state.

Question: I have implemented a CMDB, but my people spend too much time populating and reconciling the data. The overhead is diminishing the value of the CMDB so much that many intended beneficiaries are revolting. How can I minimize this work and save the CMDB effort?

Answer: Automation is the key to simplifying ongoing CMDB/CMS maintenance, including initial mapping and ongoing population updates. The category of automation products is discovery tools. We explain discovery in detail in Chapter 4. A CMS without discovery is doomed, so it is wise to implement discovery as soon as you can.

Question: You imply that ITIL v3 is the end of the CMDB, but it too references a CMDB. What is the truth here?

Answer: On page 68 of the ITIL v3 *Service Transition* book, the CMS diagram contains an "Integrated CMDB" and Physical CMDBs within the mix of parts. Note that the diagram is just an *example* of a CMS, not a definitive description. Also note that this section of the book on Service Asset and Configuration Management (SACM) is rather vague on CMDB. This is intentional, as the ITIL v3 authors share our critical view of the CMDB term. They talk extensively about CIs and their interrelationships, which is all good. The ambiguity about CMDB is also good because it marks the beginning of the end of the CMDB, not the instant death of the term. We continue to foretell that the end is coming, but it will take a while. The CMDB portions of the CMS diagram can be more effectively represented in the view taken by the CMDBf Working Group. Both CMDBf and ITIL v3 were developed simultaneously and a bit isolated from one another. This question is related to the next one, so please read on.

Question: If the proper, forward-looking term is CMS—and not CMDB—why does the groundbreaking CMDB Federation Working Group even call it a CMDB?

Answer: The CMDBf Working Group began its work long before the release of ITIL v3. During this period, CMDB was still the prevalent term and gaining momentum. ITIL v3 outlines the overarching purpose and principles of the CMS, whereas CMDBf clarifies the technology needed to make the CMS work. They both address the same challenge and align very well with each other. Each is an important innovation that together drives us forward from the CMDB of yore and the CMS of the future. One major intent of this book is to bridge the gap between these two brilliant developments. The CMS is an evolution and will continue to be. Neither CMDBf nor ITIL v3 is perfect, nor is this book, but all are forward steps in the ongoing continuum of the CMS.

To eliminate confusion, we encourage a simplification that generalizes the "CMDB" parts of both initiatives according to the hierarchical structure presented by the CMDBf. We call each individual part an MDR, and the whole system is the CMS. We expand on this structure much more in Chapter 4.

We prefer to euthanize the CMDB term, but we realize that will take time. A growing number of other influential members of the IT service management community agree, including authors of both CMDBf and ITIL v3. It is indeed uncanny how many people enthusiastically agree when we express our disdain for the CMDB term!

Summary

At this point in the book, we hope we have conveyed a clear picture of the macro-level challenges and opportunities of the CMS. In this chapter, we explained the enigma that is a CMDB. The CMDB is many things, but it certainly is not a single database. The CMDB is bound by the limitations imposed on it by rampant misinformation. Although we dislike the term, the CMDB's woes are more a product of culture than definition. We strongly endorse the transition from discussing CMDB to the more flexible and powerful CMS. CMS is fresh, and we all have a profound opportunity and duty to get it right.

Leading thinkers and practitioners have embraced the principles of the CMS. The publication of ITIL v3 was a catalyst for this inflection. It will take a long time, probably years, to abandon the CMDB term, so we will all continue to use it in conversation. For the purposes of this book, we call the entity a CMS. This is the future. Because we encourage its use, it is our responsibility to follow our own advice. We use CMDB only in a historical context throughout the remainder of this book.

CHAPTER 3

Planning for the CMS

It seems like everyone is always planning these days, but never doing all that much. We plan budgets, projects, programs, resource allocations, finances, and millions of other things. So why does it appear that some people refuse to plan for the Configuration Management System (CMS)? One answer might be that the existence of a CMS can drastically change the power structure in a company and expose longtime deficiencies. This might drive some of those impacted to sabotage the planning cycle of your effort through political means or by demanding unrealistic timelines and scope from you. Another answer might be that, it only appears that planning did not happen because it was done more secretively. Leadership might have felt that because of the anticipated pushback from detractors, they needed to deploy a large portion of the initiative before there was sufficient time to mount an opposition. We are not promoting secretive initiatives; however, you do need to understand that there are people in your organization who do not want this to happen and will cause you delays if you allow them.

In public meetings and planning sessions, you will be hard pressed to find many people openly opposing the concept of building a CMS. However, when it comes down to people stepping up and offering up their resources and repositories as the starting point for the CMS effort, the support level and attitude may change very quickly. You will encounter resistance in the form of people being unavailable, budgets not having been allocated, or managers simply saying that they can't take on the workload to change processes during the proposed timeframe. All the excuses are legitimate, but they are nonetheless excuses. They are protecting their turf, after all.

It is for these reasons that planning is so critical to the success of your CMS initiative. You need to carefully lay out your plan in a way that is the least threatening to the leaders of these departmental repositories and processes. They need to feel as though they are not losing their autonomy, but are in fact gaining from being a foundational element of the CMS. The success you have in getting these people invested in your mission at its inception will be the amount of success you can expect at the end of your CMS initiative. The other approach is, of course, doing everything in a "black-ops" manner and revealing it only when it's too late to oppose. You need to be careful if you take this approach because you're not going to make many friends. If, however, you have the support and directive of senior management to do it this way, you will likely accomplish much more in less time.

This chapter provides you with thought and decision-making guidance. Use this guidance and adapt the concepts to your own unique situation. At times, you might find that the guidance appears to be inconsistent. This is because there is no one solution that will fit every company. You need to understand who your company is, where they are on the IT Infrastructure Library (ITIL)/IT Service Management (ITSM) maturity path, and most importantly, whether the recommendation is relevant to an organization of your size. Take the guidance, combine it with the knowledge you already have of your company, and define the plans and tactics that will work for you to be successful. Remember that what works for a large company might not work for a small company, and what works for one bureaucracy might not work in another. What all of the guidance shares is an approach, one that will walk you through the same thought and decision-making process regardless of the company.

For example, if "Acme 25, Inc.," is a Fortune 25 company, its IT budget is going to be considerably larger than "Newbie 500, LLC," a Fortune 500 company. What this means is that Acme 25, Inc., is probably spending a lot more money to buy software distribution and monitoring and capacity tools. If Acme 25, Inc., is a multinational organization, it might have no choice but to invest in these technologies to stay in business. Newbie 500, LLC, on the other hand, does not need to spend a lot of money on those tools because it might only have a couple of hundred employees in two or three buildings and can do a lot of its operations manually because of its smaller size. So, when we discuss how to leverage tools and how many CMDBs you need, you will need to factor in whether your company is similar to Acme 25, Inc., or Newbie 500, LLC, to determine what might be relevant to you.

One thing that remains consistent across initiatives in all companies is this type of program cannot be managed in a traditional waterfall manner. This initiative is filled with fits-and-starts, and throughout the first half or two-thirds of the program, most of your effort is in parallel. Some elements may sit at 5% complete, then jump to 50%, then sit again for weeks with no progress. This "erratic" pattern is especially true when designing and building your federated links. Be patient with this and look into alternative project management approaches used in Agile or object-oriented development efforts.

We are proponents of automating as much of the CMS as possible because a lot of it can be performed faster and more reliably over the long run. We ask that you take the time to understand the meaning of what you read in this chapter, and not just memorize the words, so that you can apply this understanding to your unique situation. The thought process and decision points for implementing a CMS are identical, but answers may vary greatly from your peers. Even if you decide that aspects of your implementation need to be done more covertly, the process will still be the same—only how to execute will be different. Remember that the ultimate goal is to *deliver value for your company*, and only your company can define what value means to you.

Do You Need a CMS and Why?

If you are still asking the question of whether or not you need a CMS, it means that you still do not fully understand what a CMS is. The reason we can say this with relative confidence is because if you are already operating an IT department, you must have repositories in place that enable you to do so. They may not be perfect, efficient, or aggregated through a singular portal, but they are in essence the foundation of your CMS. The data you have today is the start of your CMS, but you just don't call it that. Remember that the definition of a CMS is a repository or collection of repositories that are used to store configuration records throughout the items' lifecycles. What the definition is telling you is that an organization needs to be able to efficiently access data about objects in the IT environment, and if you are operating an IT department today, you should already have a variety of repositories around to help you. The lack of quality or incomplete nature of your data in the current repositories might be your biggest challenge today, and that is where the ITIL processes and CMS Governance will help you increase the efficiency and comprehensiveness of the data.

To take the CMS definition a step further in maturity, the CMS must tie in with your IT Service Management efforts; otherwise, it is simply just another repository. Like any other expenditure, the reason you want to venture into implementing something like a CMS is if there is value to the company in doing so. Therefore, if you want to provide service-based value to your business, you need to be able to provide information about items in your environment that might impact the services and products that your company delivers.

There are no company leaders today who can honestly say that they are perfectly content in how they deliver IT services to business partners, mainly because this effort never ends and is always changing, just like business. IT leaders have talked about "running IT like a business" for years, but many of them are not business savvy and hence never really got far with that mission. Pressure from business partners to run more efficiently and transparently has forced these IT leaders to look at ITIL, ITSM, and Service-Oriented Architecture (SOA) as a means by which to finally deliver on the demands from their business partners. In order for this to happen, however, a lot of information about how the IT operation runs is needed. With that available, you can then work to detect trends and gaps in your IT operation that need to be addressed.

The CMS and supporting CMDBs are the foundational elements that will lead to a successful ITIL/ITSM implementation. *"Once in place, they can also be used in support of SOA efforts if your organization heads in that direction. We don't want to get into details about SOA because it is a topic worthy of its own book, and we could not do it any justice here, especially with a debate still going on about what it really is. What we can say is that we're confident that the data aggregated in your CMS will provide a wealth of information for your SOA initiative."* As mentioned previously, every company has data, but not all companies are able to transform it into useful information. The disparate data sources currently in use need to somehow become interwoven with each other to provide a clear picture of the environment from a business perspective. For example, the spreadsheet that contains the inventory of servers can be tied in with the MS Access DB used by the networking team to track the network topology. That then needs to be tied in with the application development team that builds and deploys applications. Finally, that collection can then be tied into an Asset Management system. The result is a collection of data that, once interconnected, can provide the operations area with a map of what servers and network devices support a particular application.

The ITIL purists reading the previous paragraph might have clamored that "applications are not services" and "you have to define your services before you do anything else." Although we do wholeheartedly agree with that philosophy, we are also realists who recognize that there is a tremendous amount of value to be reaped well before reaching ITIL utopia. That is partly why we chose to write a book in this pragmatic instructional manner versus an academic style that would leave the reader asking once again, "What is it that I am supposed to do next?" If yours is a small company just starting out, which does not have a lot of structure in place, maybe you can start with defining services and driving the remainder of your CMS. However, most companies already have a lot of processes and infrastructure in place, so they don't have that luxury.

If your company has not invested heavily in technology and does not have many sources to cultivate the necessary data for your CMS, you might be better off with the services approach because you will have to focus on specific services rather than an enterprisewide initiative. If you need to generate all or most of the data to create the image of how your infrastructure items impact your business, you will likely start with defining your most critical services and then determining how you will acquire the data. On the other hand, if you already have the majority of data available in existing sources, you can provide value very quickly by piecing together the infrastructure items that make up your applications. Similarly, you should have separate teams working on defining the services that your organization delivers and determining which applications help to deliver that service. If your software engineering maturity is high enough, maybe you can even determine which components within the applications help to deliver the service. This is where SOA comes into play with the CMS and how they can support each other. The more mature you are in either of these areas, the more successful the other will be.

The short answer to whether or not you need a CMS is yes, you do need one; however, everyone needs to recognize that they may not look the same, especially if the companies are of different sizes and in different industries. The reason you need one is because it is the only way that you will be able to truly understand the IT components that can impact a business service. A fully populated and managed CMS enables you to prevent outages and increase your Mean Time Between Failure (MTBF) through assisting the change activity. It also helps to minimize the impact of outages and decrease your Mean Time To Resolution (MTTR) by providing the Incident Management personnel with information about the business service that is out and all the IT components that might cause the outage. Besides helping Problem Management with root cause analysis and trend analysis, your architecture teams, as part of Availability Management and Continual Service Improvement, can leverage outage information to determine if certain designs or equipment are failing under certain conditions versus other conditions. This is again an area where SOA would benefit tremendously from having a CMS in place.

Reality: What Is the State of the CMS Market?

At the time of writing this book, the CMS market is in the midst of a major growth spurt, fueled by intense interest in the CMDB. Much of this dynamic is unfortunately being steered by misguided interpretations of exactly what a CMDB is and into what form it should evolve. We have been clear that a

CMDB in its traditional form is not viable for the comprehensive requirements of ITSM.

We intentionally avoid identifying vendors and products as much as we possibly can. The market is shifting rapidly with mergers, acquisitions, and failures, so some names will be obsolete by the time you read this. As a substitution, we offer the following current and emerging classifications for CMDB and CMS products. Whether true CMS tools or not, all are positioned at some level in this market. We present our vision for the future of each:

- **Asset databases in CMDB clothing.** These CMDBs currently capture the most mind share because their vendors are large and recognized the CMDB demand as it grew from existing Asset Management databases. Like any good vendor with a large marketing budget, they launched intense campaigns to establish their leadership. It paid off for two vendors worth identifying: BMC Software and Hewlett-Packard (HP). No CMDB landscape discussion can omit these two companies because of their heavy influence on the early CMDB market.

  BMC acquired the Remedy business from Peregrine Systems[1] in late 2002.[2] Although the big prize with Remedy was the Service Desk automation software, hidden inside was an asset database. Remedy users became enamored with the asset database and began using it as a rudimentary CMDB. As BMC saw ITIL accelerate soon after the Remedy purchase, it started to reshape the asset database into something more in line with ITIL's CMDB. On January 24, 2005, BMC announced Atrium,[3] arguably the first major CMDB.

---

1. Peregrine Systems was a high-flying management software vendor that became a symbol of corporate malfeasance along with WorldCom and Enron. Peregrine's accounting scandal was smaller than these other icons of greed, but it was forced into bankruptcy in 2002 and was charged with "massive fraud" by the SEC on June 30, 2003 (see http://www.sec.gov/litigation/litreleases/lr18205.htm).

2. BMC's press release announcing the closure of the Remedy acquisition is on the web at http://www.bmc.com/corporate/nr2002/111902_2.html.

3. BMC's press release announcing the introduction of its Atrium CMDB is on the web at http://www.bmc.com/BMC/News/CDA/hou_PressRelease_detail/0,3519,8573740_8630060_34366855,00.html.

HP acquired the remaining assets of Peregrine Systems in 2005.[4] Similar to the BMC-Remedy deal, the main attraction was Peregrine's ServiceCenter product for Service Desk automation, but ServiceCenter came with a companion product called AssetCenter. Like Remedy, AssetCenter became a CMDB of sorts in many IT organizations and has evolved into a key component of what HP now calls its Universal CMDB.

We violate our vendor-agnostic policy just a bit more by mentioning something about CA and IBM because they are the other two vendors in what has become known as the "Big Four" family of management software vendors. Both are also building significant CMDB product capabilities, albeit via different paths than BMC and HP.

CMDBs born of an Asset Management heritage are not the exclusive domain of the management software behemoths, but the larger vendors have understandably garnered the most attention.

This class of CMDB currently represents the most popular category. As such, its momentum will carry them forward as leading CMDB elements. Their role will morph from monolithic models to become aggregation points for the coming CMS. The vendors are already promising federation in line with the CMDBf specification and accept the reality that other vendors' data sources will also be included in the overall CMS. This is to be expected because the largest are all CMDBf founding members.

- **CMDB aggregators.** A newer class of vendors is delivering impressive technology for genuine federation. Most are small emerging vendors with more innovation than marketing muscle. They all call their products CMDBs, but they are the early vestiges of CMS, complete with object-oriented models and federation. As aggregators, these products embody the higher-level service abstractions needed to complete the CMDB federation we describe in Chapter 4, "The Federated CMS Architecture."

---

4. HP's press release announcing the closure of its acquisition of Peregrine Systems is in this December 19, 2005, press release: http://www.hp.com/hpinfo/newsroom/press/2005/051219xa.html.

Because these products represent the future of the CMS, we expect these vendors to be acquired. Suitors could replicate their innovations, but their most logical path will be via acquisition. Delays from internal development will prove prohibitive to meeting timely market demand.

- **Monitors.** Management tools such as network and server monitors have been commonplace for over a decade in most large organizations. To perform their monitoring and alerting functions, they must possess some level of understanding of the systems they monitor. This data can be viewed as a very crude, but temporary, CMDB for the narrowly focused domain that the tool is monitoring. Do not expect this to serve the CMS into the future.

  You can leverage the tools you've been using for the last 10 years as you build your CMS, but the market will transition away from capturing configuration data natively in the monitor. Whereas the configuration data is now hard-coded in the monitoring tool, it will eventually need to be decoupled. Future monitors will use modular configuration interfaces, taking data from the CMS instead of relying on the former proprietary, rigid internal data.

  Monitors require a subset of the data needed for full CMS purposes. This limits the value of internal data from monitoring tools. It is better to migrate the data capture from internal to external sources. The monitor will reference the data it needs from the CMS—no more, no less. By decoupling the configuration data from the monitor, the monitor becomes yet another use case for the CMS. This is exactly as it should be.

- **Discovery tools.** Automated discovery tools come in the form of traditional monitors and dedicated configuration discovery tools. As we pointed out previously, discovery by traditional monitors is rapidly becoming obsolete. The dedicated discovery tools offer much richer data, and their developers have already anticipated the need for these products to serve as distributed CMDBs, more appropriately known as the federated Management Data Repositories (MDRs) of the CMS. These products tend to be newer market introductions, appearing on the market around 2003 and only beginning to reach beyond early adopters by mid-2008.

  The real beauty of discovery tools is their ability to maintain an accurate portrayal of reality. These tools will tell you the truth about your environment because by their very name, they are discovering the existing elements and their attributes.

Discovery will become increasingly popular and useful as the CMS lens into the truth. Today, many are standalone products, especially in the application domain, but they will become absorbed more and more into software modules that focus on both Configuration and Change Management. Discovery becomes a much more powerful proposition when it is combined with the ability to actually help execute changes to configuration items.

- **Domain-specific configuration and change automation.** These tools incorporate both configuration discovery and the ability to automate varying levels of changes to the discovered CIs. Some of these are called provisioning or release management tools especially in the respective domains of servers and applications. These tools will become similar in function across technology domains and their categorical identity will be Configuration and Change Management (CCM). CCM is the automation technology embodying the Configuration and Change Management processes of ITIL.

This normalization of the CCM tools will occur slowly through 2010, whereupon converged CCM products will appear and enjoy a short but bright spotlight in the greater CMS market. This period will be bright because converged CCM will offer incredible benefits to service operations. Indeed, the more narrowly focused server (SCCM) and network (NCCM) products are already popular because they eliminate a lot of the time-consuming and error-prone labor. When the function is applicable across an entire business service, the benefits will compound and funding will flow liberally to the vendors who can deliver them.

The limelight of the independent, converged CCM market will be short-lived (three to four years) because the basic CCM capabilities will commoditize quickly, and they will be absorbed into broader operational automation products. This doesn't mean that an incident resolution tool will have a full CCM embedded within it and a capacity management tool will have a separate but equal CCM. These and other tools will share a common CCM module. It will be a sophisticated module by today's standards, but merely a shared module nonetheless.

One fact remains constant throughout all of this evolution: Value lies not in raw data, but in what you do with that raw data. The incident resolution and capacity management tools encode more intelligent processing of the data, so these will offer the greater value. The CCM will be included as a "free" part of the solution. If the module already exists, that existing CCM can be used in lieu of installing a new component. Again, this elaborate view of the CMS and "free" converged CCM is a vision for the 2013 to 2015 timeframe, not 2009.

- **Software distribution.** This is a product category that is quickly being subsumed into CCM products. Software distribution is just another term for Change and Release Management, but one whose obsolescence is already in progress. This category will effectively disappear by late 2009 or early 2010. Change Management is used for the controls including approvals and oversight of Release Management, which handles the building, testing, and deployment of the software.

    Just look back a few years to 2001 and 2002, when patch management was all the rage in the management software market. In those days, security breaches were making headlines because the cause of the breaches was inadequately maintained software patches. Patch management was a short-lived phenomenon because the pain point was not limited to patches; it was a general CCM issue. What applies to patches applies to all software configuration issues, since a patch is just another form of software configuration change.

    Software distribution is nearly identical to patch management, so it faces a similar fate.

- **Business intelligence.** Where the CMS is reflecting the highest levels of business services and business processes, we are currently limited to manual population of the models. Many management software products offer business-level modeling, and these models will soon find their way into the CMS. The hurdle to overcome is how quickly the vendors can deliver an automated discovery solution that will detect the services with minimal ongoing human intervention. Most business processes do not contain instrumentation that can present configuration data in a format consumable by a management tool, or a CMDB for that matter.

    Technologies do exist that already contain this data, but they are not commonly used in a way that benefits the CMS. Business intelligence tools have been used by business process planners for years. Business application platforms such as SAP have business processes already encoded within them. These systems are used for fundamental business automation, so the data exists. We just need a mechanism to access it.

    Political barriers trump technology as the culprits for this dilemma. IT operation functions and business functions have historically been islands unto themselves. Not only was data exchange not performed, but the two entities were also so diametrically opposed that they didn't even know they could benefit from one another.

ITIL, and especially ITIL v3, are finally changing this institutionalized opposition. Common sense is finally starting to prevail, although many of you will find that cultural inertia will make this a slow metamorphosis. As you build a tighter relationship across the IT and business frontier, explore ways to capture business-level information in the CMS.

Newer application technologies such as SOA and web services hold some promise here. They inherently hold value as the building blocks of business services. They also incorporate instrumentation that can be tapped to understand the structure and behavior of the business services and business processes. Older application technologies shrouded these details from view, forcing us to revert to elaborate discovery tools to reverse engineer the applications and obtain what we need. It is far better to have the application itself tell us than it is to require us to ask. This is what we achieve with SOA and web services. There is little hope for legacy applications beyond rewrites in the SOA world or continued development of the reverse-engineering tools.

- **Good old-fashioned databases.** As much as we prefer to view the CMS or even a CMDB as more than a relational database, many traditional databases do and will play a role in the CMS. Many of these will continue to exist in products that are currently (and incorrectly) called CMDBs. Some will reside in homegrown databases that may have existed for years. Some will be in the form of other business data that was and will always reside in databases.

  A great example of this latter category is an HR database. Products like PeopleSoft are pervasive and hold a generous amount of data about the human elements in the CMS. All of these are technically accessible. The mission is to work the political angles with the HR department. Thankfully, the HR department guards our personal information tightly (at least we hope they do!). Gaining access to the right data for the CMS may be difficult. You will need to establish trust with the HR guardians and extract only the tiny subset of data needed to establish unique personal and organizational identity for the people involved with business services (everyone in the company). Anything unrelated (such as social security numbers, medical history, and home phone numbers) should remain locked down and inaccessible. This personal data then ties into the CMS to assist with authentication, authorization, and accounting (AAA), as well as reporting structure to determine notification hierarchy and escalations.

This is the state of the CMS market as of late 2008. Significant evolution of CMS products and the vendors themselves will occur through 2015. Federation is just starting to gain some recognition and will take about two years to reach a point where you can realize its full benefits. It is unwise to wait for stability, however, as you can take measures now (get education, start planning, and research discovery tools) that will help you greatly as this all unfolds.[5]

Acceptance: Selling the CMS to the Organization

There are multiple selling activities that you need to plan and execute because there are a variety of audiences that need to be sold on the idea, and each one needs to be approached differently. You need to take on a used car salesman sort of approach to it because the story needs to change with each audience. This does not mean that you are lying to any of them or telling half truths, but more importantly, you are changing your approach and tactic because each audience has different interests and desires. Just remember, the Service Desk person won't care if it costs millions dollars to implement a CMS if it saves him hours of difficult research, whereas the first thing your senior executive will probably care about is how much it will cost up front and save in the end. Target your message and deliver it clearly.

There are possibly more than four areas that you need to sell the CMS to, but if you target the Service Desk personnel, Subject Matter Experts (SMEs), business partners, and management, you should be able to define a marketing and sales campaign to cover your entire basis. We mentioned marketing because that is exactly what you are going to have to do a lot of. Marketing builds the demand for the CMS and can be the difference between being funded or not—without the demand, senior management might not feel the pressure to fund your CMS initiative. We are not sales and marketing professionals, so please don't expect this to be a how-to guide for marketing and

---

5. The June 30, 2008, Forrester Research report, "A Federated CMDB Remains Distant, But Start Now," by Glenn O'Donnell (http://www.forrester.com/Research/Document/0,7211,46149,00.html) covers the issues, opportunities, and guidance to developing a CMDB strategy based on federation.

selling your CMS initiative. We strongly urge you to seek out someone in your organization who has some knowledge in this field and ask that person to lay out a strong strategy with you. What we do cover is some background on the three groups and why you should be selling the CMS to them.

Service Desk Personnel

The Service Desk personnel should be your easiest sell because they are the major benefactors of a CMS. Once deployed, the CMS will enable them to more quickly assess incident situations, make more effective impact assessments, and generally reduce their manual data investigation activities, allowing them to work on more productive and stimulating tasks. In most companies, these individuals spend a large portion of their time hunting for data they believe exists so that they can make a five-second decision once it is found. By a large majority, their time is spent trying to get the information to make a simple decision or recommendation, and that is just not effective nor a career path that most people would want. Convincing these people that you are trying to build a CMS that may reduce their manual efforts by orders of magnitude should be a very easy sell, and you would expect them to be the first on board to help.

This group is generally the most excited about the promise of a CMS, but it is also the group that can bury your ambition before you start if you don't sell the purpose and potential properly. The reason is that these roles are generally scripted in nature, and any deviation from that script is not typically well received. You need to make sure that they are on board with your initiative. The key to getting them on board is to make sure they believe that the technology changes that come with the CMS will affect their processes in a positive manner. We have seen numerous times where the "What's in it for me?" question is not answered because the individuals are not thinking about how they could change the way they work for the better. For example, shaving off 15 seconds per call at 40,000 calls per month allows a Service Desk to redeploy one agent and save the business partner the same in Full-Time Equivalent (FTE) costs. In theory, the requirements to build a CMS should come from each process owner, but we have found that for some reason, process owners don't often know what they want—especially from a future state perspective—and they need help shifting their paradigm.

You need to be conscientious about how the CMS can impact this group and ensure that new routines can be easily adapted around the CMS. You may think that one extra click of the mouse to access a data element is not a big deal, but for the Service Desk person who has to do it hundreds of times per day, it becomes a big deal quickly. Be sure to include these individuals in your design session when you lay out the end-user interface and the steps they'll need to perform in order to do their work. Include them in the testing and have them work with you on defining the testing requirements. Get them involved early, and make sure they feel that they are an integral part of the design and build of the CMS. This ensures that they buy what you are selling. Remember that these individuals are generally not technical, so you need to keep the information at a technical level that is appropriate for them. Do not overload them with too much information or intricate details that you, as a technologist, would want. They are not technologists, so providing too much technical information might simply confuse them and decrease their ability to do their jobs.

The following are Service Desk selling points and cautions:

- Reduce time manually researching possible solutions.

- More easily determine what services and/or users might be impacted by an outage.

- Reduce call time/increase volume of calls handled.

- Be sensitive to the procedural/scripted nature of their work.

- Ensure that you get buy-in during design and development.

- Be sure to deliver data at an appropriate level of technical expertise.

Subject Matter Experts

SMEs are the second group of individuals to whom you will sell the CMS. You will be working with many of these individuals in two different roles. In one of the roles, they provide data to you to use in the CMS. In the second role, they act as consumers and users of the data aggregated in the CMS. This makes your selling tactic more delicate because it is likely that some of these individuals will lose authority over data that they currently control. They may see this as an attack on their fiefdom and oppose all efforts to weaken it. What you need to convince these people of is that in the end, even if they lose authority over some of the data, they will still perform their jobs more efficiently. They will also gain access to data from other areas of the company that is already sanitized and merged with the data elements they provided.

The process integrations that leverage the CMS enable these SMEs to possibly receive notifications of changes and incidents in their domains sooner; as Tier 2 or Tier 3 support personnel, they will be able to respond more quickly. These individuals are obviously technically savvy, so try to entice them to join your effort by demonstrating the value of having all the data available through one interface rather than multiple interfaces. For example, remind them that they might no longer need to search and cross-reference multiple sources to determine what application is running on the server. Use this sort of logic and sales tactics to get them to support the CMS initiative.

The following are SME selling points and cautions:

- Reduce time manually researching faulty item by narrowing down area of research.

- Better understanding of what services and/or users might be impacted by an outage and thereby able to better prioritize workload.

- No longer maintain certain types of data themselves that is not specific to their domain.

- Ability to leverage data from other domains that can help to supplement the information they already have.

- Be aware that the SMEs may be reluctant to share their data because it would mean that the data would need to be placed under the rigor of Change and Configuration Management control.

- SMEs may perceive you as a threat to their fiefdom and thus downplay the comprehensiveness and quality of their data to avoid inclusion and disruption.

- You will encounter a lot of finger pointing about how good/bad sources are. Stay out of those discussions and stay on message about the value you can deliver to them.

Business Partners

Your business partners are ultimately the people you need to sell to because they are the true benefactors of a CMS. Having a CMS that can provide a decomposition of the services and applications you support for them, and presenting that with a financial perspective, is a tremendous accomplishment. Leveraging a CMS to provide them with visibility into the cost of services is a gold mine. If you were to approach them as if they were external buyers of your services, you would need to demonstrate detailed costs and a level of operational transparency that most internal IT organizations are not capable of doing today. Our collective inability to demonstrate this transparency to our business partners could be the reason why we are seeing a lot of senior management changing jobs, and not always voluntarily.

The following are business partner selling points and cautions:

- Reduced Mean Time To Resolution (MTTR)/outage duration.

- Transparency of costs.

- Association between expenditures and business service delivered.

- Potential of providing end users with a "heads-up" on imminent outages.

- Ability to operate in a more "provider-consumer" model.

- Cost savings are "soft" and not always "bottom-line" or tangible.

- Exposure to uncomfortable questions about current inefficiencies and expenditures.

- Business partners might decide that they can "purchase" services from external provider for less.

Management

Selling the CMS to your leadership is an interesting topic because most times, you actually begin the CMS journey in response to their request. Now you find yourself trying to sell the concept and asking for budget from the same people who asked you to implement it. It's a strange dynamic, but one that we have seen often. The reality is that there are a lot of unknowns and even more gray areas when it comes to implementing process efficiency initiatives partly because there is no real end to the initiative. This is where the selling actually begins with this group of people. You must, without ambiguity, provide very clear milestones with equally clear Critical Success Factors (CSF). It goes without saying that you need to meet these milestones to stay funded.

For you to propose CSFs, you need to establish a baseline of where your organization is so that you can measure your progress and present it to senior management. This baseline will help you establish a starting point with your senior management so they know very clearly what the current state of the organization is. Be careful with this one because the owners of the areas that you are trying to baseline might not like the results and may make it difficult for you to get good metrics. Find out from your senior management what their major objectives for the initiative are and establish Key Performance Indicators (KPI) around those objectives to measure your progress. Make sure your leadership fully understands and appreciates the demands and needs of the Service Desk personnel, Subject Matter Experts, and business partners as well. If, for some reason, your leadership does not agree with these requirements, go back to these groups and make sure that they understand that your senior management does not agree with them, and thus you will not be delivering that capability. You must set the proper expectation, or else you will not succeed in their eyes regardless of how good or bad your solution is.

The following are management selling points and cautions:

- Enable management to talk with business partners in nontechnical terms.

- Ability to "price" services more accurately and based on real data.

- Opportunity to show business partners that it is operating efficiently.

- Ability to deliver more stable and reliable services with fewer and less disruptive outages.

- May try to drive initiative as primarily a "cost-savings" project.

- May not have strong enough will to ride out up-front costs and changes to their organization and thereby not fund it long term through full transformation.

- Day-to-day issues rise on the priority list; they no longer see the CMS initiative as high priority, allowing the organization to go back to their old ways.

Unfortunately, we have all seen great technology projects that have failed because of poor salesmanship and the mediocre technology projects that were hailed as tremendous successes because of the sales and marketing spin. The reality is that it is part of the equation, and we have to deal with it. As technologists, we see the purity, purpose, and value but sometimes can't appreciate the cost-benefit aspect. The same holds true in reverse of the nontechnologists. They determine a certain cost-benefit ratio, and that is all they see. The really successful people and projects find a way to meld the two together in an acceptable balance that delivers value to the organization. This balance is what you need to seek in your own organization and initiative.

Structure: How Will the CMS Fit In?

ITIL v3 and its explanation of the CMS helps dispel the many misconceptions about the CMS and its predecessor, the CMDB. These misconceptions can make it difficult to determine how a CMS will fit in to the organization or business. The misconceptions are primarily rooted in the use of "DB" as part of CMDB name in ITIL v2 and then secondly reinforced by the marketing efforts of vendors. The label CMDB was replaced by CMS in ITIL v3, and many of you who have studied the v3 books have a better appreciation for the CMS, what it truly is, and how the "CMDBs" support it. We believe we're stuck with the second reason, unfortunately, and it is unlikely that the vendors will stop marketing products using sales-enhancing techniques regardless of the potential confusion it might add.

As mentioned previously, ITIL v3 addresses the role of the CMS in a much better manner than in v2. Unfortunately, however, ITIL v3 cannot do anything about the marketing departments of the software vendors in the IT Service Management space. Their job is to catch your eye with their fancy trifold, lure you in, and turn you over to the salespeople and account managers to close the deal. They've done this primarily by rebranding their products to mimic the ITIL glossary. This is sort of a harsh statement, but we have all seen examples where an Asset Management system suddenly became a CMDB and software distribution products became Release Management tools. In all fairness to the vendors, they are not all the same, and many have added functionality to at least get close to the functionality needed to deliver on the promise made by their new ITIL branding. What this does mean is that everyone contemplating the purchase of software to fulfill an ITIL project must be vigilant in putting forward the requirements they want in a very clear manner and to some extent, disregard what the vendor has named the product.

A CMS fits into your operation much in the same way that your current repositories that maintain your IT data do. The difference is that the CMS has more control, audit, and verification processes surrounding it than do your current repositories. A statement that we have always liked using is, *"A CMS is no different than any other database if it does not have the rigor and control of the Change and Configuration Management activities surrounding its contents. What makes a database a CMS is the process governing its content."* This statement cannot be taken literally or word for word because it implies that the CMS is a singular database, which it is not; however, we think that the point is clearer when we state it that way.

The information utilized through the CMS by the ITIL processes will become invaluable. It will, over time, replace the need for the operations teams to go to other sources for reliable data. In some cases, they will actually still be utilizing the data that originated in the smaller departmental source but through the CMS in a federated fashion. Where the CMS benefits those users is where it has aggregated and verified data from that source, enabling the end user to forego the need to access the originating source and attain more of a "one-stop-shopping" effect by going to the CMS only.

Over time, as the scope of your ITIL initiative grows, so too will the demands that you place on your CMS. The depth and breadth of it will have to expand in order for it to meet your ITIL needs. If you leverage the power of federation, you will be able to make this transition more smoothly for your end users. Remember that the purpose of the CMS is to provide the end users with fast access to reliable information so that they can perform change impact assessments, monitor the lifecycle of components affected by a change, and assist in the Incident and Problem Management space as well as others. You can reduce the number of repositories that these end users access every time they perform their jobs by aggregating and federating the data they need. This alone will entrench the CMS in their daily routine, and they will make sure that it fits in exactly where it needs to.

In the ideal world, the CMS will also fit in by eliminating the need for some of the smaller ancillary repositories that are currently in place. You can make an argument that once the CMS is in place and you are acquiring all the data you need for your ITIL processes through it, there is no need for the smaller ancillary repositories that aren't contributing. We fully understand that there is no ideal environment and that the CMS is not supposed to be a data warehouse or data-mart. You must understand, however, that every organization is in the business of running as efficiently as possible and is seeking to maximize profits. That means that at times, you might need to part ways with the ITIL utopia path, be a realist, and leverage the CMS as a quasi data-mart.

Time is money, and people spending time searching for data to do their job are costing the company money. It might be directly, because they cannot resolve an outage as quickly as they'd like, or indirectly, because they are spending two hours performing a change impact assessment instead of one hour doing the impact assessment and the extra hour reviewing and closing changes. Reviewing and closing changes unfortunately is not done as often as needed typically because people are overloaded with other work. This can cause errors to repeat themselves and never get detected in the request for change documentation upon submission.

The controversial aspect of the ancillary repositories is whether or not the CMS should ever engulf one in its entirety. First, let us state again that the CMS is not a data warehouse; however, from a business perspective, you need to make a very strong argument as to why you would want to pay for and maintain an ancillary repository when the majority of its data is already in the CMS. We do *not* recommend that you do this as part of your primary ITIL initiative. We do recommend, however, that if there is a cost savings—directly or indirectly by replatforming a small ancillary repository to the CMS without negative impact—you consider it a separate project. We also recommend that you fund and manage it separately from your ITIL CMS initiative simply to ensure that no one gets confused as to the purpose of the CMS. There is no question that there are many opportunities to streamline operations by replatforming or retiring small ancillary repositories. Leverage the CMS platform to deliver value where it makes sense, even if it is not pure ITIL.

Quantity: How Many CMDBs Are Needed in the CMS?

The number of CMDBs or repositories that you need for your CMS frankly is irrelevant. What you need to focus on is how you can most efficiently obtain all the data you need for the CMS. Whether this takes 3 or 30 data sources is not of any relevance; what is relevant is that you need the data to satisfy your business requirements, and if it takes 30 sources, that's what you need to use.

Let's take, for example, an organization that is well organized, has invested millions of dollars on operational excellence initiatives, and has reduced the number of data repositories needed for the operational areas by 50% in the last 10 years. This company might need only a handful of sources, such as your Asset Management and human resource systems, the type of systems that you can't eliminate. Additionally, you need a few other essential operational systems that have all of your services, applications, IT equipment, and monitoring information. The opposite of this is the company that is of identical size, but decided to not implement an operational excellence initiative, and therefore has a different repository for every different type of network device and has multiple Asset Management and human resources systems. Both companies could be identical in size and produce the same widgets, but if they were given the same ITIL requirements to execute, there is absolutely no possible way that they could deliver it utilizing the same number of repositories. The second company described would obviously need to leverage many more repositories than the first. It would cost more for the integration, take longer to implement, and be more prone to failure due to a higher number of integrations.

Now that we have successfully not answered your question, let's focus on "what kinds" of CMDBs you need versus "how many" CMDBs you need. The first driver is, of course, your business requirements. Because we can't determine that in a book, we address all the different areas of data that you might need in your implementation. After you have your requirements, you can reference this section to help remind you of whether or not you have identified all the possible Configuration Items (CIs) you need to deal with based on your business requirements. As mentioned previously, you need to determine whether you can get all your information for a specific CI from one source or aggregate it from multiple sources.

Creating three groups of objects might help to simplify things, so let's say that everything in the IT environment has to be of one of these three types, as follows:

- Hardware

- Software

- Services

Within hardware, you need to make sure you address information for servers, workstations, network devices, storage, displays, logical and physical components, frames, racks, chassis, printers, and telecommunications. You may also choose to manage the components within these objects such as hard disks, disk arrays, network cards, graphics adapters, processors, and memory. Fortunately, the hardware hierarchy is relatively straightforward compared to software.

For software, it is more difficult because the hierarchies are ambiguous. If you do not manage the software elements any lower than your business applications, you do not need to spend a lot of time designing a complex software hierarchy to suit your needs. Besides your business applications, some other software you might want to consider tracking is operating systems, DBMS, application servers, collaboration and email software, and middleware, depending on the criticality of these components in your environment. Remember, though, that you need to be able to track and manage everything you decide to put in the CMS, and every element needs to have a single owner identified.

Services are trickier in some ways and simpler in others. Your organization must first define all IT and business services that will be managed under the ITSM initiative. Without this, you will not be able to define a structure or identify the sources from which you can pull the information to satisfy your requirements. If, however, you have defined your IT and business services, you should be able to integrate with that repository and leverage the existing work. The problem you might encounter is figuring out what hardware and software actually support each service. Because most of the current-day software was not written under an SOA model, your applications are probably not segregated into modules that can be neatly mapped to a service.

There are many more objects, categories, and subcategories of both hardware and software that you can choose to place under the control of Change and Configuration Management than were mentioned previously. Every object and/or data element you place in the CMS must undergo the full rigor of these processes, and the owners of these data elements must ensure that they can provide the level of data quality that the CMS needs. Also, you must be careful that your end users are able to perform the duties as defined by the processes to maintain the data in the CMS as it moves through its lifecycle. You might want to place a hundred different types of elements in the CMS, but do you really have the human resources to manually maintain it or the technology investment to automate the maintenance of it?

If you are looking for more help on what sort of objects exist and how they are composed, we suggest you look into the efforts of the Distributed Management Task Force (DMTF). They have been working for many years with technology companies to create the Common Information Model (CIM), which is an effort to provide "a common definition of management information systems, networks, applications, and services, and allows for vendor extensions."[6] The CIM as it stands is too detailed for a CMS, but there are some efforts within the DMTF to adapt a version of the CIM so that it can be used as a CMS model. These new DMTF efforts are discussed in more depth in Chapter 4.

Accountability: Who "Owns" the CMS?

The CMS, once fully established, aggregates information from a variety of sources and disseminates it to multiple destinations in both an active and passive manner. The data contained in the CMS and maintained by the Change and Configuration Management ITIL control activities will be leveraged by most of the IT organization in some fashion. In order for it to be reliable,

---

6. Distributed Management Task Force, Inc., Common Information Model Standards (http://www.dmtf.org/standards/cim).

however, there needs to be a clear owner of the platform, as well as of each element it governs.

The difference with the ownership of the CMS is that it cannot be one single individual or department; it has to be a collection of people who come together to form a governing body over the CMS. The Configuration Control Board is this governing body. It should have equal representation from both contributing and consuming disciplines. As with any governing body, it needs to be small enough to be productive, but large enough to factor in the needs and concerns of the entire organization. For a higher likelihood of success, tie a portion of each member's annual financial incentive, like their bonus or salary increase, to the overall success of the CMS platform. This forces them to think more globally than locally.

Instead of spending too much time on explaining how to form a governing body, which we assume most companies know how to do, we want to spend some time on explaining in our words what the function of the Configuration Control Board should be and provide some guidance on the participants. We recommend that you refer to ITIL v3 Service Transition 6.3.2.3 for the official definition of the Configuration Control Board and other roles associated with the CMS. It is not crucial, in our opinion, who the chairperson is, as long as that person is well versed in all the ITIL processes and has a strong technical knowledge to be able to challenge requests to change the contents or operation of the CMS.

The function of the CMS governing body is to ensure that

1. The CMS contains all the necessary data required by all the implemented ITIL processes.

2. The contents of the CMS are managed on entry by the Change Management process.

3. The contents of the CMS are periodically verified and audited by the Configuration Management activities.

4. The contents of the CMS are updated in a timely manner in accordance with the Change and Release Management processes.

5. Data discrepancies identified in the CMS are routed to the data element owner for verification and remediation.

6. Requests to modify the CMS model are scrutinized to ensure the following:

   • The requests are legitimate and in support of the ITIL processes.

- The owners of the operational processes have been notified of the changes and have signed off that they will not impact their process or are modifying their process because of the change. Close coordination with the impacted process owners will be necessary for any rollout of CMS changes.

- The operational teams can handle the additional workload that might be imposed on them because of the change to the model.

- The request identifies who will be accountable to ensure that the new data is of sufficient quality and remediate data-related issues identified during business operations.

The potential participants on the board will not vary considerably from company to company. You first need to look at the primary stakeholders of the CMS. These are going to typically be people from the Change, Release, Incident, Problem, and Asset Management groups. There is also an argument that could be made as to the inclusion of someone from your IT Financial Management area because of the importance of cost models and charging. If you have a designated Configuration Management process owner, he will also be on the board and likely be the chairperson, although it is not necessary if he is not the most qualified to do so.

In addition to the people mentioned, we suggest that you include individuals from your larger technology units whose data will be on display in the CMS. This element is critical to your success because if they are not part of this group, they have no vested interest in helping you succeed. You should also look to have representation from your operations, networking, server, mainframe, and application development areas all involved in the governance of the CMS as well.

Finally, if you are already at a high maturity level in ITIL and CMS, or once you get there, there are certain groups that we would recommend you also add to the governance board. As your maturity grows, you continue to place more data elements in the CMS and under the rigor of the Change and Configuration Management control activities. As this happens, and especially once you implement the ITIL Information Security Management process, you should include your Security, Risk Management, and Architecture domain exerts to the governance board.

The addition of these individuals will broaden the scope and utilization of the CMS greatly. Take, for example, the implementation of an identity management system in your environment. If you already have a highly functional CMS that enables you to quickly identify all IT components that support various applications within a business service, the addition of the identity management system enables you to almost instantly identify every individual who was or could be impacted by a service interruption. Just think about how your business partners would respond if you could proactively contact them about a pending outage before their people were impacted. Right now, the impact occurs with little warning, but in the future, you might actually be able to take proactive measures to minimize the service interruption at the end-user level.

For all this to happen, the CMS governing body must work together to establish a CMS structure that will grow and adapt to all the changes an organization might encounter. You cannot be shortsighted or make decisions that will hamper the growth of the CMS or reduce the efficiency for the people using the CMS. This governing body must also be the central point of communication and project coordination for any enhancements that are made to the supporting repositories that might affect the operation of the CMS. There will be times when repositories feeding the CMS cannot perform their duties. The owner of the supporting repository must communicate this interruption of service to the governance body immediately so that it can be addressed. The governance body must then communicate how end users might be impacted so that they can modify their processes if necessary.

Up until now, the discussion has been why you need this governing body, but what might happen if you don't put one in place? First, it is very unlikely to get the buy-in from your server, networking, or Asset Management organizations because they might feel as though all you are doing is exposing their data to be scrutinized by the entire organization. Next, you are not informed ahead of time when your federated CMDBs are being updated, modified, taken down for routine service, and so on. This alone undermines your credibility and feeds into CMS reliability. The excluded groups will not just resist helping populate or maintain the CMS data; they will avoid using it altogether because it is unreliable and unstable. The bottom line is that if they are not on board, you are simply wasting your time and your company's money.

Reuse: What Incumbent Tools Can Be Leveraged?

Any investment that you have made in technology is a candidate for being leveraged. There are few reasons why a tool you currently have in place cannot be potentially used to supply information for your CMS. Some of those reasons might be because you cannot directly access the tool's data repository or there are no APIs to access the data. Instead of being concerned about whether or not a specific tool can be leveraged, focus on what value there is in the data that the tool generates or maintains and how it might benefit the CMS.

The value and stability of your CMS is largely based on the quality of the data that you bring into it, not what tool generated it. Depending on your implementation of an incumbent tool and the control processes you have in place around it, the data it contains could be spectacular or horrendous. This variance will greatly impact the quality that results from your implementation versus an implementation of the same tool at a different company. So again, do not blindly rule in or rule out any tool until you perform an evaluation of the quality that you can reap from your incumbent tool. There are, of course, some tools that most professionals agree are generally unreliable, but we don't want to start listing those here and upset the vendors, so stay focused on the quality of the data your particular tool implementations can provide the CMS.

The types of tools you should leverage also vary from company to company depending on your size, industry, or regulatory issues. As discussed previously, there are certain types of information that everyone will need to bring into the CMS. You should investigate your technology implementations to determine which of those technologies you should consider for inclusion or integration with the CMS. We are strong proponents of automating as much of the data aggregation, validation, and audit activities of your ITIL processes as possible. Do this only if you can ensure that the automation or leveraging of technologies is not coming at the expense of lowering the quality of data that is introduced into the CMS.

Every company will be faced with hard decisions on whether to use an existing tool or not. You should ask yourself these questions when you are considering leveraging an incumbent tool:

- What is the level of data quality that I must have before I can use it in the CMS?

- How often must the data be refreshed?

- What alternative tools are available in my organization?

- What are the alternatives to using the incumbent tool?

- Are there alternative tools that I can purchase and implement (within my program timelines)?

- Can the data be generated and maintained manually as an alternative to technology?

- Is the quality of the data generated and maintained manually better than the available tools?

- Is the depth and breadth of the data manually generated and maintained more extensive than the available tools?

- Is the depth and breadth of the data manually generated and maintained more reliable than the available tools?

- Is it more cost effective to generate and maintain the data manually versus using technology to generate and maintain it?

- Am I better off using lower-quality data in the CMS when my only alternative is to not have it at all? For example, the only data available for network devices is at best only 75% accurate. Do you use network device data that is 75% accurate or implement a CMS with no network device data?

- Can I increase the quality data generated by an incumbent tool by adding or modifying processes around it?

There may be additional questions that you ask yourself when making these decisions, but hopefully these have provided you with a starting point. The underlying question to them all, however, is: "Am I providing value by making this decision to include or exclude the technology?" In some cases, due to the regulatory nature of your industries, such as the financial and pharmaceutical sectors, you may not have as much leeway to include or exclude a data source. However, in less-regulated industries, we would argue that your end users are well served when provided with data that is 50% accurate when the alternative is to not have any data. Obviously, you need to be prepared to increase that data quality shortly after the first deliverable.

There is no sense in getting too far into what tools you should or shouldn't use because the aspect is too broad to adequately discuss in this chapter. As discussed before, a large company may have invested millions of dollars in Asset Management and software distribution tools out of sheer necessity to operate their business on a day-to-day basis. Besides not having budgets for tools like that, small companies, for example, might simply not have the need to acquire them. The amount of users or pieces of technology in their environment might be managed more cost effectively by implementing manual processes. The end result, for both the large and small organization, is that you are delivering value to your end users with your CMS.

Schedule: What Timelines Are Realistic?

The sad reality is that no one timeline is realistic, and anyone who comes into your organization and tells you otherwise is taking on an unmeasured risk. There is no way that anyone can go into an organization without understanding the technological or political environment and guarantee you that they can implement ITIL/ITSM and CMS in any given timeframe. It simply is not reality, so be cautious when an outside consultant gives you a timeline without some intensive investigation of your environment. Their accuracy will also vary depending on the size of your organization because, obviously, the larger organizations will have more bureaucracy to overcome than the smaller ones. Since we all know that you do need to put timelines around projects, how should you go about it?

First, you need to establish the level of active participation you're going to get from your senior leadership. The reason we say "active participation" is because just getting buy-in from them will not be enough. What you are embarking on is much more of a cultural transformation than a technological one. Typically, if you're a smaller organization, you will have far less cultural change to deal with than if you are a large Fortune 100 company that has been in business for 50 or more years. These large companies are successful in part sometimes because they do move slower, and sometimes that prevents them from getting too caught up in the hype of a passing trend. Some of it is surely their inability to react quickly, but some of it is their experience. Unfortunately, some of it is also the cultural resistance to change.

That mentality exists whenever significant change is proposed to the way things are done today. ITIL/ITSM and CMS are significant changes to the way things are currently done for most organizations. This is why you need active participation from senior leadership. The level of this senior leadership has to be high enough that everyone impacted by the impending changes ultimately reports to this one individual. Problems arise if the people impacted by or contributing to the effort report up through different management structures. If they do, a time will come when the two senior leaders disagree on the priority of the different workloads or initiatives.

In some cases, perhaps the senior leaders can work out their differences and agree on an acceptable priority to both. In other cases, however, one of those leaders is going to direct his or her people to no longer participate in the initiative or participate only after they complete their other work. A good way to determine what they really mean is if the directive is ever written down and communicated or if it is just verbally instructed. In either case, the workers find themselves in a difficult situation where senior management for the initiative is asking them to do one thing and their management is telling them to do something else. This is where it is ideal if everyone ultimately reports up to the senior leader sponsoring the initiative. All the budgeting and resource allocation goes through this one person, and all the accountability is his or hers.

The reason why this senior leader has to be actively participating in the initiative is also because this is not a short-term build and deploy technology project. This is a long, multiyear, cultural transformation for your IT organization, and in many regards, also for your business partners because they will ultimately be the benefactors. The senior leader must be out on the road with you regularly, evangelizing that this is not a passing fad or something that will be deployed and then forgotten about. They must make it clear to everyone that this is the way of operating IT, and everyone must adapt to this new philosophy. The senior leader cannot just kick off the initiative and preach its importance to the team running the program because those are the people who already believe in it. If they disappear from sight and only surface to ask why things aren't progressing or to promote their other number-one priority, you will not succeed. If senior leadership is not there visibly with you at large presentations and sending corporate-wide emails about its importance, you will not succeed. If they are not backing that all up with their daily actions and decisions, you have a senior leader who is not actively participating, and it will be very challenging for you to succeed.

We cannot stress enough how implementing ITIL/ITSM and a CMS is so much more of a cultural transformation challenge than it is a technological implementation. You need to understand that technologically, implementing a CMS is, relatively speaking, not complex. It is simply a matter of identifying data sources that contain the CI information you plan to place under control and establishing a link between the CMS and that source via SQL, Web Services, Perl, CSV (Comma Separated Value), and so on. Technologists do this every day, so it is not that complex. If the CMS were simply a technological implementation, there would be no reason why you could not, with a team of five or six strong technologists, implement a complete ITSM platform, including CMS, in less than nine months. Because it is not just a technology implementation, you will be challenged to implement a complete ITIL/ITSM and CMS environment, including the process rollout, in less than three years. The size of your company and entrenched processes greatly impact this number, however, and only you know how resistant to change your company is. Please do not view this as a contradiction to our statement about nobody being able to guarantee the delivery in a certain timeframe. All we are trying to bring to light is that once you have your process require- ments, and assuming you don't have political or resource constraints to still overcome, the initiative is much like every other technology implementation.

Because a three-year project is unacceptable, you need to get something done while the larger effort is being worked on. It is hard for us to provide a generic amount of time that it will take to get all of this done that is both accurate for a small regional organization (Newbie 500, LLC) and a larger international organization (Acme 25, Inc.). What we can do, however, is give you some guidance on all the things that you must do in order to reach your goal of delivering a CMS that meets your organization's ITIL/ITSM require- ments. One comment that we would like to make is that we have seen many companies lose sight of the fact that ITIL/ITSM and CMS is a program that has no real end because of the Continual Service Improvement element. Use that to your advantage and deliver as much value to your end users as you can on a regular basis, even if it is not completely in line with ITIL utopia.

Your program will need several ITIL processes to be designed and in place to some extent before the CMS can be integrated and so that the data can be placed under the control of Change and Configuration Management. You will most likely need to expend some effort on doing data source consolidation and data quality improvements for your CMS as well. Instead of waiting for processes to be designed, people to be trained, and processes to be rolled out, why not make the data source consolidation and data quality improvement efforts something that the end users can benefit from while waiting for the processes. You have to remember that the end users, a large portion of whom are Service Desk employees, spend a tremendous amount of time researching multitudes of data sources to do their jobs and frankly do not care at all about a CMS unless it helps them. What they care about is answering the call and resolving the incident or submitting the Request For Change (RFC). If they can do it with a makeshift repository that has quality data in it, and it elim- inates their need to go to five other sources, they will be thrilled; they will be your strongest supporters when you get ready to roll out your CMS. Deliver *value* to them as often as you can, even if it is not the actual CMS, as long as it is helping you take another step closer to delivering the CMS. That step, remember, can be from either a technological or cultural perspective, and in some cases, the small technological functions you provide early will buy you a tremendous amount of cultural shift in that population.

By now you're probably asking, are they ever going to give us any timelines? The answer is yes, but with the caveat that they are only guidelines, and they are not representative of every company—as we've said, we don't know the complexity of your IT environment or your leadership's willingness to make the tough choices that will undoubtedly directly affect fiefdoms and silos.

Table 3.1 shows some of the larger functional activities that you need to perform as part of your CMS development effort, and some conservative estimates about how much time might be spent on performing them, assuming all resources, budgets, people, hardware, and software are already allocated. It also assumes that you have already defined your Change, Incident, Problem, Asset, and Release Management processes, in addition to the Configuration Management activities associated with each of those processes. The items are not necessarily listed in sequential order and, in some cases, can be performed in parallel, assuming resources are available. Some of the functions listed are not likely performed by the CMS team, but the CMS team needs to ensure that they do get completed. For example, the CMS team is not typically responsible for improving the data quality of an external source, but it has a vested interest in making sure that the data quality is improved. Finally, the estimates vary by your ability to allocate a large development team (5+) versus a small team (2–3).

When looking at the data in Table 3.1, note that first, resources are full-time at some stages, and then part-time at others over the time period specified in the table. For example, the initial design of the CMS model can start based on a traditional relationship approach of IT components. These individuals then need to wait for requirements to be gathered to supplement the design to accommodate the requirements. The period between finishing the initial pass and when the full requirements become available is unknown at a generic level. Second, we do not factor into the table data how long it takes for you to receive management or budgetary approvals. Finally, all the major decisions you make with regards to the design and direction must go through the CMS governance body for approval. The governance body not only approves your decision and direction, it communicates those decisions out to the appropriate communities so as to make sure everyone is on board with your direction. Remember that at the end of this, your job is not done; you have simply completed the first iteration of your Continual Service Improvement lifecycle.

TABLE 3.1   CMS Functional Activities

Activity	Small Company		Large Company	
	Time	Resources	Time	Resources
Gather CMS requirements from processes.	1 Month	1-2	3 Months	5+
Initial design of CMS model. (The model will be continually revisited as new requirements are gathered or discovered.)	3 Weeks	1-2	2 Months	2-3
Identify available data sources.	1 Month	2	3 Months	3-4
Rationalize data source contents and determine quality.	3 Weeks	2	1 Month	3-4
Document data source precedence and data element merging criterion.	2 Weeks	1-2	1 Month	4-5
Design strategy for data source consolidation, data quality improvement, integration approaches, and "value" deliverables.	1 Week	2	1 Month	3
Develop integrations between CMS and data sources.	1 Month	2-3	3 Months	5+
Develop and test data element merging software.	3 Weeks	2-3	2 Months	3-4
Develop and test end-user interface for CMS (including integration with relevant processes).	1 Month	2-3	2 Months	5+
Approximate total if sequential.	7 Months		18 Months	
Approximate total with parallel efforts.	3-4 Months		9 Months	

Frequently Asked Questions

Question: I have a database schema, so isn't my CMS/CMDB already modeled? Aren't they the same?

Answer: A database schema is a technology design used to store and retrieve data from a relational database, whereas a CMS/CMDB model is a conceptual picture of objects and the relationships between them that are under the control of the Change and Configuration Management ITIL processes. The CMS/CMDB model is technology neutral. A database schema is not a CMS/CMDB model.

Question: I have a database that is already supporting my ITIL toolset and processes; isn't that the CMS/CMDB?

Answer: The database(s) that is supporting your ITIL toolset and processes is only a repository that contains the data needed to operate all your ITIL processes. A subset of that, typically a small subset, is what would be considered to be in the CMS/CMDB. This subset is the data that is under the control aspects of the Change and Configuration Management ITIL processes and is represented by the CMS/CMDB model.

Question: Is it true that the only data that I should put in the database is that which is in the CMS/CMDB?

Answer: If you are starting from scratch and plan to have a separate and distinct database that houses only your CIs, data controlled by the Change and Configuration Management ITIL processes, then yes— the only data that you would put in that repository is CMDB/CMS data. However, this is not typically the case. Most implementations leverage a data repository that comes with their service management tool. This data repository and the vendor's tool cannot function if you put only the CMS/CMDB data in it. Do not confuse the entire data repository as being the CMS/CMDB.

Summary

As with all initiatives, planning is essential if you want to succeed. The saying has taken many forms over the years by different writers, but the essence still holds true: "If you fail to plan, you should plan to fail." There are far too many pieces to deal with in this type of initiative to think that you can "wing it" and do things off the cuff. You need to have a strategy, a very clear vision on where you are going, and a strong resolve to keep the initiative on track toward that vision despite the opposition. You should consider using Agile, Spiral, or any other iterative style of methodology over Waterfall because this initiative is not one that lends itself well to sequential thought patterns or development cycles. You need to stay focused on the goal, but it is very unlikely that you will follow the shortest path between points A and B to deliver on this initiative. You will surge and pause with each area over the lifecycle of the initiative, and only toward the end will they all begin to converge on each other. You, as the visionary for it, will see it much sooner than everyone else, but for most, they will not be able to see that vision until it is right in front of them in a form that you can demonstrate.

CHAPTER 4

The Federated CMS Architecture

The word *federation* is most often associated with a form of national government. In these political federations, local entities have a certain amount of autonomy, but a strong central national government acts as a unifying force that forms a collective national identity. Examples are the United States, Russia, and Mexico.

The correct approach to the CMS follows a strikingly similar model. We touched a bit on the federated CMDB in Chapter 2, "What Is a CMDB?," but here we present the full details of federated configuration information and how you can benefit from this innovative architecture.

Turning Data into Useful Information

We often confuse data as information and vice versa. In reality, they are very different constructs of content and knowledge.

Consider the following set of characters:

```
I N F A O L A P R N E N I D G N K M T A E O
```

This is data. It is raw chunks of content, but the relationships between the characters are virtually absent. There is a bit of organization to it in the sense that they are human-readable characters and they lie in a certain sequence, but that is where the meaning and usefulness end. Using a different set of relationships, we can arrange them into words that convey a bit more meaning, as in this example:

```
DALMATIAN GRAPE NEON FINK
```

Because the characters are now clustered into actual English-language words, they have more meaning. Still, the four words are gibberish when arranged in this manner. If we rearrange the characters in yet another order, this ana-grammed data becomes the following:

```
ONE GIANT LEAP FOR MANKIND
```

This is much more meaningful and conjures up the iconic image of Neil Armstrong as he stepped off the *Apollo 11* lunar lander. Each of the three lines contains the exact same set of characters (the raw data), but the last one is the only one of the three lines that is recognizable. This example points out the difference between data and information.

Data is the raw collection of elementary pieces of the message. There is no inherent structure, and the relationships are either weak, arbitrary, or missing altogether. Information, on the other hand, is meaningful. It is data, but data that has been rearranged and connected in a particular way to convey some-thing useful to the consumer of the data. It is a higher-level abstraction of the data. This structural assembly model is extremely important in the discus-sion of CMDB and CMS. Just as the DNA structure in all living organisms is based upon the same four fundamental data elements (recall this from Chapter 2), IT services use many of the same basic data elements arranged in different ways.

In the context of the CMS, information can exist in multiple levels of the structural hierarchy. Its relevance depends on what you plan to do with it. To the system administrator responsible for managing a farm of VMware servers, information can be as narrow as memory pools on the virtual machines. To business users, such data is meaningless. Their information needs are at a much higher level, and details such as memory pool size are merely bits of data hidden beneath the cloak of complexity that comprises the business service.

The Relationships Are Critical

Raw data has little actual value. Information emerges only when this data is linked by relationships (see Figure 4.1). *The relationship is the most impor-tant single facet of the CMS.* This is why we devote so much of this book to understanding, mapping, and using the near-endless array of relationships that exist in the real world. Storing data is easy. Linking that data to produce information is a harder, but much more valuable, task. The CMS is the vehi-cle by which you convert your data into information. After the data is linked by the relationships, as demonstrated with the puzzle pieces of Figure 4.1, the pieces become aligned and interconnected in such a manner that there is meaning to it. Without it, there were only puzzle pieces with no meaning.

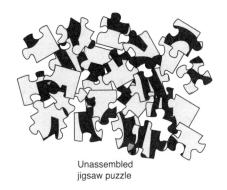

Unassembled
jigsaw puzzle

Assembled pieces
based on relationships

FIGURE 4.1   Relationships create meaning.

Relationships can be obvious (for example, RAM in a server) or more obscure (such as a storage device that holds a specific end user's email). Relationships can be physical (for example, a network switch PHL12C port 1 connects to router PHL01B port 6 using gigabit Ethernet over multimode fiber). They can also be logical (server SFO68R exchanges email messages with server DFW22P). There are far more logical relationships than physical in the IT environment. There are still other relationships that seem less relevant, but they are indeed even more important as we apply the CMS to genuine business problems. These are the variety that capture organizational, business process, and business service relationships, among others.

There are hundreds of dimensions to the relationship matrix. It is easy to become overwhelmed by the sheer magnitude of understanding, let alone mapping, this labyrinth. The human brain collects components of images such as color, space, shape, and so on, and combines these to formulate a visual image. It collects that raw data about an image and then puts it together through the relationships it has defined within it in order to perceive the entire image. If we can't visualize something, we struggle to comprehend it. The tools are here to help us understand this, and they are getting much better at this task. Software tools don't care how many dimensions to the relationship matrix we have. If we can identify a relationship, the tools will gleefully fulfill their designated function without complaint.

A good CMS maps all of these relationships and then enables navigation along the many possible paths. These paths adapt to reflect reality, changing as needed. Navigation follows whichever paths are appropriate for the individual use cases. For one use case, a certain set of paths is followed. For another, a different set of paths is followed, even if the CIs are the same. The navigation is performed for a purpose. It is within the jurisdiction of these use cases where the CMS shines. It is, after all, the use cases that make the CMS worthwhile. Unless the CMS serves a purpose in the operation of the business, it is merely a great intellectual exercise with no authentic value.

Just as Configuration Items (CIs) have attributes, relationships have attributes. The reason for this is because they are both objects with their own characteristics. This aspect could be somewhat confusing to database experts because at the database level, relationships are built between attributes. In an object-oriented world, they are themselves entities. One can even view the relationships as CIs unto themselves. This is one reason object-oriented technologies are so useful in the CMS space. By treating every possible uniquely identifiable entity—relationships included—in a similar manner, the object technologies can reuse many of the same methods and modeling constructs across Management Data Repositories (MDRs). This greatly simplifies the software used to manage the CMS and the tools that benefit from this CMS.

Note that just as in the DNA example of Chapter 2, the same basic data elements can be connected in different ways to produce different applications, business services, and so on. This is what separates a CMS (or even a CMDB) from a mere asset database. The asset database is just the collection of CIs. A CMS includes these same CIs, but with the relationships woven throughout. The CMS can be navigated from any point to any other point (from end to end in an application transaction, for example), but an asset database cannot. As we show in Chapter 9, "Leveraging the CMS," an asset database snapshot of the CMS is useful, and Asset Management is a prime use case for the CMS.

Where Is the Data?

In a federated CMS, data is potentially scattered all over the enterprise. It is extremely unlikely that everything is captured and maintained in a single place. This is the true essence of federation—to spread the data around. This data distribution may be difficult to grasp for those who have been molded in the traditions of legacy relational databases, but the CMS presents a new perspective to data management.

The raw data should be as close to the source as possible. By "close," we are suggesting physical proximity, but it also implies a syntactical match (that is, models that closely match the actual elements). In the CMS discussion, these local data stores are what we call the MDRs that we introduced in

Chapter 2.[1] An MDR contains the basic CIs and relationships that link to other MDRs and CIs. The MDRs are considered to be the most basic storage elements of the CMS because they reside in software tools that hold the authoritative data (the truth) about the objects included.

There is one level even closer to the truth than an MDR, however. That level is the element itself. In the network domain, it could be the SNMP agent on the device. On a server, it can be the agent or embedded intelligence that resides on the server. For the human CI, it is the actual person. In many cases, instrumentation enables us to capture this raw data easily (for example, infrastructure and some applications). In others, there is no instrumentation, so manual population is needed (done via business processes and humans). This element level often does not play into a CMS or CMDB discussion, but we show you how this most elementary data can be used in a federated CMS. You do not always need to go to this level, but sometimes it makes sense (such as with real-time actions and diagnostics).

MDR Linking in the CMS Chain

The MDRs are then linked according to the relationships inherent between them. Figure 4.2 illustrates a typical chain of MDRs that forms a useful assemblage of information. Here, we can see the various tiers of the service chain from infrastructure and other lower levels right up to the business process level. At each level, there are MDRs that represent this level's objects (more on this later in this chapter). The logical progression from one extreme of the chain to the other is based upon the relationships between the tiers. Note how one of the MDRs is a human resource database. Personal identity is important, yet it is often an overlooked element of a CMS. Here, the raw element is a person, and the attributes about these people are represented in this database.

This chain involves MDRs at different levels of the service hierarchy. Each level can be deconstructed into a number of CIs and their attributes. The attributes can be raw data (for instance, 4GB of RAM in a server), an upward relationship in the hierarchy (such as server PHX97G hosts application XYZ), a downward relationship (for example, the online product ordering business service uses the custom J2EE application known internally as "Sunrise"), or a sideways (peer-to-peer) relationship (for example, a network switch LHR29C is

---

1. In a CMS discussion, this is the only appropriate time to use the CMDB term, as even ITIL v3 tends to use them somewhat interchangeably. We much prefer to use *MDR* and to eventually phase out *CMDB*.

connected to switch LHR29D). By connecting the MDRs in this manner, we can navigate the most accurate information when we need to make a decision.

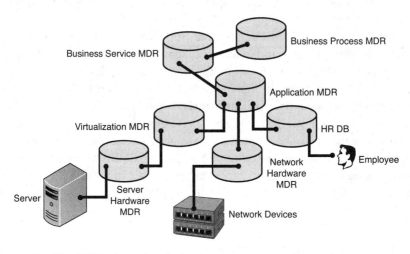

FIGURE 4.2   The CMS information chain

Note how the tiered layers of the MDRs create some interesting observations about data consumers and data providers. A data consumer can also be a data provider to the next higher layer in the chain. This dual role is important to the discussion of a federated CMS, as many MDRs will feed data to other MDRs. Processed information at one level becomes raw data to the next higher layer, which generates its own abstracted information. The information chain is created through a series of interactions between data consumers and data providers. A consumer is not necessarily aware of the makeup of the data it consumes. Each link in the service chain can be unaware of its role in the broader perspective. As long as mechanisms exist to assemble the data elements into the right information elements, the chain works well. A common service chain analogy, shown in Figure 4.3, helps us understand the relationships in the chain.

In this analogy, a new bride and groom need a wedding cake. From their perspective, the provider is the baker and the delivered product is the cake itself. From the baker's perspective, the relationships are different. The newly wed couple is the consumer of her product, and her provider is the grocer, whose products are the ingredients she will use in the preparation of the cake. We can follow this chain back to the farmer who provides raw produce to the grocer.

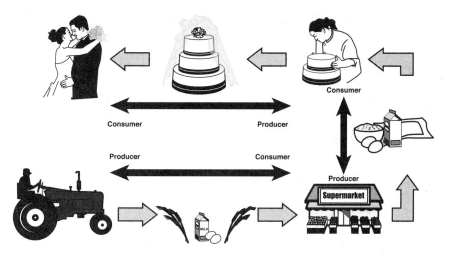

FIGURE 4.3   Transactions in a service chain

What if the groom is also the farmer—or the grocer? We get a recursion in the chain, a feedback loop of sorts. Such recursion is unusual in a CMS, but not impossible. In fact, as more sophisticated applications emerge, recursive CIs may become more common. The CMS must be able to account for these situations as they evolve.

If we take Figure 4.2 and apply the same consumer-producer chaining to the MDRs, we see the situation in Figure 4.4. The federated configuration data is organized and linked in this fashion.

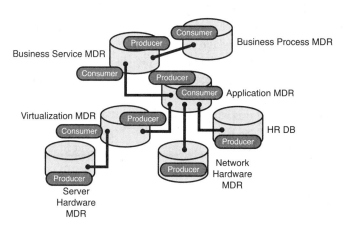

FIGURE 4.4   MDRs in a CMS chain

Note how one MDR consumes data and then presents processed information as a producer to other MDRs that are consumers. This seemingly dynamic nature of the MDRs is not only acceptable, but fundamental to the success of the CMS. It reflects the reality of hierarchical composition, similar to our wedding party and the DNA example in Chapter 2.

Link Data into Information Using Metadata

Metadata is commonly known as *data about data*. In a data model, there are attributes that define the characteristics about the object (or CI, as we call it in the CMS), but metadata adds more to the meaning and utility of the model. The data about the data enables us to attach behavioral aspects to the data (for example, associated methods, performance constraints) and to reference related data, even if that related data resides elsewhere (such as a URL to the related CI rather than a database relationship).

Metadata is what enables federation. Sure, other mechanisms can connect remote data (for example, RPCs and CORBA), but metadata-based object modeling is the modern equivalent of these alternatives. Standards built upon object-oriented (OO) software models, like J2EE and .Net, and XML integration offer all the benefits of OO design.[2] The metadata in CMS federation instructs the information-consuming management tool how to navigate across the chain of MDRs. Although data describes the basic characteristics of the object, metadata adds more meaning to this data. In the case of relationships needed to navigate through the service chain, the metadata describes the connective behavior of the objects. It informs the navigating tool how to follow the links. These types of dynamic links are the crux of federation, enabled by the metadata.

As you assemble data into higher-level models, more metadata is used (see Figure 4.5). Every layer of the service chain benefits from metadata, but the higher layers in the chain will use more. The lower layers will consist of tremendous amounts of discrete raw data (for example, network MAC address, physical memory), but as we move upward, there is less need (indeed less desire) to manage this type of raw data. The data we need at these layers is

---

2. A good thesis on object-oriented data modeling, *A Conceptual Approach to Object-Oriented Data Modeling*, was published by Gerald B. Barnes of the Naval Postgraduate School in 1994. Although quite old now, this document is a great tutorial on good concepts of object-oriented data modeling. It can be found at http://oai.dtic.mil/oai/oai?verb= getRecord&metadataPrefix=html&identifier=ADA286048.

more in the form of processed and assembled information, not data. The metadata offers a clean mechanism to represent this information by combining data and metadata from the lower layers into something meaningful at these respective higher layers.

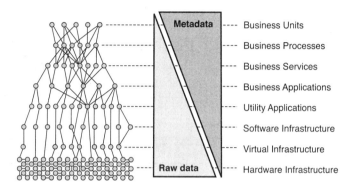

FIGURE 4.5   Metadata increases with service layer.

To illustrate the mix of data and metadata, we build upon Figure 2.4 (from Chapter 2) in Figure 4.6 with values in place for the attributes. A1t this lower layer of the infrastructure, all attributes have explicit values entered. The data types are also shown for these attributes. In this expanded example, you can see how the data types are similar to databases or object classes. Not all possible data types are used in the example.

server		
attribute	**type**	**value**
hostname	string[20]	DEN002B
manufacturer	string[30]	Hewlett-Packard
model	string[40]	HP ProLiant DL360 G5
serial number	string[15]	PDQ1010202
cpu architecture	string[15]	Intel Xeon E5420
physical memory	integer	4000
operating system	string[20]	Red Hat Ent. Linux 5
ip address	ip_address	192.168.51.78

FIGURE 4.6   Expanding the CI example

The atomic types of string and integer are shown, but you can also see a data type called ip_address. This is a more complex data type that a programmer would create in yet another class; what we would call another CI. Ideally, the ip_address class would also have an attribute of a version that reflects IPv4 (32 bits long) or IPv6 (128 bits long) and possibly other attributes. The data model should therefore link the server CI to the ip_address CI, not just have ip_address as a simple attribute. This is done by adding metadata to the model. Figure 4.7 shows some of this metadata. For simplicity, we show only two attributes with metadata. The server has 4000 set for memory, but four thousand what? Metadata tells us the unit is megabytes, so this server has 4,000MB, or 4GB of memory.

server			
attribute	type	value	metadata
hostname	string[20]	DEN002B	
manufacturer	string[30]	Hewlett-Packard	
model	string[40]	HP ProLiant DL360 G5	
serial number	string[15]	PDQ1010202	
cpu architecture	string[15]	Intel Xeon E5420	
physical memory	integer	4000	unit:MB
operating system	string[20]	Red Hat Ent. Linux 5	
ip address	ip_address	192.168.51.78	class:ip_address

FIGURE 4.7   The CI example with some metadata

As we look at the ip_address attribute, the metadata says the class is also ip_address. Internal to the MDR software, this has special meaning, as does all metadata. The special meaning here is that the class now points to another CI of type ip_address where the additional attributes of an IP address are managed. If the ip_address class resides within the same MDR, the link is straightforward and handled by the MDR's internal software code. If the ip_address class resides in a remote MDR, the metadata must refer to that remote MDR instead of just a simple class type. The metadata will be much richer for these situations, but this is where the power of federation becomes real. You can link remote data in other ways, but metadata offers much more flexibility, simplicity, and control because the metadata can theoretically and easily tailor each of these aspects of the data linkage. There is a wee bit more overhead to process the metadata, but the CMS should not emulate a trans-action processing system in its resource demands anyway. Extreme perform-ance is not the goal. The goals are flexibility and accuracy.

Metadata for Remote Information Linking

To drive home this point of reflecting the federation aspects of the metadata, it will help to do two things, as follows:

- Convert the server CI to XML, because this is how the metadata is represented. It also becomes difficult to portray complex data models in tabular form.

- Expand on the network interface to show how a relationship is mapped in a federated environment.

First, we show Figure 4.7 as it would be represented in XML (see Figure 4.8). The same attributes are shown, but the format is more flexible and consistent with XML tagging. This is just a fragment of a much larger XML listing. We truncated it to just this CI for brevity.

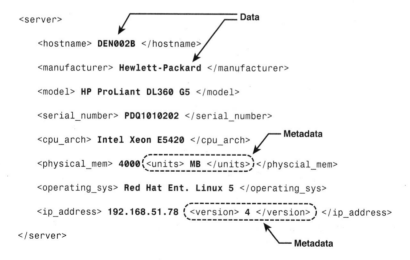

FIGURE 4.8   The server CI example expressed in XML

Here, you can see the same attributes, but there are a few notable differ-ences. First, we need not be explicit about the data types. The model attrib-ute, for example, was previously defined as a string of 40 characters. Some programming languages and databases require us to set a finite limit on the length of an attribute, but XML doesn't need to specify data types. We just represent it in a human-readable form and the MDRs take care of the rest. Each MDR must address the local formatting issues of whether there needs to be a finite length and how the CI will be stored either in memory or on disk.

In federation, we are more concerned with the *exchange* of the data, not so much about the data itself. The MDR can internally store the data as a text file, a SQL-Server database, an in-memory Java class, or scribbled notes on a stack of napkins. As long as the data is exposed and received according to the rules of the XML format, federation works well in all of these cases.

Metadata for specifying the linking mechanisms can come in many forms. Metadata tags can contain a URL, or more specifically, a Uniform Resource Identifier (URI).[3] When a URI is specified, remote data can be referenced instead of local data. Herein lies the essence of federation. A data model can include both local and remote data and metadata. Combined with the web services interface software, the model allows this "magic" of federation to happen. If we federate our server CI example, the ip_address line may appear as follows:

```
<ip_address>
        <query>
                <recordConstraint>
                        <propertyValue
                        namespace="http://cms.mycompany.com/dns"
                                localName="hostname">
                        <equal>DEN002B</equal>
                        </propertyValue>
                </recordConstraint>
        </query>
</ip_address>
```

This is some additional XML code, but you should rarely need to worry about the XML itself. Software tools that embody the MDRs and the data consumers perform all the complex functions associated with the XML. In fact, a full reference for the ip_address record involves even more code than shown here.

---

3. A URL is a Uniform Resource Locator, whereas a URI is a Uniform Resource Identifier. The difference is that a URL, the string we commonly type in as a browser address, is only one part of a URI. As such, a URI is more specific in what it references. For more information on URLs, URIs, and more, visit the World Wide Web Consortium (W3C) site: http://www.w3.org/TR/uri-clarification/.

This expanded code supports the ability to query the DNS MDR for all of the IP address information affiliated with the server DNS002B, the server we focus on within the configuration record in our example. The MDR holding the DNS data resides on the web at the URI http://cms.mycompany.com/dns, and the XML server interface on that system presents the desired data requested in this XML code segment. The XML code specifies a query operation, similar in nature to a SQL query in a database. Within the XML standards, we can tailor the response according to our needs. The actual MDR may even contain a SQL database, and the XML query is merely translated by the DNS MDR into its corresponding SQL query.

Web Services for the CMS

When federating data repositories, the best approach to linking remote data is through the use of web services.[4] A *web service* is a software connection that leverages XML-based communications and dynamic component locations. Rather than hard-code these connections as one might do with an RPC,[5] web service connections are identified and linked on demand. The functional component needed by the requestor is the *service* in question here. The *web* part comes from the fact that the service is found and linked through web-based software technologies such as HTTP and XML.

In fact, the CMDB Federation Working Group's standard is based upon web services. The reason is one of flexibility and simplicity. In Chapter 6, "Integration—There's No Way Around It!," we cover more specifically how the CMDB Federation specification uses web services. A web service exchange involves registering particular services (that is, each MDR) and then when other CMS consumers need the data, they can simply request the data from the MDR registered to provide the relevant data.

Web services are flexible because they enable dynamic shuffling of MDRs. An MDR request might potentially be answered by more than one MDR. This can happen where parallel MDRs serve similar data, but they can be segmented by business unit, geography, or some other logical demarcation boundary. The same data request is made, but the precise target of the data

---

4. A good tutorial on web services is available from the W3C at http://www.w3.org/TR/ws-arch/.

5. Remote Procedure Call (RPC) is a mechanism to connect two software components over the network. Deemed an anachronism by some critics, RPCs remain valuable, powerful, and widely implemented. The current version of the RPC specification can be found at http://tools.ietf.org/html/rfc1831.

may be different based on context that affiliates it with one of these logical segments. The context directs it to one MDR or another, even though the data schema is identical across the two. MDRs can even act as failovers for one another, and the web services can adapt to point requests to one or the other.

A full explanation of web services is outside the scope of this book, but we present a short tutorial here. There are at least three major elements to a web services architecture: a producer or provider of the service, a consumer of the service, and an optional broker used to register services and requests for the service (see Figure 4.9).

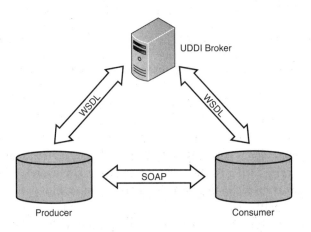

FIGURE 4.9   Web services architecture

New communications protocols layered atop HTTP are used in a web services communications exchange. The two most relevant are Simple Object Access Protocol (SOAP)[6] and Web Services Description Language (WSDL).[7] The producer and consumer exchange information using SOAP. WSDL is used by both to communicate with the broker.

The web services broker is the registration authority governing the location and access to the services. A service provider (producer) registers with the broker, informing the broker that it is providing the specified service. When a service consumer needs to use a service, it issues a request to the

6. SOAP originally stood for Simple Object Access Protocol, but the acronym is no longer relevant. It is the communications protocol for exchanging XML messages. The formal W3C specification for SOAP version 1.2 can be found at http://www.w3.org/TR/soap12-part1/.

7. WSDL (Web Services Description Language) is a W3C specification for modeling web services. You can see the Web Services Description Working Group's official documents at http://www.w3.org/2002/ws/desc/.

broker, asking where the desired service can be located. The broker then acts as a matchmaker between the consumer and the appropriate provider. Once introduced, the broker steps aside and the provider-consumer exchange commences. This negotiation with the broker is built upon WSDL and SOAP.

Universal Description, Discovery, and Integration (UDDI)[8] is a common registration specification used by brokers. It is used by web services to mediate the location of and connections to web services. Both public and private UDDI registries are used in web services. We point out UDDI because it is important to web services, but CMS federation takes a bit of a different approach. We cover how the CMDBf standard addresses registration when we go into more detail on the CMDBf standard in Chapter 6.

The Distributed CMS in Practice

Much of what we presented in this chapter represents the ideal approach to federation, and some of it is theoretical and still emerging (the CMDBf standard). The logical question that arises is, of course: "How much is real?" One answer is, "Not much," when it comes to what has been done so far. Federation is very new. Virtually all CMDB implementations in existence are more rigid than the federated model. These implementations have most of their CMDB contained in a single database. For these organizations, federation is a goal, but one that is not yet reality. Very few can claim to be a true CMS.

The other answer to the reality question is much more optimistic. That answer is, "Everything discussed in this chapter is now possible!" This is great news for everyone because it means your journey can now commence. Do not become overwhelmed by the challenges ahead of you. Many vendor offerings still need to mature, but others are readily available. Nobody can honestly tell you the federated CMS is easy, but it is finally within grasp.

Integration Is Not Necessarily Federation

Data integration is nothing new, of course, but federation is something very different. This is one reason federation is so exciting. It represents a more evolved form of integration, one that is much more flexible. Integration involves data exchange. Federation goes another step further because the

---

8. Universal Description, Discovery, and Integration (UDDI) is an OASIS standard for XML-based registries. The full specifications can be located at http://www.oasis-open.org/committees/uddi-spec/doc/tcspecs.htm.

data is referenced, not exchanged. The difference is whether a copy of the data is made or whether the data remains in its original location and is just referenced on demand. The latter scenario is used in true federation.

Many CMDB "federation" efforts provide integration adapters to extract data from one source and import it into a "CMDB" in a central point. This exchange results in a copy of the original data being transferred to the CMDB. This copy is then used by the CMDB and all of its derivative process uses.

Making copies of data is contrary to the ideals of the CMS and of good data management in general. When you have copies, it is highly likely that data discrepancies will occur. You can ensure consistencies across these data stores, but the overhead costs and resources to maintain them will be extreme, especially as the data stores grow in number and in aggregate size. Raw storage needs are higher, but this is not the real concern. Storage has gotten very inexpensive, and the CMS data does not amount to an enormous data set anyway. The reconciliation processing and the constant exchange and checking of the data is absolutely a concern. Even with highly rigorous and demanding reconciliation engines, the data still remains subject to corruption. Remember, corrupt data is worse than no data at all!

The main task of the adapter is to translate objects and attributes into the raw form needed in the CMDB. The following discrepancies in data types and the represented attributes are examples that must be reconciled by the adapter:

- A source attribute is an integer, but the CMDB expects a double-precision floating point number.

- An attribute exists in the source, but is not in the CMDB. The adapter will ignore this attribute.

- An attribute cannot be provided by the source, but exists in the CMDB. The adapter cannot import this, so it remains empty in the CMDB.

The adapter facilitates this exchange and reconciliation, and the import is performed at periodic intervals to keep updating the CMDB. There are many imperfections to this approach because the data is subject to inaccuracy, especially if the interval is long (greater than several hours), which is usually the case. Most data imports are performed daily in the best case and sometimes only weekly. Demands on the CMDB server and other resources (for example, network, data source, and storage) are intense during these imports, so longer intervals are needed just to avoid resource collapse. Ad hoc imports are usually possible, but rarely performed.

Figure 4.10 illustrates this copy mode of integration. Before the integration, the CMDB's schema is set up to accept the data in its original form, and the space for it is allocated in the CMDB repository. This is sometimes hard-coded in the CMDB, requiring the adapters to perform more translational work. Tailoring the CMDB to more efficiently accept the data takes more up-front effort, but it streamlines the periodic imports.

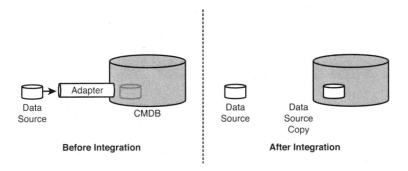

Data Source   CMDB   Data Source   Data Source Copy

Before Integration   **After Integration**

FIGURE 4.10   CMDB integration adapters

In Figure 4.10, the *before* picture shows the segment of the CMDB set aside for the imported data. In the *after* picture, the two copies of the data are shown. The adapter is only invoked on the import.

We kept referring to this copy integration in the context of a CMDB because it is much weaker than true federation and is therefore not characteristic of a CMS. Discussions about federated CMDBs sometimes cover actual federation (as in the CMDBf standard), but it is often just copy integration misrepresented as federation. Although copy integration is the only option in many situations, as noted earlier, we recommend against this in your longer-term strategy.

Discovery Tools

We keep stressing the need for accuracy and timeliness of the data in an MDR. This is irrefutable, especially as we expand the complexity of our environments. Manual population of any portion of the CMS is wrought with pitfalls. Some manual population is unavoidable, but every iota of manually populated data becomes dubious when compared to its discovered counterpart. You can employ systematic checks and balances, but they quickly become cost prohibitive. Our ability to manually keep data up-to-date can never match automated discovery. In Figure 4.11, we demonstrate how manual entry or weak discovery documents only three of the potential six entities and changes in the environment. With a strong Active-Passive Hybrid auto-discovery approach, you are much more likely to capture all six entities and changes. Auto-discovery tools are not perfect by any means, but they will advance your ability to maintain your CMS accuracy by orders of magnitude. Some programmatic solutions can also be employed, but only to the extent that the data and technology allows. For example, if you rely on manual input of all new servers into your environment, you must ensure that there is only one mechanism for their introduction, which is rarely the case.

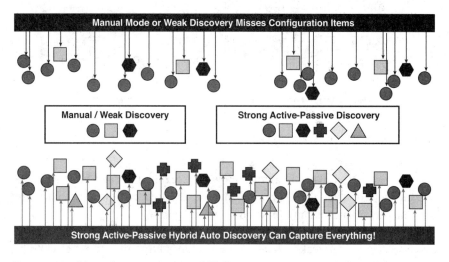

FIGURE 4.11   Manual versus automated CI discovery

Discovery tools are among some of the most valuable innovations in the whole CMS story because they not only automate the function, but they also can do so much to dig into the real-world environment, producing a level of accuracy never before seen. Discovery tools come in many forms, and they have actually been in use for many years, but they are becoming more sophisticated. Traditional management tools always performed some level of discovery because their fundamental operation required it.

Network monitors are a perfect example to highlight this point. Among the most mature of all management tool categories, network monitors must discover the network devices and then commence monitoring them. To effectively monitor a network device, it needs to be known, of course, but then we must learn more about it. After discovering it, we then check to see if it responds to SNMP requests. Today, every enterprise class network device is SNMP-enabled, so it will respond to SNMP requests. Once the tool knows

SNMP is available, it then commences navigation of the MIB structure, learning more detail as it traverses the MIB tree. In the process, it discovers a rich amount of data. None ever claimed to be a CMDB (nor could they), but all store the CI and its attributes, at least temporarily. They did, however, set the stage for CMDB tools to come.

In these earlier tools, the discovery function was (and still is) integrated into the main tools. This is beginning to change as vendors realize the value of decoupling discovery and moving it to a dedicated CMS role. The main tool (the data consumer) then uses the CMS discovery instead of its own proprietary discovery. CMS discovery has many advantages, including the following:

- It allows the consumer tool to focus on its added value. In the case of a performance analysis tool, the vendor can focus on the more difficult and valuable analysis, not on the discovery.

- It allows for better discovery. No user tool requires every bit of data, so integrated discovery restricts the richness of the data. The discovery developer can be free to expand beyond these restrictions.

- A dedicated discovery engine can be more aggressive about discovery timeliness, yielding more accurate data. Because it need not share resources with the consumer tools' main function, the divide-and-conquer structure philosophy can be applied to the tools themselves, as it should be.

- It allows the discovery to be reused beyond the needs of the consumer tool. Other tools can benefit from the same data. This reuse is a fundamental principle of federation.

Network Discovery Example

To understand how discovery works, it is valuable to use an example. In this one, we examine how network discovery works. It is a relevant example because networking is a well-understood concept among IT professionals. The instrumentation (SNMP) is widely deployed, and many have at least cursory knowledge of its purpose and maybe even a bit of its model. The network CI is populated not only with the attributes of the individual devices, but thankfully, the designers of most embedded SNMP agents had enough vision to also include attributes that tell us something about relationships. This proves to be extremely helpful.

As a discovery tool examines the SNMP agent, it follows the Management Information Base (MIB) tree, but it will do so in a guided fashion. Without some guidance, it will collect the enormous number of MIB objects that are not needed in the CI. For this example, it helps to know a little about SNMP and how it works. Many excellent books and other resources on SNMP are readily available for those wanting to learn more about SNMP.[9] We touch on the salient points relevant to our discovery example.

At the heart of SNMP is the MIB—in effect, the data schema. The MIB defines the various objects and attributes available in the network device.[10] A MIB follows a hierarchical structure, with enumerated object IDs (OIDs) representing the attributes. For example, sysDescr is an attribute that holds a descriptive text string and is represented numerically in the MIB as 1.3.6.1.2.1.1.1. This sequence of numbers is the navigation path through the tree that gets us to the sysDescr_value. Other MIB values are referenced the same way, with different number sequences.

Most of the MIB values are actual attributes, but others contain MIB number sequences themselves. These act as pointers to other data and enable the relationships we need within the MIB structure. As a result, the MIB appears less like the tree that it is (the left side of Figure 4.12) and more as an interconnected partial mesh of related data (the right side of Figure 4.12).

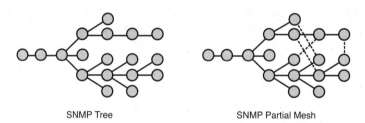

SNMP Tree   SNMP Partial Mesh

FIGURE 4.12   SNMP navigation topologies

Another type of relationship mapped in the MIBs is addressing that offers connectivity data. A MIB for a network device interface will likely contain a few important addresses that allow the discovery tool to know just how two

---

9. SNMP books are too numerous to mention, but there are even more extremely valuable web resources to examine. Arguably the most definitive source for SNMP information is SNMP Research (www.snmp.com), the company founded by Dr. SNMP himself, Jeffrey Case. Go to the "Technology" tab at the top of the SNMP Research web site to learn more about this pervasive protocol that launched IT into the age of automation.

10. SNMP is not just limited to network devices. You will find that it is extensible to any CI type you can imagine, and many of these have been standardized by the IETF. For example, the host resource MIB for hosts such as servers is defined by the IETF as RFC 2790 (http://tools.ietf.org/html/rfc2790).

devices are connected (that is, the physical link relationship between the two). Most important among these are link-layer addresses, such as the 48-bit MAC addresses for Ethernet, which we usually represent in the 11:22:33:44:55:66 format. We show this linkage in Figure 4.13. We eliminate the OIDs for brevity, and for these purposes, they are not relevant.

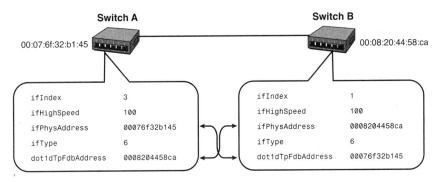

FIGURE **4.13**   SNMP MIB data indicating connectivity

We show just a few of the many MIB variables (CI attributes) of the two connected switches. Port 3 of switch A is connected to port 1 of switch B. We know this because the MIB details tell us. Each switch port shown is a 100Mbps Ethernet port.[11] The important information is in the addresses. The ifPhysAddress attribute is the physical address of the port, the lowest layer of identification for a network device. The last line in each sample is part of the standard Bridge MIB in nearly all enterprise class switches. The dot1dTpFdbAddress attributes indicate physical addresses of other devices reachable via the selected port on the local switch. There will usually be several dot1dTpFdbAddress entries in the switch for each port.

Discovery tools can use a number of methods to "connect the dots" across the data. Using the Bridge MIB[12] is one method. If interface 1 of switch B is

---

11. In IETF RFC 1213 (http://www.ietf.org/rfc/rfc1213.txt?number=1213), the Interfaces MIB represents the units of the ifHighSpeed object type as 1,000,000 bits per second, and the ifType of 6 represents any variant of Ethernet, regardless of speed. This is defined by the Internet Assigned Numbers Authority (IANA) at http://www.iana.org/assignments/ ianaiftype-mib.

12. The Bridge MIB is specified in IETF RFC 1493 (http://www.ietf.org/rfc/ rfc1493.txt?number=1493), which has been superceded by RFC 4188 (http://www.ietf. org/rfc/rfc4188.txt?number=4188). Although it describes bridges, a switch is essentially a multiport bridge, so the MIB can apply to all switches.

in one of the dot1dTpFdbAddress entries for interface 3 of switch A, there is a *likely* physical connectivity relationship between the two. If the data for interface 1 of switch B concurs by telling us that its dot1dTpFdbAddress table contains the address for interface 3 of switch A, there is a *definite* relationship. The tool can map this connection with confidence.

A good discovery tool navigates through these links to obtain the most accurate representation of the network, and it populates the CI object model appropriately. The discovery tool knows how to put the right links in context to represent network connectivity maps. Our example shows physical topology relationships, but logical relationships (for example, TCP virtual circuits or OSPF routing) can be mapped in a similar fashion using different MIB variables.

Most modern network configuration tools also support a front-end to the command line interface (CLI) for the network devices. By establishing a telnet or secure shell connection to the router, the tools deliver the commands to gather the desired data, and then parse the returned text stream. The end result is similar to the SNMP method with a rich and accurate model of the network.

Application Discovery

Discovery tools in actual use focus on the more mature infrastructure (such as a network or server), but the application domain is the new hot focus in discovery. In just the past few years, application discovery and dependency mapping have become not just viable, but quite good. These tools perform discovery, but must take different approaches than networks or servers. There is very little, if any embedded instrumentation built into applications. In short, there is no "SNMP MIB" for the typical application, and therefore, we cannot just poll this instrumentation to tell us what we need to know. In the absence of instrumentation, the discovery tool must employ other techniques for data visibility and collection that we cover later in the chapter.

There are a few notable categories of application discovery that must be considered, and all are necessary in the full picture of the CMS. These are discussed in the next sections.

Application Instances on Servers

Each application component resides on a server somewhere, so one of the functions of server discovery should be to determine which applications reside on these servers and how their local configuration parameters are set. To do this, the discovery tool must scan the file systems for patterns that indicate the presence of application elements (/usr/local/jboss probably suggests the presence of a JBoss application server component). The tool should also scan the process table and registry entries for evidence of installed (and running) applications.

We stress the difference between installed and running applications to emphasize an important point. A server can be configured to host an application, but for many reasons, these applications may not run. Maybe they are sitting there in "standby" mode waiting to be called into action, possibly loaded at startup but not executing. Maybe they were part of a standard build but have yet to be activated. Maybe they are leftover from a previously executing system, but they were never fully removed. Whatever the case, they are not running, and they are therefore not relevant to the real-time perspective of the application and how the application fits into a more comprehensive business system. These dormant applications are important to the overall CMS discussion, but not to the real-time view.

The real-time view is concerned with what is actually happening—that is, which applications actually participate in business systems. In many of the CMS use cases, such as incident analysis, we don't care what is installed; we only want to know what is running now. This is where the different modes of detection (file systems, registry, process table) make a difference. File systems, configuration files, and registry settings only tell us what is installed, for the most part. To understand which applications are truly running, we need to peer into the process table. Discovery tools must examine all of these and distinguish which are installed and which are running.

Consider the varying methods to gather this information. Access to the process table and other raw data sources will be different across operating systems (OS)—in some cases, even on different flavors of the same OS (for example, RedHat versus Debian Linux). The discovery tools should address this by implementing the right mechanism for the job, but check to be sure.

For more complex applications, server-side application discovery is more likely to discover application infrastructure, those distributed components of the broader application (such as a JBoss application server that acts to serve one or more distinct complex applications). For the more complex, distributed applications, these server-side components represent puzzle pieces that have not yet been assembled. In the example, JBoss is application software, but it is not the application itself that is seen from the end user's perspective.

Application Dependency Mapping

This is the exciting new field of application discovery. It is exciting because Application Dependency Mapping (ADM) represents the automated capture of the relationships that enable us to assemble the puzzle pieces. It is the glue" that binds infrastructure (including application infrastructure) into a meaningful application. For the first time, we can now automate the creation and population of application-level models.

Application dependency mapping tools use one or both of two general discovery modes to gather the necessary data, as follows:

- **Active Mode:** Active mode employs a polling mechanism to periodically query servers for the desired data. The typical execution of the query remotely logs into the server and then runs a script to present the details.

  On a Linux or Unix server, the common method logs in using secure shell (SSH) and shell commands are run. The command ps -ef, for example, produces resulting output lines like those shown in Listing 4.1.

LISTING **4.1**   Process Table Extract on a Linux Server

```
$ps -ef
UID          PID  PPID C STIME TTY          TIME CMD
root           1     0 0 Jul29 ?        00:00:04 /sbin/init
root           2     0 0 Jul29 ?        00:00:00 [kthreadd]
www-data    3993  5118 0 06:25 ?        00:00:00 /usr/sbin/apache2 -k start
www-data    4013  5118 0 06:25 ?        00:00:00 /usr/sbin/apache2 -k start
www-data    4015  5118 0 06:25 ?        00:00:00 /usr/sbin/apache2 -k start
mysql       4857  4817 0 Jul29 ?        00:00:05 /usr/sbin/mysqld
root        5118     1 0 Jul29 ?        00:00:00 /usr/sbin/apache2 -k start
nagios     21973     1 0 Aug12 ?        00:00:15 /usr/local/nagios/bin/nagios
```

Listing 4.1 is parsed according to the rules encoded in the discovery tool. Each executing process gives a clue as to the application represented by that process. In the preceding truncated list (the actual output is dozens of lines long, maybe hundreds), we can see the server is running the Apache web server, MySQL database, and Nagios, a network and server monitoring tool. Collectively with the other bits of data parsed, we can glean a highly accurate and detailed perspective of the application components and how they interact.

Active mode requires the appropriate login credentials to execute the data-gathering scripts. In most cases, the desired data is restricted to system administrators only (root, on Unix/Linux systems). This is frequently worrisome to security staff. We will expand on this issue later, but it is worth mentioning here because it is an important factor to the overall success or failure of active-mode discovery.

This is fine for applications on the server, but what about the most critical need for applications that span servers? These cross-server interactions can be identified using several methods, but the most common is the netstat command (see Listing 4.2).

LISTING **4.2** An Extract of a netstat Command

```
$netstat -a
Active Internet connections (servers and established)
Proto Recv-Q Send-Q Local Address       Foreign Address     State
tcp        0      0 *:nfs               *:*                 LISTEN
tcp        0      0 *:48290             *:*                 LISTEN
tcp        0     60 moe.com:mysql       larry.com:3892      ESTABLISHED
tcp        0      0 moe.com:ipp         *:*                 LISTEN
tcp        0      0 *:38680             *:*                 LISTEN
tcp        0      0 moe.com:www         localhost:53054     TIME_WAIT
tcp6       0      0 *:ssh               *:*                 LISTEN
tcp6       0    660 moe.com:ssh         curly.com:4440      ESTABLISHED
udp        0      0 *:32770             *:*
```

As with our ps command, this listing is truncated and formatted for brevity. It tells us some detail about remote application connections. We see that our server moe has established a connection to larry, which is accessing moe's MySQL database. Another host called curly is also connected, but using secure shell, probably a remote login, and maybe the session that requested this listing. Other applications are listening for remote connections, but they have not yet been established.

The larry host is using TCP port 3892, which is not a well-known port. Remote systems often choose a random unused port for their connections. As such, it is hard to tell precisely which application on larry needs the MySQL connection. To complete the picture, the discovery tool must query larry and ask which application is using port 3892. Note that the same condition exists for curly, and the tool must also query curly for similar data. After all three stooges are discovered, the more complete distributed application environment is known.

On Windows servers, active mode commonly uses Windows Management Instrumentation (WMI)[13] supported by almost all

---

13. WMI is Microsoft's Windows Management Instrumentation, its implementation of the DMTF's WBEM specification. More detail is available at http://msdn.microsoft.com/en-us/ library/aa384642(VS.85).aspx.

Windows server software. The resulting data doesn't need to be parsed as in the command-line methods on Linux and Unix servers because its architecture is designed for data retrieval from the ground up. The method using command-line scripts and parsing the output is an inefficient option, but usually the only option for those servers.

- **Passive Mode:** In contrast to active mode, passive mode does not need to log into the servers to obtain its data. This mode captures the data by observing application activity. Instead of relying on inquisition to get what we need, we watch the actual running applications.

There is no single instrumentation technology used because there are multiple points in the application and infrastructure where relevant data can be collected. Each gives us a slightly different perspective, but they all give us similar results with differing pros and cons that include the following:

- **Server agents** observe activity from the server. They can tap into the network interface driver, observing packets as they arrive and depart. They can also tap into the kernel to examine software connections internal to the server itself.

- **Client agents** act in a similar manner, although from the other end of the transaction. They are effective for understanding the application from the end user's perspective, but they are blind to the activity inside the server.

- **Network traffic capture** works in the middle, watching traffic traverse the network by tapping into the network and "sniffing" packets. The packets are examined and assembled to form information streams that tell us about the applications encapsulated within the packets.

- **Embedded application instrumentation** is the best approach, but also the rarest. This method is best because the application itself is telling us what we need to know. It is the rarest because almost no applications are instrumented to do this. As web services and SOA technologies become more popular, applications built atop these technologies offer more promise to use this method of data access.

Ideally, both active and passive modes would be used because either mode alone gives an incomplete picture. Active mode offers server-side configuration details not available via most passive modes, but passive mode can give us detail in real time. Technologies converge on a hybrid of the two, benefiting from the best of both modes.

When choosing active or passive, you also have to examine the resource load imposed by one or the other. Generally, passive modes require fewer resources, but this is not always the case. Active mode resource demands are usually high in the initial discovery, trailing off for subsequent discoveries. As discovery technologies evolve, the polling methods become less viable, because their intervals can never shorten to the lengths necessary for the coming dynamic technology needs. We address this problem in Chapter 7, "The Future of the CMS," posing a novel, but not revolutionary, solution that will overcome the dilemma of resource requirements in any discovery mode.

Network traffic capture requires the lowest overall resources because it is only observing network packets. The resource demands are then placed on the device doing the observation. If it is a dedicated appliance, the appliance absorbs the load, and production systems never notice any impact. If the capturing system is a shared system with other services, the capture will obviously impact that system's performance. We do not recommend this mode. Dedicated appliances are designed to handle the load.

Application Behavior

The CMS is not just about how the data is related structurally (it's not just that the foot bone is connected to the leg bone). It is also about behaviors because changing behaviors should be viewed as Configuration and Change Management issues. As the CMS, and especially its use cases, mature, this view will become more common. One of the great mistakes with the common perception of the CMDB is a pervasive misconception that it is only structural data. This will change, but it may take a few years.

Security Concerns with Discovery

Any time discovery tools are deployed, someone objects about security issues. There are good reasons to be concerned, but there are also good reasons to deploy the technologies. The solution, of course, is to address the concerns with sensitivity and commitment to succeed on both goals. Effective security is not negotiable; however, by exercising care with implementations and coordinating planning with security staff, an acceptable solution can be attained.

Discovery tools may emulate security breaches. The method of trolling for CIs and then digging deeper for attributes is similar to common security attacks like port scanners and distributed denial of service. Security breach detection tools need to be configured to ignore scans and other discovery methods from the authorized discovery tool. Of course, stringent security practices on the discovery tool are mandatory. In fact, discovery tools can actually keep watch over each other to ensure compliance with security policies. This becomes more a use case of the CMS than a function of the CMS itself, as we explain in Chapter 9.

Login credentials to discovered servers, applications, and other systems are often needed to properly perform discovery. To make matters even scarier, the login accounts are often privileged accounts with potential to inflict serious damage. To quell these fears, discovery must be well defined, well controlled, and well monitored. Here again, the compliance use case can help keep discovery and the CMS secure. Any deviations in the configuration of discovery must follow good Change Management practices, just like any other technology of business system. Out-of-process changes need to be detected and appropriate staff notified.

This points out a great area where everybody in the security discussion wins. Security staff who may initially worry about credentials will be thrilled to have irrefutable visibility into the state of the environment and how it changes. Detected changes might be benign, but they can also be malicious or even accidental. We should all scrutinize any change that happens outside the Change Management process. Even if it's not hackers attacking, such changes institute unacceptable risk. After all, good security practice is just another form of risk management, not necessarily a war between the "good guys" and the "bad guys" of the world. Very often, it is the "good guys" who inadvertently pose the bigger risk!

Discovery can also result in what we call the *Big Brother* effect. With discovery tools (especially passive tools) constantly watching activity, people feel the natural discomfort that their sensitive data is being consumed and stored by a third party: Big Brother.[14] Access is necessary, especially as we move higher up the service chain (applications and business processes) if we hope to properly manage these services. Like those with access to any sensitive data, the CMS owners and maintainers must exercise extreme care with the power endowed upon them. We can relate this in some way to health care. Physicians require access to sensitive personal information to offer proper

---

14. The Big Brother in this reference is (as science fiction buffs know) the always-watching totalitarian authority in George Orwell's 1949 book *1984*. The book was released as a popular movie of the same name in 1956 and again as a less-popular film titled—not surprisingly—*Nineteen Eighty-Four*, naturally released in 1984!

patient care, but with that access comes an incredible responsibility to protect that confidential information.

Perimeter security (for example, firewalls) is pervasive and for good reason. Perimeters require tight ingress and egress controls to maintain a secure environment. If all CIs are within a single perimeter, discovery is straightforward. Business services have become more complex, however, and a single perimeter is no longer appropriate for these situations. Multiple perimeters are now common in many enterprises, especially in financial services firms, but we also need to consider scenarios with business partners.

These perimeters make data collection more difficult (see the left side of Figure 4.14). Communications between the management station and the managed elements is necessary, so this communications path must be opened in the firewall. XML-based communications makes it all easier because it rides atop HTTP, and HTTP is often open. Proprietary protocols require more negotiations with the security team.

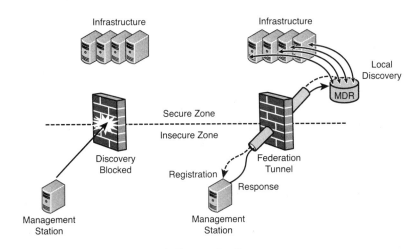

FIGURE 4.14   Security perimeter challenges for discovery

Directionality—that is, direction of the data request, interrogation, or flow—is also a consideration. The firewall may allow HTTP outbound but prohibit it inbound. Such a rule is not typically negotiable. The only way discovery can work in this scenario is to have instrumentation in the more-secure zone initiate outbound connections to the CMS elements in the less-secure zone (see the right side of Figure 4.14). This may require installation of a management server within the tighter zone. The MDR initiates communications by registering its services to the management station using web services. The management station then knows how to communicate through the firewall tunnel to obtain its desired data. All management systems should reside in a high security zone because of the aforementioned sensitivity of the data they house. That said, it may be unacceptable to install a management system in the most secure zones. If instrumentation is unable to initiate outbound communications in these zones, the CMS will be blind to the zone's contents.

Many aspects of management raise security concerns, but security must be balanced with the ultimate object of management. That purpose is to attain more effective control over the business technology environment. This control is needed to optimize service quality, so although it is foolish to be lax about security, fears cannot be irrational. Pragmatism must prevail over dogma when it comes to security. The two should not be seen as contradictory. Both goals can be achieved. Both sides can (and should) win. The way to achieve this alleged paradox is to engage the security staff. Cooperation is the answer, not conflict. Security staff must have good knowledge of the discovery tools, what they are querying, and maybe most importantly, the benefit to *them*!

Agent-Based Discovery Versus Agentless Discovery

Management instrumentation has long been subject to an argument about whether the instrumentation requires an agent or whether it is agentless. The word *agentless* is actually yet another misnomer, but it has become part of the management vernacular. All management—CMS included—requires an agent of some form. In this context, an agent is instrumentation that can collect and present data. Without an agent, there is no data. We will briefly discuss agentless aspects to help set the record straight.

A bit of history might help. Management agents of the late 1990s came into prominence to offer performance and availability monitoring visibility into infrastructure such as servers and databases. The network already had an agent technology in SNMP, but these other infrastructure elements did not. Once the agents were deployed, users learned that the agents often caused more problems than they solved. They placed an inordinate load on the server (as high as 30%–40% of CPU and memory consumption) and sometimes even made the servers unstable. Agents therefore gained a poor reputation—warranted, but poor nonetheless.

The term "agentless" has since come into use to identify systems where we do not need to load a third-party agent. There is still an *agent*, but it is already included as part of the standard installation. SNMP and WMI are both examples of agentless instrumentation, since they come preloaded by the manufacturer. Agentless discovery usually involves a management system querying the embedded instrumentation. The active mode of application discovery typically leverages this embedded (agentless) instrumentation.

System resources have improved considerably since those adventurous early days of management, and agents have become far better with their stability and performance. Although still less desirable than agentless, sometimes agents are beneficial.

Ideally, the instrumentation should be smart enough to present its own data instead of requiring remote queries. Agentless instrumentation will eventually evolve to this level, but it will probably require an additional agent while the industry pursues such a model.

The correct resolution to the agent versus agentless debate is as it often is—somewhere in the middle. It is desirable to use agentless technologies wherever possible because of costs and simplicity, but some level of agents (the additional ones) will be warranted where more detail is required (see Table 4.1). Eventually, most management will be agentless, but whenever a new management capability emerges, it appears in agent form first. We hope that many of the next innovations will include management designed into the managed entity itself, but we expect that few innovations will realize this ideal state anytime soon. If we all apply pressure to the vendors, however, it will indeed happen.

TABLE **4.1**   Pros and Cons of Agent-Based Versus Agentless Approaches

Type of Approach	Pros
Agent-Based	Fewer network-related access privilege issues
	Can be scripted to query more details about device
	Fewer network traffic-related concerns
Agentless	No need to install on each device
	Can detect new devices without being told they exist
	Can be used to detect rogue devices that weren't already registered

Type of Approach	Cons
Agent-Based	Must be installed on each device
	Cannot detect new devices without being told/installed on
	Must be monitored to ensure healthy operation and regular reporting
Agentless	Increased network traffic
	Potential security risks when firewalls modified to allow agent to query devices
	More difficulty in acquiring all necessary access privileges to traverse entire network

Distributed Domain Managers

In the divide-and-conquer approach to the CMS, the divided parts are best when aligned with configuration domains (for example, network, application, people, server). We highlighted this segmentation earlier, but it is important to stress the point and explain how it works. Your ability to establish, align, and leverage this structure weighs heavily on the success or failure of your CMS. We call these pockets of the CMS *domain managers* because each covers its own domain effectively (see Figure 4.15). These become, in essence, the MDRs.

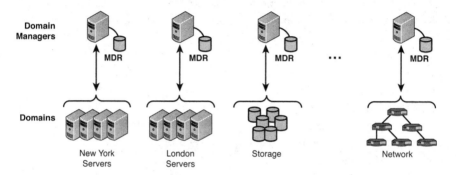

FIGURE 4.15   Domain managers

We show two server domains to emphasize how multiple MDRs can be used for the same purpose—in this case, for coverage of distinct geographies. It is perfectly viable to do the same for any domain, including storage and network. As you plan your own CMS, consider which divisions of the CMS make sense for your scenario and which do not. Certainly, technology domains are likely demarcations, but there can be others that conform to geography, business unit, or any other segmentations that are viable. You want to minimize the number, but minimizing to a single MDR is not always the wise move.

To avoid confusion, we must point out the difference between a domain manager and an MDR. The domain manager is the tool that contains the data. It may be a discovery tool or some other tool that performs a specific function, such as a provisioning tool. The domain manager contains the MDR, which is technically just the data store, not the tool itself. The distinction is important from an architectural perspective, but in practice, the domain manager becomes the "face" of the MDR, and therefore they are nearly synonymous. The domain manager may be an automated discovery tool or something more manual, like PeopleSoft for the HR MDR.

Domain managers are effective because they are optimized to the specific domain, and they are closer to the domain itself. By closer, we mean they can be dispersed geographically, by business unit, or by whichever division makes sense in your environment. Automated discovery works best when the discovery tool has the most straightforward possible access to the domain. This more easily keeps the MDRs within the discovery tools up-to-date. In manually populated domain managers, this "proximity" is less important.

The optimized fit of the domain managers is naturally a good thing, since a network CI and a server CI are very different, just to give an example. Each domain manager has to be tightly focused on its specialized domain so it can address the unique challenges and idiosyncrasies of its domain. Any attempt to cover two or more disparate domains requires multiple schemas and APIs for population and access. This is one area where the difference between a domain manager and an MDR becomes pronounced. The data management (that is, the MDR) is not inherently complex; however, trying to perform all the integration and processing functions (the domain manager) is indeed complex.

The cleanest structure for domain managers is to assign one per domain, but circumstances such as business unit structure and geography may dictate otherwise in your situation. You might actually have a few for a domain. For example, you might have four large data centers full of servers, and a domain manager in each of them. The proximity enables you to maintain timely, accurate data on all your servers, especially if the data centers are each protected by security perimeters. More MDRs is more complex. By now, it should be apparent that we discourage complexity whenever possible, although every situation has different requirements, and parallel MDRs may be beneficial. The higher-levels of abstraction that reference the MDRs should not care where the MDRs reside nor whether they are siblings to others. The referential negotiation that takes place will resolve the right links.

High-Level Abstractions

By now, it should be clear that there are many possible levels of abstraction in the CMS. We keep building abstractions from the elements in the layers below, with many that are abstractions of abstractions. Most of these layers are not implemented in CMDBs. Many are actually not even possible in the available CMDB products. Because a genuine CMS uses object-oriented federation, there is significantly more flexibility to support any possible abstraction. This is a key differentiator between the CMS and a mere CMDB.

The most common abstraction layers in common practice are the application layers, including application infrastructure. These abstractions can be embodied in many tools, but until recently, these tools required manual construction and maintenance of the application models. The new development that provides highly automated construction, population, and maintenance of the models is ADM tools.

These ADM tools use the application discovery modes we explained earlier in this chapter. They perform this discovery for many applications and application components and then assemble the various discovered parts into a map that reflects how all these parts are connected. These maps are, in effect, the models needed for the application layer abstractions. Every person or automation tool that requires visibility into applications will benefit from this map of reality.

Above the application layer, in business services and business processes, abstractions are built with the various modeling standards, most notably Business Process Execution Language (BPEL) and Business Process Modeling Notation (BPMN). There is no commercially available discovery product to automate the population of these modeling layers, but the standards will allow auto-discovery in the near future.

Identifying a Successful CMS

When you have finally achieved a genuine CMS, it will bear the following traits that clearly tell you that the CMS has become a reality:

- Genuine federation, as described in this book, of the data elements is in place. It will not be copy-based integration, but truly referential linking built upon XML and metadata.

- Abstraction models represent higher-level applications, services, and business processes, and these models leverage the data and the abstractions below it in the service chain hierarchy.

- Automated discovery is in place to maintain the accuracy of the CMS.

You need not have 100% of your environment covered in such a way. Indeed, as a moving target, this may never be fully attained. These traits should start to emerge, however, indicating that you are making the right kind of progress.

This progress may not even be recognizable without deeper inspection of the traits because it will happen gradually. There will be no great revelations or revolutions along the way, but at some point, you will understand that you have made the transition. It is a bit like a fitness program. You know you are making progress, but you might not know how far you have come until you walk up that long flight of stairs and you no longer feel short of breath!

Navigating the CMS Information Chains

Use cases query the CMS for the desired information, but they will each initiate and traverse the service chain in different ways. Those that focus on the highest layers (for example, business process monitoring) start at the top and navigate downward, but only as deep as necessary. Those that focus on a specific technology domain (for example, network performance analysis) usually begin in the relevant lower layer and remain there.

Sometimes, a use case will demand navigation right down to the live element, even below the lowest MDR level in the hierarchy. Diagnostic tools and processes are a good example. Network diagnosis may need to drill down through the MDRs and right to the SNMP instrumentation on a router. Tools can do this easily as long as the federation architecture is in place to enable it. Few commercially available tools exist to navigate in this way, but the work in the standards bodies is now fueling rapid development and expansion of the tools for such scenarios.

Navigation is not necessarily just downward. Use cases can navigate upward (for example, business impact analysis of a server consolidation exercise) or parallel (for example, desktop Asset Management). In fact, the relationships go in so many different directions that our minds, accustomed to visualizing only three dimensions, struggle to visualize them. Navigation across the CMS can follow any of these dimensions in any direction. How the relationships are traversed is governed by the CIs and the attributes of the relationships themselves. Recall that everything in the CMS has attributes, even the relationships.

When we cover some of the more popular use cases in Chapter 9, we go into more detail about how each navigates the CMS.

Why Federation Makes More Sense Than a Monolithic CMDB

We have laid out federation of the CMS, but why is it better than the previous notion of the monolithic CMDB? Many argue that their CMDBs are delivering value, and they are probably right. We argue, however, that to realize the full potential of IT excellence and ensure future organizational viability, the monolithic model poses an impediment. Federation in the true spirit of the CMS is the correct path to excellence.

Efficiency: Distributed Processing Reduces Resource Demands

A single CMDB is a monstrosity for any organization with significant size or complexity. Even in smaller instances, resource demands can be prohibitive. The inescapable fact is that an incredible amount of data is maintained in a CMDB or in a CMS. This data places a heavy load on the server, the database, and peripheral resources like networks, storage, and yes, people. The monolithic CMDB winds up collapsing under its own weight! The only way to overcome resource bottlenecks is to distribute the load.

It is possible to distribute load without federation, but the weak linkages make the distributed system fragile and difficult to manage. As an example, typical remote database connections cannot easily adapt to the different MDR locations that are needed in the complex modeling used in federation. They remain largely fixed in place, not flexible. True federation, as spelled out in this chapter, offers local controls and management while preserving strong unity with the other elements of the CMS. Federation bonds the CIs in a way that doesn't require cumbersome relational database (RDBMS) connections or duplication of raw data.

The referential method of data access ensures tight linkage while still remaining flexible enough to adapt to changing conditions. There is admittedly much more sophistication and therefore more overhead to maintaining the labyrinth of CIs and relationships, but automation tools make it look easy. All complex systems require automation to simplify their management. A well-federated CMS is bound by the same requirements, and tools are evolving very quickly to address this challenge.

Discovery is significantly more efficient in a distributed, federated model. If all data is being pulled into a single point, discovery intervals must be set to ridiculously long interval lengths. If each discovery poll takes 12 minutes to complete (this is extremely generous as an average) and you have 6,000 devices to cover, that suggests a minimum discovery interval of 1,200 hours. That's 50 days! To be truthful, discovery tools use many tricks to improve this, sometimes dramatically, but long intervals are unavoidable. Federation divides this discovery across multiple tools, further improving the timeliness of the data.

The end state (or at least the stable state, as there is never an end) of the CMS contains many MDRs, domain managers, discovery tools, and CMS consumer tools, all linked by the federation system. Servers are scattered across the enterprise and maybe even outside the enterprise. Data stores exist in memory, in relational databases, and in many other forms, and the network is the plumbing that ties it all together. Parallelism is the savior of resource demand, and federation is the key to parallel execution and access.

Accuracy: Raw Data Is Optimally Accurate and Closer to the Source

A monolithic CMDB is a proverbial "jack-of-all-trades, master-of-none" situation. It contains all the details of the various domains, and it can therefore become a maintenance nightmare. Trade-offs are often made in the data to make it fit the generalized CMDB. You can customize the CMDB to adapt to your needs, but this gets you back to the maintenance nightmare because you need to exercise care to avoid corrupting other data elements.

With federation, the data is maintained in an MDR tailor made to the exact specifications necessary for that data. The MDRs for unrelated domains and objects are functionally isolated from each other, nearly eliminating any chance to corrupt one when making changes to another. The only common ground they share is the federation mechanisms needed to link them for their intended purposes. This results in a protective barrier around the MDRs, and penetration of the barriers is tightly controlled through the well-defined federation mechanisms. In the monolith, you can separate data tables, but still be vulnerable to cross-object corruption because the isolation is much weaker than in a federated model.

By dividing the load across domain managers and MDRs, you can also locate them closer to the actual managed domains. A data center MDR can actually reside within the data center. You can split MDRs by business unit, by geography, or any other segmentation that makes sense. The monolith sits in one place, and all domains suffer from an equally mediocre compromise.

The benefits of being "close to the source" are many, but the best reason is to minimize resource consumption and response time to gather data. You can get more granular with timeliness when you are closer. Tighter granularity is more accurate.

Flexibility: Information Is Easier to Use and Reuse

With partial thanks to the efficiency and accuracy reasons described previously, we also gain superior flexibility. If the access is more efficient and the data is more accurate, we can do many more things with the same copy of the data. One use case can access the data for its purpose, and another can use the exact same data for a very different purpose. This is the principle behind data reuse, whether it is in an object-oriented software application or in the CMS. We need to have confidence in the authenticity of the data if it is going to be the catalyst behind our most significant decisions.

Confidence in the data is gained by initially verifying that what the MDR is capturing is indeed correct. Most often, this is performed manually, comparing reality to the contents of the MDR. After several such verifications, we tend to become more confident in the MDR, trusting it to be the definitive data source. Depending on your quality control needs and previous verification results, we should periodically revisit this verification to ensure that the MDR remains within the accuracy tolerance acceptable to your organization. It is rare for an MDR to drift away from accuracy, especially when discovery is involved. Still, it *can* happen, and the integrity of the CMS is too important to risk complacency.

Data reuse is a prime benefit of federation. Many CMDBs, especially in large environments, rely on copy integration to get their data. This immediately makes the data's accuracy and authenticity suspect. Instead of using data that is a duplicate, federation ensures you tap only into the one true source. Its authenticity is guaranteed based on its exclusivity.

In the multitude of use cases, most raw data does not need to be stored for any substantial length of time. Good use cases access the data, perform their relevant functions, and then discard the raw data. The data is not useful in the long term—only the processed information that results from the specific use case. Even in these situations, the results are then stored in their own MDR for further processing by yet another layer in the service chain. Remember, one use case's information may be another use case's raw data.

That said, certain long-term use cases such as trending and long-term pattern recognition can benefit from some of this "useless" data. Dramatically lower storage costs and multitier storage architectures now make it possible to cost-effectively retain a huge volume of data, so there is less economic incentive to discard old data. Exercise sound data retention policies for your situation to achieve the proper balance of visibility and cost.

Integrating External Domains in the Federated Model

Other than touching on it briefly in the security implications section, we have been intentionally vague about organizational locations of the MDRs in the federated model. Most will be located within the boundaries of your enterprise, but some might be located within an external partner. As time goes on, more of the MDRs will actually migrate outside the traditional enterprise.

Targeted outsourcing, tighter integration of business partners, and closer touch to customers are all factors pushing some MDRs outside. Business services are dependent upon these external relationships, and the general business trend of the flat world[15] will see these relationships expanding more. As this trend continues, we must ensure the CMS can adapt to the new model. More specifically, federation must cross once-traditional boundaries.

One of the architectural tenets of federation is the ability to link any MDR regardless of where it resides. In theory, this is true. In practice, additional measures are necessary to allow federated communications across these boundaries, but to do it in a responsible manner. Just as business applications can securely exchange data with business partners using XML messages, the federated CMS can follow very similar methods and technologies.

The end result is a CMS that doesn't really care where the MDRs reside. Certainly, the architecture, design, and implementation of the CMS will need to account for these situations. Once operational, data federation will refer to CIs and attributes in very similar ways. In the next chapter, we cover the actual implementation of the CMS. This is where much of the CMS theory becomes practical and useful.

Frequently Asked Questions

Question: Federating the data is too complex, so why is it worth pursuing?

Answer: Federation is indeed complex, but that's why we need tools with a high degree of automation. One of the best benefits of automation is the ability to hide complexity under the covers of the tools. They can map complex relationships and link to remote data sources far better than manual methods. Without automated modeling and discovery tools, federation would be impossible. The entire CMS is embodied in many cooperating tools, all working together in harmony to serve the many use cases.

---

15. The flat world is a concept popularized in Thomas Friedman's groundbreaking book, *The World Is Flat*. The flat world is one where traditional corporate and geographical boundaries are becoming meaningless. New social and economic models, with fuzzy, radically different boundaries, are becoming the norm, and our world is irreversibly changing as a result. You can visit Mr. Friedman's web site at http://www.thomaslfriedman.com/bookshelf/the-world-is-flat.

Question: The CMDB we now use is working well. Why would I want to interfere with this success?

Answer: It may be capable for basic Asset Management, but the CMDB of the past cannot support the process integration of the future. You should work with your CMDB vendor to migrate toward a federated model with support for the CMDBf standard. The work you put into your CMDB should be preserved as much as possible, but you should expect to carve CIs out of the central CMDB as you move them to MDRs in a genuine CMS. The work that should be preserved is the modeling that has been done to represent your environment and the continued management of manually-maintained CIs and attributes. Other CIs and attributes that can be automatically maintained by discovery should be migrated away from existing monolithic CMDBs to become MDRs in the federated model.

Question: My RDBMS can be distributed. Isn't this the same as federation?

Answer: Database distribution is very different because it is unable to adapt to the changing needs of the CMS. You can "bolt on" federation code to turn a database into an MDR. In fact, many MDRs do just this. The database alone (that is, without the federation code) is too static to act as an MDR.

Question: All that metadata and XML is too much overhead. Wouldn't an RDBMS be simpler and more efficient?

Answer: It is true that metadata adds complexity, but just as in our first question, automation technologies can make this so transparent that it's virtually invisible to most CMS users. What metadata gives us, that an RDBMS cannot, is flexibility. Data types need not be explicitly defined, and the referential pointers allow much easier remote access of the data. To this end, metadata makes life much simpler, not more complex.

Question: Isn't ADM too invasive and resource intensive?

Answer: Few can legitimately argue that ADM is not invasive or that it doesn't consume more resources; however, you must balance these issues with the benefits gained. ADM is a major step forward in the automation of CMS construction, population, and maintenance. The benefit of having such a trustworthy perspective of the applications gives us unprecedented visibility into the number-one trouble spot for IT organizations today—application behavior. To obtain this visibility, we must more closely examine some corners of the environment that have previously been off-limits. This can be done securely, and it can be done with minimal impact on resources. The resource demands are determined by discovery architecture, configuration, and implementation. As with all good ideas, poor execution negates the value. Execute properly, and ADM offers significantly more gain than pain.

Summary

We hope we have made the case for how information is constructed from the many dimensions of relationships among the CIs. The federated structure for a CMS is superior to the monolithic model, with several MDRs making up the typical CMS, and the most basic data residing in the MDRs and only in these MDRs. The protected integrity of the MDR data is a hallmark of the CMS, as is the sophisticated linking established and leveraged through federation.

The truly useful objects in the CMS are abstractions of the raw data, built using web-based metadata and object-oriented modeling technologies. A hierarchical organization is developed where abstractions are built using other abstractions, all of which reflect the actual services in place in the business technology environment. Services themselves need to be properly defined based upon the producers and consumers of those services. Once defined, they can be modeled and accurately represented in the CMS.

The CMS must be accurate. You will deploy numerous discovery technologies to help maintain this accuracy. The discovery technologies feed the MDRs or become MDRs unto themselves and then participate in the hierarchical federation to produce the multiple levels of services that make the CMS useful.

Now that we made a strong case for the federated architecture and explained how it works, we can move on to some practical guidelines for actually deploying the CMS.

CHAPTER 5

CMS Deployment Strategy

When most of us buy a book like this one, there is usually that one chapter you look for in the table of contents in which you hope to find "The Answers" to your questions. Although our questions are different, we still all seek "The Answers" to them. We hope that you find your answers in this chapter, but we aren't naive enough to think that we can provide every reader with the answers to all of their questions. What we hope to do is provide answers to some of your questions and, for the rest of the questions, a pathway to find your answers.

Building and deploying your CMS is going to take a lot of careful analysis and planning so that you ensure you deliver a platform that can grow with you as your level of ITIL[1] maturity grows. As you gather specifications from your business partners, service owners, and process owners, you will reach a point of saturation where you realize that you will simply not be able to deliver everything they want in your first or maybe even second and third release. It is vital, however, that you capture their utopian desires because it is the only way you will be able to design and architect a platform that can grow with you if the organization wants it to. The reality is that you will never reach utopia and you'll never build the perfect system, but if you design and architect the platform for only your first release, you will likely be looking for work elsewhere after you propose structural changes to a system that

---

1. ITIL® is a Registered Trademark, and a Registered Community Trademark of the Office of Government Commerce, and is registered in the U.S. Patent and Trademark Office. It is an abbreviation for the *IT Infrastructure Library*, a collection of IT operational best practices developed by an agency of the British government (now called Office of Government Commerce, or OGC) in the late 1980s and enriched over the years by a global coalition of IT professionals. To learn more, visit the official OGC ITIL web site at http://www.itil.co.uk/. The IT Service Management Forum (itSMF) also provides a wealth of information. Their web site is http://www.itsmf.org.

was just deployed. This should be common sense but sometimes, in an effort to "just get it deployed," shortcuts are taken that come back to cost people dearly.

You need to ensure that you *design for the future but build for today* so that you don't get caught in a difficult situation when you deploy subsequent phases. You will not be able to envision every possible thing that might come at you, but you should be able to leverage some of the subject matter experts around you to help you with scoping issues. You will already have in your possession the requirements from the service and process owners and all the extras that the business partners would like, so use them and make some educated guesses as to how they might use the CMS in three or five years under ideal conditions. If addressing these ideals is not going to increase costs significantly and is not going to impact your deployment schedule, you should design them into your solution. It is a calculated risk that you are taking that won't have a negative impact if you don't use it. If you need to leverage it in the future, you will not only be saving your business partners a lot of money by avoiding the need to re-architect the entire platform, but you will be able to deliver their new requirements in a much shorter timeframe because the platform will be capable of scaling to satisfy the new demand.

The actual deployment of your CMS will require a lot of coordination with your business partners, IT staff, Service Desk, service owners, process owners, and just about anyone else who might interact with it. If your initiative is part of a project to replace an existing Service Desk tool and you have redesigned your processes, this becomes even more challenging because all the people will need to be trained on the new processes as well as the new tool. Do not underestimate the amount of training that will need to be done. Although the CMS is an enabling technology for others to use, you need to be deeply involved in supporting the people who design the training materials and courses to ensure that they are instructing people to access the CMS information in the most efficient manner and according to the work instructions for that particular process. This also helps you capture feedback that you can incorporate into future releases. The individuals going through the training, especially those who currently have a tool in place, will typically be very candid with you if they don't like something or if the data is too cumbersome to access. Don't ignore their comments, but also don't compromise crucial design decisions that you may have made either. Be sure to understand what they are seeking to do and why. This will allow you to either find alternatives or develop a different way to access the data without compromising the original design.

Although it has been stated already, we want to remind you again that one size does not fit all when you are building and deploying a CMS. The approach that is taken and the amount of work needed will vary from company to company depending on the technologies you have in place, the amount of redesign that your processes are going through, and the amount of manual data collection/entry you need to do. You will need to assess your particular situation to determine how these things factor into your environment. They will, without question, impact what you will need to do and how you will do it. So again, read the text, but more importantly, be sure to understand its meaning before setting out on your initiative.

Getting Your Hands Dirty

As much as we would like to automate everything and have technology accomplish all the tasks we need to perform, the reality is that there are some things that we will have to do manually. For some companies, the amount of manual work required to automate is a large factor when it comes to deciding what to do or not to do with regards to a CMS solution. Depending on the company, they might need to do a tremendous amount of manual work that may just not be cost effective. On the other hand, a company may be small enough that they can more easily justify the reallocation of some Full-Time Equivalent (FTE) hours to manipulate data manually instead of a large capital expenditure for new technology.

Companies that have invested heavily in automating things like their software distribution, monitoring, change detection, event alerting, and capacity allocation processes have available to them a wealth of information and technology that reduces their need to manually generate and maintain this type of information. However, they most likely had to make these large financial investments because they are too large and complex to operate using only manual processes. A Fortune 100 company, for example, may have thousands of servers in multiple data centers that get replaced at a rate of hundreds per month, whereas a small company might have only a couple of hundred servers on one data center with a replacement rate of 50 per year. You can easily see that maintaining the changes in the small company manually is much more manageable than in the Fortune 100 company.

In some cases, you may choose to start off using a manual process for some aspects of your solution until you iron out all the details of how the technological solution will be implemented. Of course, you may not be able to address the full scope of the requirement manually as you would technologically, but you can use it to demonstrate the process and flush out any issues that the process might have. For example, the tool you use for your Change Management process might not be able to capture the granular detail of the modification that is being requested in the RFC. If this is the case, you might need to implement a process that requires individuals to check a small sample of RFCs for the details being requested and manually validate that those requirements were fulfilled. Once your tool has the ability to capture the granular detail, you can automate the validation and perform it on all the RFCs, not just a small sampling.

As discussed in the "Building Service and Application Infrastructure Models—It's What Matters" section later in the chapter, these models require a significant amount of manual effort and will likely be the largest amount of manual effort required for your entire initiative because there are no real alternatives. If your organization is small and doesn't have a lot of automation in place, you will likely have to begin by manually defining the business service models and manually documenting the technology components they are comprised of. You will then need to notify everyone who might interact with those components that they will be placed under strict Change Management Control, and the models associated with them must be updated whenever a change is made to any of the components. What is also very important for you to communicate to them is that not all technology components in the environment will be under the same level of Change Management Control. Only those components associated with a controlled business service model will have that level of scrutiny. This can become a very delicate and confusing situation because identical technology components will be handled differently depending on whether they are a part of a business service model or not. Make sure that everyone also understands that the data quality of the components under control versus not under control could vary significantly. In order for the operations personnel to perform their work with the proper level of scrutiny, they need to be fully aware of the data quality they are dealing with every time because it will influence their decision-making process.

Regardless of whether you do things manually or with technology, the controls and processes still need to exist and must pass the same level of audit scrutiny. In many cases, you may begin with a manual process out of necessity to address a need, and in other cases, you may not be able to justify the technology expenditure. Be sure that you document the manual process carefully. You will need to perform a more significant amount of manual auditing on the data than you would if it was an automated solution because you are relying on humans to enter data and verify it, making it more prone to random errors than technology solutions. Also, be conscious of the fact that manual processes cannot handle the same volume as a technology-based one, so you need to drastically reduce the depth and breadth of your initiative if you must rely heavily on manual intervention.

What Comes First?

The big question everyone always has is: "What do I do first?" That, of course, depends on a variety of questions that you need to ask yourself. They will not give you a specific answer, but will help you gather your thoughts about what needs to be done, where you might have some foundational gaps, and any other items that need to be addressed before implementing your CMS. The following are some, but not all, of the questions that will help you determine where you should begin and what needs to be addressed:

- **Business Services:** Do you have business services defined?

- **Resolving Problems:** What problem(s) are you trying to address with the ITIL initiative and CMS?

- **First Timers:** Are you implementing a Service Desk solution for the first time?

- **Maturity:** How mature are your Change Management and Release and Deployment Management processes?

- **Existing Technologies:** What technologies do you already have in place for things like monitoring, software deployment, Asset Management, and Network Management?

Let's look at each of the questions independently and get a better understanding as to why they will impact what you do first. After reading each one and getting a better understanding of them, you should have a better feel for where your CMS initiative should begin, or more specifically, what data you need to target for your initiative. Regardless of where you begin, however, the end state of each cycle is always Continual Service Improvement (CSI), which essentially brings you back to the beginning to assess where you can enhance the process or its supporting technologies.

Business Services

Business services are vital if you hope to deploy a CMS that will fulfill "all" aspects of the ITIL framework. Business services enable you to move past the application infrastructure model and get at the real core of what your business partners care about: the customer experience. Unfortunately, most companies have not developed their software in a way that they can easily parse out a business service from the application to determine whether the service is down versus the whole application. Object-oriented applications in the mid '90s promised this, but were not able to become fully entrenched for a variety of reasons. Service-Oriented Architecture is the latest attempt to try and push the software engineering maturity to that next level. Regardless, however, of its success or failure, you must be prepared for business services by designing the capability into your CMS.

Although most companies have not fully matured in the delivery of service-based software, some have been able to make significant headway with regards to listing the business services they offer. The services might not map one-to-one with a discrete software module, but it is a step in the right direction—defining a catalog of business services is a great first step. Don't be discouraged if you can only define your business services at a high level initially. Define the business services as best as you can and associate them with the applications that ultimately deliver them and technology that enables them. As your software engineering matures and enables you to become more granular with your software modules, you can revisit your business services and bring them to the next level of granularity. At that stage, you will be moving closer to identifying exactly what pieces of technology support and impact the service. If you have no business services defined at all, map the technology pieces to the applications and treat the applications as the services until you can formally define the business services. Remember that it is better to make some progress in a less-than-ideal situation than to sit around waiting for the ideal situation to arrive. Figure 5.1 illustrates, from a business service perspective, a simple flow that should help you get over some hurdles when starting out on your CMS design.

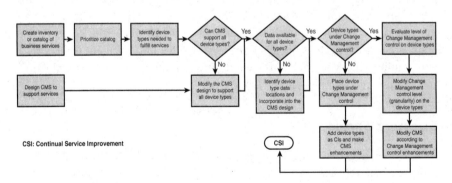

FIGURE 5.1   CMS design consideration: Driving design from business service perspective

Resolving Problems

Like all projects, your ITIL initiative is being performed because there are some issues with technologies or processes in your environment that your management has decided are unacceptable and need to be addressed. You need to fully understand those problems in order to deliver your project and meet their expectations.

Besides regulatory requirements, the two main areas that most companies are trying to address, in very generic terms, are Mean Time Between Failures (MTBF) and Mean Time To Resolution (MTTR). These two things are metrics that identify the frequency that outages occur and the amount of time that it takes to remedy an outage when it does occur. The two general areas are tackled in very different ways and by different processes.

The Change Management, Problem Management, Availability Management, and to some extent Knowledge Management processes are the major players in increasing your MTBF metrics. They collectively help assess modifications to your environment for impact on your services and potentially prevent those RFCs from being approved as is. With information about the success of previous RFCs, the historical stability of the equipment in question, and your business cycle, you will be able to put together a strong assessment of the situation. The information for this assessment must come from your CMS, and you need to have a full understanding of what information is available and its reliability.

The Incident Management process in conjunction with Knowledge Management is a primary factor for an MTTR-driven initiative. These processes need accurate and targeted data as quickly as possible to help assess the current situation. They provide workarounds and potential remedies, as well as possibly alerting others of pending outages if they can access relevant data. They can only do this if they have a complete picture of the segment of the environment that is experiencing the outage. If they are notified that a specific network device is not performing up to its standards, they could potentially identify downstream ramifications if it is not resolved in time and proactively alert those individuals or support personnel to take action in the event that it does impact them.

When you are designing your CMS, as shown in Figure 5.2, you need to take these aspects into account so that you can narrow down and prioritize the data that your processes will need. In some companies, it may be that they have an immediate need to increase the quality of service and uptime of the applications and services. In other cases, perhaps there is a feeling that they need to stop inflicting outages on their business partners, so they want to get their Change Management processes under better control. Neither one is wrong; it is all a matter of what is more important to your company.

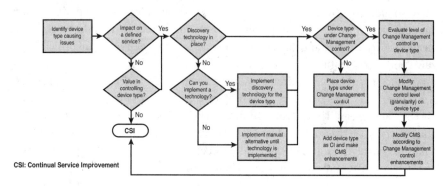

FIGURE 5.2   CMS design consideration: Initiative driven by desire to resolve existing problems

First Timers

If this is your first foray into Service Desk- or Service Management-related implementations, it is sort of a double-edged sword. If you have no formal processes or system in place, you don't have to convert current processes or integrate existing systems. On the other hand, if you have nothing in place, you have to start from the very beginning, and it will feel like a triathlon to you versus a marathon for everyone else. We prefer to be more optimistic and believe that although some aspects will be very challenging to get started, you have the luxury of doing it the right way with no legacy mind-set to drag along. You won't have to listen to the "but we don't do it that way" or "we've always done it this way" type of statements.

Although this might be your first time implementing a Service Desk-related solution, you should have some data already available to you unless you are a startup or a very small company. You might have only a minimal amount of automation in your environment if you are small. If you are a little larger, you have likely implemented some of the basic monitoring and operations tools in order to support the business. Regardless of your size, find out what technologies you have in place and determine their reliability. While you are doing that assessment, also document all the spreadsheets, notebooks, or whatever people use today to help them get their job done.

As you are doing your assessment and gathering information, begin to think about the overlaps between these spreadsheets and notebooks and how you might be able to facilitate efforts between the respective owners to work together to merge their data sources. Use the flow diagram in Figure 5.3 to help with some of the decisions. Facilitate these meetings and conversations but do not take over the ownership of the effort because they might feel as though they are losing their autonomy. Empower them to be part of your initiative as foundational members and contributors. Assist their efforts by providing a data or meta model of how the data should be organized and how you will be able to aggregate their efforts into your larger CMS initiative. Share your vision of the CMS with them and let them help you mold that vision into a design that will grow with your organization.

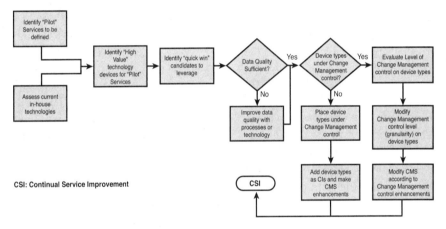

FIGURE 5.3   CMS design consideration: First time deploying Service Desk or Service Management solution

Maturity

The maturity of your Change Management and Release and Deployment Management processes are fundamental to your ability to control the data in your CMS. One of the key purposes of the CMS is to understand what your environment is supposed to look like and the modifications it has undergone or is undergoing. Without these processes in place, the CMS only has the ability to describe "what the environment looks like at that point in time" versus "what it should look like." The difference may be subtle, but it is crucial to your organization's ability to fully understand why things are or are not happening. They help you to understand where the issue may reside, such as the following:

- Was the change request documentation inaccurate?

- Was the release package flawed?

- Did errors occur during the deployment that went undetected?

- Did the submitter of the change request simply make a mistake?

- Did the implementer of the change request make a mistake?

There are many things that can happen during the cycle of a change, and only if you capture the planned/proposed state in your RFC do you stand a chance at understanding what may be happening in your environment.

The Change Management process acts as the CMS gatekeeper and captures all the modifications that take place in your CMS. In theory, there should be absolutely no data modified in the CMS unless there is a corresponding RFC to that same level of detail. This topic is very sensitive among the ITIL idealists, so we won't get into too much detail on it. The pure ITIL theory will have you controlling every data element in your CMS, from origination through retirement and every step in between, with the help of the Change and Release and Deployment Management processes. Change Management documents what the purpose and goal of the change is, and Release and Deployment Management carries that request through to production all the while updating the CMS with the intermediate steps and CI status changes. We agree with this and believe it should be done this way. We also recognize, however, that for most companies, the volume of changes is so great that it is not realistic to believe that every jumper setting and configuration modification on a server or laptop can be managed to this level of granularity.

So what can you do? What you do is make a calculated, risk assessment-based decision on how deep into your CIs you can realistically manage and control data to that level. But first, you need to make sure that your Change Management and Release and Deployment Management process can do that. If they are not able to do that, you have to either back off on the level of granularity even more until you reach the point where your Change and Release and Deployment Management processes can handle it or allow the data to go into the CMS without the controls. There is an obvious issue with allowing uncontrolled data to be part of your CMS, but you have to make a judgment call based on the following:

- Is there value to your end users to include uncontrolled data in your CMS?

- Can you somehow flag the uncontrolled data in a way that the end users can clearly distinguish the controlled from the uncontrolled data?

- Are there any manual processes you can implement in the short term to help increase the quality of the uncontrolled data while your Change and Release and Deployment Management processes mature?

- Are you introducing risk to your business by providing uncontrolled data to the end users?

- How accurate do you believe your uncontrolled data to be and can you demonstrate its accuracy?

The bottom line is, how accurate does your data have to be before you would consider including it in your CMS without the controls provided by Change Management and Release and Deployment Management? In some cases, due to regulatory requirements, it is not an option; in others, it may be perfectly acceptable as long as you can denote what is controlled versus uncontrolled. Regardless of the situation, however, you need to push your Change Management and Release and Deployment Management processes into high levels of maturity if you want to solidify your CMS design long term (see Figure 5.4). You may be asking yourself, "What is a high-level of maturity?" Unfortunately, it is a relative term, and there is really no set level that deems you mature or not. This is one area where you will likely need to engage an external service provider to understand where exactly you stand as compared to your industry peers. You will want them to perform a complete assessment of your environment and provide a relative comparison to your industry peers. The alternative to engaging a consulting firm is to establish a strong network of peers where you can share ideas and accomplishments. Local Interest Groups (LIGs) and online interactive sites/blogs can also be a good way to get a feel for where you stand as compared to your peers. The thing to remember is that you need to achieve a level of maturity that works for you, not anyone else. If it works for your company and is the right balance of cost and value, then you have achieved the level of maturity that you need. Don't forget that ITIL Continual Service Improvement (CSI) will keep pushing you to become more efficient, so wherever you decide is the right level of maturity is the point at which you will begin exercising your CSI efforts.

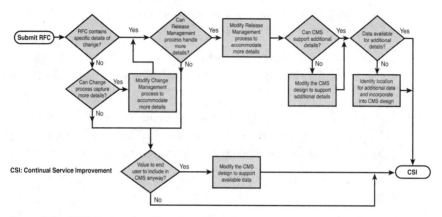

FIGURE 5.4   CMS design consideration: Maturing process captures details to match CMS capability.

Existing Technologies

The reason for understanding what technologies you already have in place is because this helps you scope the amount of work that needs to be done to gather information for your initial load, as well as data that helps with your Verification and Audit activities to ensure that the CMS is accurate. If you have a mature technology environment with regards to monitoring, software deployment, Asset Management, and Network Management, you will have many of the potential CIs already being gathered and maintained for you so your energy will not need to be directed in those areas. You can instead focus on gathering data for additional CIs or apply that energy toward the automation of aspects within your Change and Release and Deployment Management processes to support your maintenance of the CMS. Figure 5.5 walks through, at a high level, the flow of CMS design decisions that you should consider when assessing your existing technologies.

We have stated on several occasions that we are big proponents of leveraging technologies wherever you can and wherever it makes sense. Technology implementations, besides running faster and longer than people, are typically more reliable and consistent over the long haul than people performing the same function. If you are able to deploy a technology to perform some of these repetitive tasks, you can redeploy those individuals in areas that can't be automated, such as building application and service models. Everything comes at a cost, and if you don't leverage technology to automate the repetitive tasks, you will likely not have the resources available to perform the tasks that cannot be automated.

We would be surprised if you could sell the idea of buying these technologies exclusively for a CMS effort, so try to work with your domain experts to procure the technologies. Work with your Release and Deployment Management managers to see if they want to jointly propose a project to implement an enterprise-wide software distribution tool. Put together the requirements you both need and build your business case together. The problem you will encounter is that these projects tend to be multiyear and will significantly impact your CMS timeline. So, you need to promote and actively participate in their acquisition and implementation, but at the same time, design short-term alternatives until the technology is available.

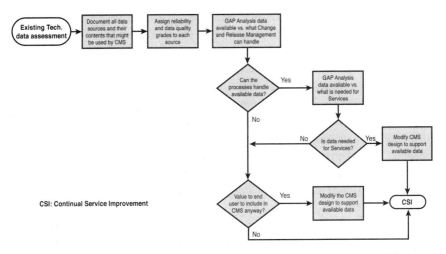

FIGURE 5.5   CMS design consideration: Leveraging existing technologies to deliver "value"

These five areas of thought are by far not the only things you need to consider when determining what to do first or how to go about designing your CMS. We hope they have provided insight into some of the moving parts that affect your CMS implementation and helped you begin to formulate your own plan of attack. Another thing that we hope you were able to get out of it is that there are any number of areas that could be worked on that provide tremendous benefit before you even start your CMS project. These are especially critical if, for whatever reason, your project is delayed—you can work on improving these areas while you fight your political or budgetary battles, and once approved, you benefit from them being in better condition to support the CMS initiative.

One controversial element in Figures 5.1 through 5.5 is the notion of including data in your CMS, even if your Change and Release and Deployment Management processes can't manage it and if your defined services don't require it. This is not an ITIL recommended option, but from a practitioner perspective, your job is to provide value to your end users. We would argue that if the value of using data that is not managed by the ITIL control processes outweighs the risks of using the unmanaged data, you should strongly consider including it in your CMS design. We would recommend that you somehow flag the data that is managed by the ITIL control process versus what is not, so that it is clear to your end users what data is being audited and verified and what is not. You could do this with visual indicators on your ITSM tool, comprehensive online help documentation, end user training, or some combination of any three. The point is that a mechanism needs to be in place for the end users to determine the difference, and the technology must be able to support your desire to denote which elements are controlled and which are not.

The remainder of the chapter digs a little bit deeper into specific areas you need to address during your CMS implementation. They are loosely ordered in the manner that you would tackle them, but do not hold steadfast to the order we describe if you can achieve more value by modifying it. For example, if you already have well-defined application and service models, and want to focus your CMS implementation on only the most critical applications in your environment, you may choose to "attack the domains," but only for the components (that is, server, router, SAN) in those models. On the other hand, if you don't have the models well defined, you might want to target all your servers, regardless of what services and applications they support, and ignore routers and SAN. Your approach might be to assemble them into groups that support your services and applications and use this as your first crude attempt at defining a service or application infrastructure model. Again, focus on the areas your company will get the most value from and direct your energies to deliver on that.

Building Service and Application Infrastructure Models—It's What Matters

After everything is said and done, the end users and your business partners will not be very happy unless you can associate all the technology items discussed into a form that means something to them in terms that they understand. That form is a business service model, and the terms are business, not technological. This is one of the main efforts that define whether your initiative is seen as successful or not and is vital in order for you to fulfill your CMS initiative. Unfortunately, it is also one that cannot be significantly automated and requires some manual intervention. Remember that you can design the best CMS and populate it with the most complete and accurate data, but if the business partners cannot understand it or the end users cannot use it, it will not be viewed as a success.

Up until now, the discussion has been very technology centric, and there is a lot of value in it in order to establish a base of information to work from. However, there comes a point where the CMS solution needs to be wrapped in a layer of information and terminology that is intuitive to the end users. The CMS will be used extensively by nontechnologists, and they do not want to interact with things that are called servers, routers, and network cards. What they want to work with is a simplified picture, at a higher level than a technology item, which represents their business service model. The graphical representation you build in the CMS should illustrate, in layman's terms, the technology components that help to deliver that business service to the customers. They don't generally care about all the bits and bytes; they just care that their customer is being serviced and their investments in the technology are being used efficiently. Your focus needs to be on developing a way to shield them from all the technological details you have collected and deliver a graphical representation of the business service model they are interested in. When the technologists get involved in the RFCs or incident tickets, they will need all of the details, but the end users and business partners do not.

Let's first briefly describe the difference between an application infrastructure model and a business service model. An application infrastructure model is still somewhat of a technology-centric term. It refers to a technology solution or collection of technology components, which is comprised of both software and hardware elements. It is represented graphically and will generally contain icons of servers, workstations, and network devices that support the application being modeled. Software modules and architectures such as J2EE[2] components reside on these technology components. On the other hand, a business service model is technology agnostic and is graphically represented with boxes labeled with terms that represent functions of the service or process the customer interacts with or would recognize. Figures 5.6 and 5.7 represent a simplified sample of each so that you have a sense of what they

---

2. J2EE, Java, and all Java-based marks are trademarks or registered trademarks of Sun Microsystems, Inc., in the United States and other countries.

might look like. The figures do not depict the software components that might reside on each technology component because it can get overly complex and will vary widely between implementations. Pure application models go one step beyond the application infrastructure model and add the next layer of granularity by including the software technology components as well. For the systems in your environment, you should already have either the application or application infrastructure models defined so that you can easily make the translation to business service models.

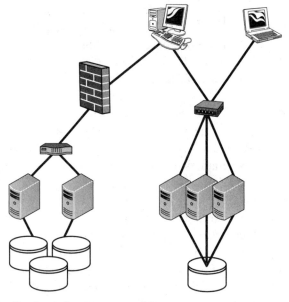

FIGURE 5.6   Application infrastructure model

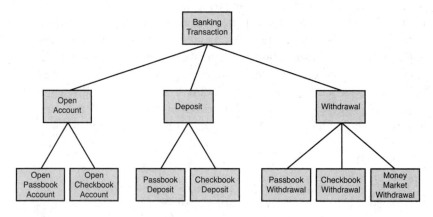

FIGURE 5.7   Business service model

Now that the difference between an application infrastructure model and business service model has been discussed, it is important to make sure that everyone has the same understanding of what each model is and what each needs to contain. Essentially, the models represent all the components that support or deliver the service and the relationships between those components. The key in the application model is really in the relationships, because without them, you are only managing the inventory of technology items for the model. By connecting the inventory items with relationships, you are transforming the list of disparate technology items into a form that has value. This model represents a union of items that collectively mean something and will be used by individuals to make decisions about change requests and incidents so it is vital that its accuracy is managed.

Depending on your organization, you might have no choice but to begin with designing application infrastructure models if you have not yet defined your business services. These models can originate from your architecture personnel, application developers, or your monitoring and event management departments. Most organizations have some level of these models documented in binders or electronic design tools. The issue is that they are generally out of date by the time the application system is deployed to the production environment. As with the technology components, these models need to be managed and maintained. This can be a very difficult concept for you to sell to your organization because you are essentially telling them that architectural documentation for the applications under control need to undergo the same level of Change Management rigor as the components do. The main reason for this is because you need to be notified when these documents are updated so that you can modify your model in the CMS. If the model in your CMS is not updated when items are added or removed, your CMS will not present accurate information to the users. If the information is wrong, individuals using it to perform impact assessments or incident research could execute tasks that negatively impact the application or service.

In order to build the business service model, you need to work with your business partner to understand how they do business. You can look to your *OGC Service Strategy ITIL* book for in-depth details about how to go about this. Your business partners generally already have some form of a business services list available, but it needs to be defined in much more detail in order for you to leverage it. When working with them on defining the list, remind them they may want to design it with some level of financial tie factored in. If the list is somehow formulated in a way that it truly represents their business, they will be able to associate technology investments with the business services and get detailed financial metrics down to the technology component level. This assumes, of course, that you implement a Financial Management process. With the process in place, business services defined, and a CMS deployed, your business partners have tremendous insight into the value of their investments and should be able to make informed business decisions that factor in real technology value metrics. Operational transparency is a key element for any internal IT operation if they want to be seen as being a "value-add" operation versus overhead cost operation.

One thing to remember is that IT organizations and departments also have services they deliver. Think about companies that offer outsourcing solutions. Their catalog of products is essentially services that their business offers. For example, they might offer service products such as collaboration, application hosting, or systems monitoring. These are the same business services that your business partners are seeking from you and will look for externally if you cannot offer them some level of operational transparency. So, in addition to modeling the business services your business partner is requesting, begin to think about how you can start modeling the IT business services that you offer them. Do some research on the services that outsource providers are offering in their business catalogs. Look at how they have defined their services and model yours accordingly. Your business partners would rather talk to you about increasing your ability to deliver a more reliable application-hosting service than about adding 11 servers to the infrastructure.

Ideally, you will be able to merge all these models together in a way that represents what is happening in your organization. Figure 5.8 shows you how the "Deposit" Banking Transaction from Figure 5.7 could be merged with the application infrastructure model in Figure 5.6 and how an IT Service might factor into it in order to present a complete picture that would satisfy all levels of users. The models are not technologically complete, but are intended to simply demonstrate what the framework of a complete model might look like.

As you have probably figured out, there is no way that a vendor tool is going to be able to define and automatically identify all these models in your organization. You are going to have to do this manually and leverage tools to help identify the technology components. This is why we stated that the models need to be placed under the control of the Change Management process. Once defined, we suggest that you add a task to your RFC tickets, reminding the implementers that any model associated with the component being changed needs to also be updated. From here, you should be able to automate the detection of changes to technology items and whether or not the associated documents have been updated. If you have an online document management system, this will be simpler for you to do versus using file shares and relying on the file timestamp for the detection. If you have an online run-book system, you have a real opportunity to automate even more of this process by integrating it in with your Change Management system and CMS.

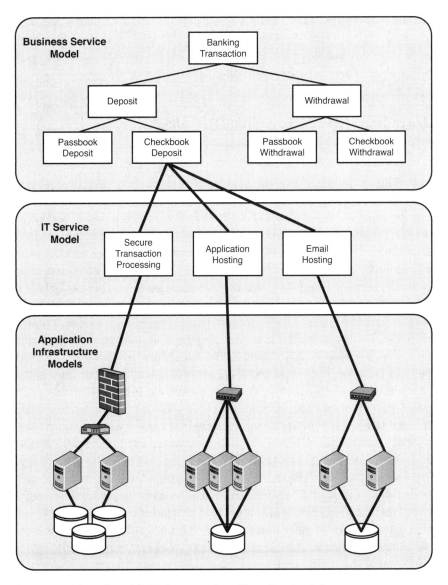

FIGURE 5.8   Merged model: Business services, IT application infrastructure

Regardless of what your level of business maturity is, the concept of business services and modeling needs to be forefront in your mind when you are designing and deploying your CMS solution. You need to design this capability into your CMS solution so that you are prepared for the future demand. If you don't design your CMS with service models in mind, you will likely need to make significant modifications to your CMS in the future. Design your CMS with the future in mind, but build it for today's needs.

Wait for the "Uber-CMDB/CMS" Technology...If You Can

Depending on the timeframe you have been given for your directive, putting off a CMS technology purchase may not be an option. If it can be put off for a short period of time, you will benefit from the vendor products and technologies becoming a bit more stable and possibly having some of them merged by way of corporate acquisitions ultimately providing a better suite of functionality. As discussed, the technologies to support an enterprise-class CMS still are being worked on, but there are some available that can help you build a foundation that will leave you prepared to take the next steps as the CMS technologies mature. There are a variety of things that you can do in the interim that will provide value to your organization over the short run and significantly reduce your workload in the long run when you do implement the CMS technology. Some of these are not traditional work that you might associate with a CMS initiative, but if you have the luxury of putting off a CMS technology purchase, your organization will still benefit tremendously from doing these things when you do make that CMS technology purchase.

First, take some time and assess your technology environment. Document all the data you already have available, where it is located, who owns it, and any controls that are already in place to manage it. Cross-reference this against your future state CMS model and document any gaps that might exist. This will give you a starting point to determine what you have versus what you need, and identify duplication of data; it should give you a preliminary understanding of data quality-related issues you may run into. After you get all of this information collected, you can begin to make plans for how you will address any weaknesses in the controls of existing systems or how you will generate any data that is not currently available. While working on these efforts, you should continue to follow the progression and maturity of the CMS technologies and time your purchase accordingly.

Once all your data sources have been identified, dig deeper into them to better understand the technologies that they are built upon and how you might integrate with them once the CMS technology is deployed. Try to get an understanding of where your existing technologies are heading with regards to maturity and functionality so that you don't spend too much time planning out strategies for them if your company is looking to move away from them. You also need to consider any plans the vendor may have in regards to significant changes in functionality or architecture. Both of these research and planning activities should help you determine how much time to invest in each source from a technological perspective. It won't always be easy to get some of this information from the vendor, but it is worthwhile to try. If they don't provide the information outright, talk with your peers at other companies to see what they are hearing about the vendor direction for the product. Next, you want to evaluate the quality of the data in each of the sources. You need to get a very strong understanding about how reliable the source technology is and if you will be able to count on it when you begin to implement your purchased CMS technology. Talk with the subject matter experts in your organization and get their input on the technology stability and potential. If possible, set up conference calls with the product managers for these technologies, not sales or pre-sale people, and explain to them the concerns you have with their product and find out if they are planning to address them in the future releases. You should be looking not only for data quality-related issues with the product but also data that might not be currently available that you feel would be valuable to have in your CMS solution.

You will eventually run into situations where you have more than one source for the same data, with the owner of each source claiming that theirs should be treated as the "authoritative source." In some cases, you might be able to resolve it by dividing up the elements that you pull from each source. For example, you might decide that Source A is most accurate and reliable for the server attributes (Name, IP, and RAM), Source B is most reliable for server attributes (Serial Number, Manufacturer, and Model), and Source C is most reliable for server attributes (Purpose and Date in Service), even though all three sources may have the same exact seven attributes. As long as the sources share a common unique identifier, you can merge them into one conceptual record in your CMS. This same exercise can be done with as many sources as you may have that share common attributes. Identifying which source should be considered for each attribute won't always be simple, and there will be times that you will need to escalate some of these contentions to upper management for their direction and decision because each source owner might be claiming that her repository should be used as the authoritative one. Regardless of how you go about deciding which sources are the authoritative ones, these situations need to be resolved quickly so as to not delay your progress. Figures 5.9 and 5.10 show how the decision flow that might be executed and what the resulting record could look like for our server example when more than one source contains authoritative data.

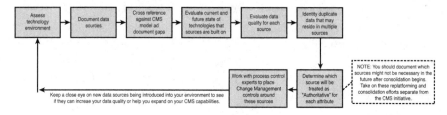

FIGURE 5.9   Authoritative source decision flow

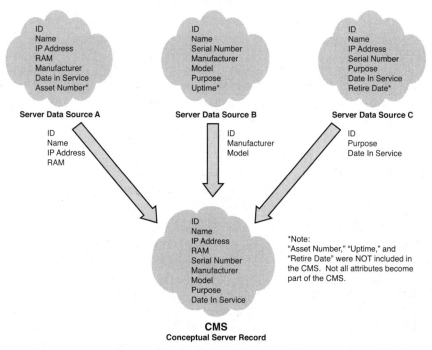

FIGURE 5.10   Sample merged server record from multiple authoritative sources

At this stage, you should have a relatively good sense of your current state environment, which includes the following:

- The technology solutions currently installed

- Available data for each installed technology solution

- Weaknesses and/or limitations of each technology solution

- Functionality enhancements needed for each technology solution

- Future release plans for the technology solutions from the vendor

Your next challenge, while you put off the CMS technology purchase, is to start identifying where you have duplicate information. This is an extension of your efforts to identify the "authoritative sources," as depicted in Figures 5.9 and 5.10. Evaluate the results of your current state assessment and document where duplicate data exists, as well as the sources where they come from. Ultimately, you want to try to identify sources that you can expand the functionality under or increase controls around. Leverage these sources as central knowledge platforms that you can merge functionality and data into while enabling the retirement of the originating sources you moved data and functionality away from. This drives immediate costs savings both before and after your CMS implementation in the following ways:

- Reduced number of data sources and platforms to maintain

- Simplification of operational processes due to reduced number of sources to research

- Improved data quality due to more people using the shared data and identifying inaccuracies and incompleteness

- Reduced number of sources for the CMS to integrate with

Efforts to merge and reconcile data should not be considered part of the actual CMS project but more of a precursor project so that people don't get confused as to what a CMS is. We have seen efforts where some of this workload is included as part of CMS projects. In many cases, it confuses individuals' understanding of what the CMS is and leads to the belief that the CMS project is a glorified data warehouse project, which it is not. This confusion eventually will lead to philosophical debates on what a CMS is, and you will end up back at the beginning with no work getting done and no value being delivered to your business partners.

The final activity for you to perform while you wait for the CMS technologies to mature is to improve the data quality in the data sources that remain and have been merged. You can do this in a variety of ways, but the most obvious is by placing processes and controls around those sources when data is added or modified. Do not forget that the data quality will already benefit from having more people see and use it than when it was a lone data source. Some data source owners may oppose your efforts because they are concerned that the level of data quality will be questioned now that it is visible and being used by a larger audience. They should instead be excited by the fact that they will now have many more people accessing it and will have the opportunity to leverage the feedback that comes with it to improve the accuracy and completeness of their data source.

If you have done all the things just discussed, you might actually have the opportunity to leverage some of these sources as CMDBs within your CMS solution. The key to doing this is making sure that you put in place the same level of Change Management rigor around these sources as you do around your CMS and Change Management system. "At the data level, the CMS may take data from several physical CMDBs, which together constitute a federated CMDB."[3] These data sources, once used as CMDBs to form the overarching CMS, must be owned and maintained by the multiple groups that access and leverage the data it contains. Each group has a vested interest in it, and therefore must have some accountability for its accuracy and completeness.

Now that you have addressed all these areas, you are essentially left with a reduced number of data sources that you expect to leverage for your CMS initiative once you begin your technology implementation. You may be thinking that you are not advancing your CMS project by these external efforts, but you are. If you follow this approach, your management and peers will likely question you about your lack of progress with regards to the actual CMS implementation, but you must not give in to that pressure. Explain the theory behind what you are doing. Demonstrate the value that is being delivered by increasing data quality and reducing the number of sources needed. Show them the savings that are possible by maintaining fewer systems and increasing productivity by reducing the amount of time needed to research data. These are legitimate reasons to perform the activities described, regardless of

---

3. Office of Government Commerce (OGC). 2007. *Service Transition, ITIL Version 3.* Ogdensburg: Renouf Publishing Co. Ltd.

whether you are deploying a CMS or not. However, if you are deploying a CMS based on this reduced number of sources, the value you can deliver will be higher and your time to market with your CMS solution will be shorter.

Attack the Domains

If you are going to drive your CMS initiative from a technology perspective, you need to clearly identify all the different domains that factor into your solution. Each area of focus will have its own nuances and challenges. You need to be very flexible in your project planning and timelines because the workload will likely be very erratic as you progress. There will be times of great progress, and times when nothing seems to get done. Jump between the different focal areas as you need to so that you continue to achieve some progress within the larger project. If you don't, and you become fixated on one specific area just because the project plan says that's where your energy belongs, you will have a hard time achieving your goal. In the end, all the areas of focus will need to be completed, and some will have predecessor-successor dependencies that cannot be ignored. Generally, however, you should be able to work on most areas independently of the others as long as your CMS model is complete, you have defined what you are looking for, and the initiative as a whole is moving forward.

Divide the contents of your CMS model into logical technology groupings that can be worked on somewhat independently of each other. Depending on your organization, your groupings may be in perfect alignment with the organizational structure or they may be more operationally structured. What matters most is that the groupings make sense to you and that they will be an efficient way to gather information about the technologies without having to go back to the same subject matter experts multiple times. Be very considerate of the time that you are spending with these individuals because they typically have very little time available to spend on activities that do not directly affect the day-to-day operations of the IT environment.

Establishing your groupings may come naturally to you, but for some people, it can be a bit of a challenge because of outsourcing arrangements, organizational structure, regional location, or possibly even regulatory-related issues. Regardless of the reason, we recommend that you study the DMTF Common Information Model (CIM) to help you formulate your groups if you are not sure where to begin. More specifically, you should begin to research the CMDB Federation (CMDBf) specification.[4] The CMDBf working group, which consists of individuals from BMC Software, CA, Fujitsu, HP, IBM, and Microsoft has been working on the specification since April 2006 and formally submitted it to the DMTF on November 27, 2007. We recognize that the CMDBf specification is still a work in progress. However, if you have not started designing your CMS yet, we believe that utilized in combination with the CIM, they should be able to provide you with a tremendous amount of information to help you get started in creating your groupings.

CIM is very detailed on the technology elements but rather light with regards to users and people information, but fortunately that is one of the elements that the CMDBf specification will help to clarify for you. We will warn you, however, that the specification is a technology specification and not a simple graphic of all the bits and pieces you need to design. For this reason, we have tried to give you a sample of one way that you may choose to group your elements and some of the types of information you will be looking to capture in each. The sample grouping is by no means a complete list nor will it fit everyone's needs. The intention is simply to help you understand how you might want to create your groupings. The details within each grouping will be different from company to company based on your industry and level of maturity. The following are some examples of the attributes/objects in each grouping that you might want to consider:

- **Users/People:** Name, phone, location, access rights/authorities

- **Computing Devices (physical and virtual):** Workstations, servers, handhelds

- **System Components:** Media device, memory, cards, BIOS

- **Networking—Devices/Infrastructure:** Switch, router, firewall, modem, VPN

- **Networking—Connectivity/Protocol:** ATM, ISO, SNMP, TCP/IP, UDP, FC, iSCSI

---

4. The Distributed Management Task Force (DMTF) produced and maintains the specification for the Configuration Management Database Federation (CMDBf). The first version of the CMDBf specification was submitted on November 27, 2007, and is currently being revised by the working group. A Committee Draft from October 22, 2007, is available at http://cmdbf.org.

- **Storage:** SAN, NAS, storage array, tape library, core/edge storage switch, Host Bus Adapter (HBA)

- **Software Products/Technologies:** Licenses, vendor information, product name, version/build number

- **Applications/Installed Software:** Name, manufacturer or business unit, install date, business owner, version/build number, function, license ID

- **Facilities:** Building, floor, bay, HVAC, location

Users/People

The data contained in this grouping will obviously be about the individuals in your company or those who interact with your applications and systems. You want to capture all the relevant contact information, as well as any additional information that might set them apart from other individuals. Things such as priority routing for top salespeople or senior executives are attributes that you will want to associate with these individuals. This type of information will be very beneficial to your Service Desk users later on after deployment when they receive calls from these individuals. With the information available, your developers could automatically route their calls to a dedicated Service Desk or bump them to the top of the call queue. Once connected, the Service Desk personnel could automatically be given a visual cue that the individual on the line has special privileges, and therefore they should provide preferential treatment. The key is that once the designation is captured, you can act on it in any manner that is needed.

A key element of data that you should associate with the user records is equipment or assets that they own, manage, or use. Again, this type of information will prove to be immensely beneficial to your Service Desk personnel when trying to route tickets and reduce their call times. If possible, you should also consider associating the access rights they have to hardware, applications, networks, and so on because these types of incident tickets are very common for a Service Desk. If a Service Desk operator can quickly identify a user calling in who is having trouble accessing a system, they may be able to determine that the person does not have the proper authority to do so. They could then direct the user to the proper ID Administration group and close the ticket very quickly, instead of wasting valuable time researching why they can't access a system when in fact they were never given authority to access it.

The types of systems containing user/people information include the following:

- Human Resources/Personnel Applications
- Identity Management
- ID and Password Administration
- LDAP

Computing Devices

These elements are likely to be some of the easier devices to get data on because most companies already have relatively good controls around introducing new servers and workstations into their environment. Handheld units, on the other hand, are still a wildcard in some organizations, but the current trend is that they will be managed similarly to servers and workstations; in some cases, they are actually replacing laptops as an employees' workstation. Depending on how your organization does its software distribution, systems monitoring, and hardware deployment, you may already have a wealth of information readily available for you to use. If you have good processes in place such as ensuring that every laptop image contains an Asset Management or other form of agent that reports back periodically, you are well on your way to compiling a reliable inventory of computing devices in your environment.

Establishing a reliable inventory of items is a key first step for you in trying to establish a reliable CMS. Be sure to evaluate the reliability of these agent-based tools because remember, "they only know as much as you tell them." For example, if the image is accidentally built without the agent, or if the computing device is rebuilt from scratch and they don't use an image, you may have no way of knowing that the computing device is on your network because the agent doesn't exit on it. A way to mitigate this risk is to use an agentless-based tool in conjunction with the agent-based tool. Chapter 4, "The Federated CMS Architecture," discussed the pros and cons of both. This enables you to compare both inventories and verify that both tools are seeing the same devices out on your network.

The types of systems containing computing device information include the following:

- Software Distribution

- Software Licensing

- Asset Management (Inventory, Procurement, and so on)

- Business Continuity/Disaster Recovery

- Security Administration

- Network Monitoring

System Components

System components are the elements within your computing devices. They are the hard drives, memory, NIC cards, BIOS, and so on that make up the computing device (see Figure 5.11). Controlling this level of object becomes more challenging because of the levels of controls that you need to have in your environment. You need to decide if it is cost effective to control these things, and if you even have the capability to do so with a technological solution. The reason is because these components tend to change more often than an entire computing device and, in many cases, are considered disposable units, so they are not tracked at a unique instance level.

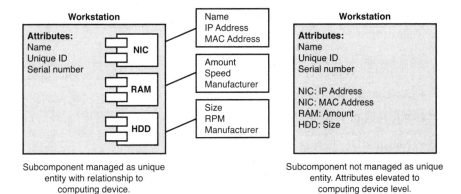

FIGURE 5.11   System Component management level

This does not mean that these objects are expendable and aren't critical to the success of your CMS. Instead, you need to find or build a technology solution that captures all the details you want on a regular basis, elevate the details in these subcomponents up to the Computing Device level, and track them as an attribute of the computing device versus a subcomponent of the computing device with its own attributes. The other option is to assign individuals to do it manually. We do not suggest the latter unless you have no other choice. It is very costly, prone to errors, and not realistic in larger multi-site organizations.

Some software agents can provide you with details about the subcomponents on computing devices, so leverage those where you can. You do need to pay close attention to whether or not your processes, in particular Change and Release and Deployment Management, can actually control the level of detail that managing subcomponents as unique entities would require. We believe that in your early phases, you will derive a lot of value from elevating the critical subcomponent attributes up to the Computing Device level and place less burden on your other processes. After some time of getting accustomed to the new processes and controls, you can revisit this area and determine if there is value in breaking out the subcomponents on their own and managing them as unique entities. Doing this, however, requires changes to your merging routines, reconciliation rules, CMS design, and end user work instructions. So, make sure that before deciding to do this, you have buy-in from everyone who will be impacted.

The types of systems containing system component information include the following:

- Technical Support Repositories
- Asset Management (Inventory, Procurement, and so on)
- Business Continuity/Disaster Recovery
- Network Monitoring

Networking

Networking can constitute a wide array of devices and concepts. It includes many different physical devices, virtual devices, and conceptual structures. We listed several different types of networking equipment at the start of this section, but it is far from the complete list that you will need to investigate for your CMS initiative. You will have to decide which ones are the most critical to your organization and prioritize accordingly. Also, you have to determine whether you will treat all devices of the same type similarly independent of the environment they are utilized in, such as production versus development.

Some companies have a highly segregated network infrastructure for their business, so they choose to incorporate all types of devices but only for a segment of their network infrastructure (that is, Production versus Development, Domestic versus International, and so on). Other companies that don't have this segregated model sometimes choose to incorporate only a few types of devices but across the entire network. There is also the hybrid approach that you can take in which you are not highly segregated, but because of the size of your environment or scope of your initiative, you may focus on only major network devices within a particular segment of your business in only the production environment. There is no wrong approach as long as your expectations are communicated clearly, everyone understands the risks with each approach, and all the stakeholders have signed off on the chosen approach. Figures 5.12a, 5.12b, and 5.12c show the different possibilities for attacking your network infrastructure.

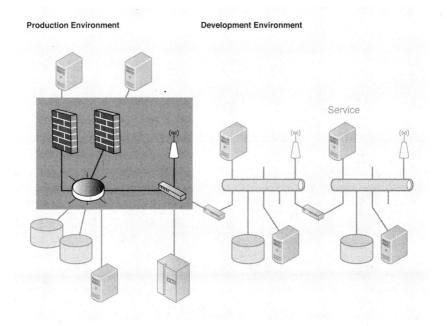

FIGURE 5.12A   Segregated network infrastructure approach

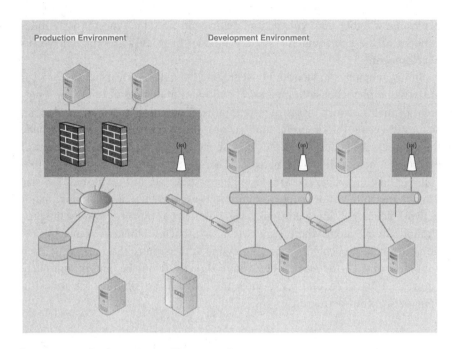

FIGURE 5.12B   Device type specific approach

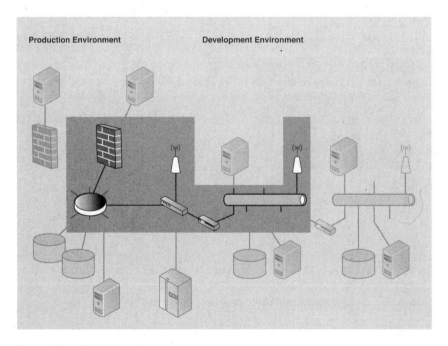

FIGURE 5.12C   Hybrid approach

Including networking infrastructure in your CMS is a very significant step forward in your initiative because it provides you with the items that form the topology upon which everything will function. It provides you with potential upstream causes of incidents and downstream impacts of changes. Having this available at the Service Desk should significantly narrow down the research target when dealing with incidents and changes. Typically, a large percentage of time is spent trying to narrow down the area that needs to be investigated, and providing the networking information could reduce that time to minutes instead of hours. Without this information, you really do not have a reliable way to identify the upstream/downstream relationships, and that will drastically minimize your ability to deliver value.

The types of systems containing networking information include the following:

- Network and IP Scanners
- Network Diagramming and Modeling
- Analyzers and Sniffers
- Trace Routing
- Network Bandwidth Monitoring

Storage

Corporations today generate and store tremendous amounts of data, and in order to manage that data, they are turning to solutions such as Storage Area Networks (SANs) and Network Attached Storage (NAS) to address their needs. These elements become more critical to your design as your organization moves more heavily toward these storage solutions. Although there are differences between SAN and NAS, we address the storage topic in a solution-neutral way for the purposes of this discussion. You will tackle both in the same manner when researching and assessing what to include in your CMS initiative. One thing to remember as you move forward in this area is the advancements that are being made with regards to virtualization of the storage and its connectivity. Be sure to become familiar with these advancements before designing your model so as to allow flexibility in your model to account for this. We suggest that you bring in some of your storage subject matter experts and have them review your design to ensure that you are accounting for the present and allowing for the future.

The types of systems containing storage information include the following:

- Storage Management Systems

- Business Continuity/Disaster Recovery

- In-House Built Storage Requisition Systems

Software Products/Technologies

Items in this grouping are probably most desired by the Change and Financial Management processes than most others. The reason is because these items are essentially the stock of products that have been purchased and are approved for installation in the environment. For Change Management, they need the ability to select one of these items in an RFC as the product that the user wants to have installed. From a Financial Management perspective, it is obvious that they want to track how many licenses were utilized and the costs associated with them.

It is not to say that these items are not important, but in the grand scheme of things, this area will likely be one of the last to implement. There is a lot of value once you get to this point, but it is hard to quantify the value until the remainder of your initiative is moderately mature. These items differ from the items in the Applications/Installed Software grouping simply because they are not yet installed and may never get installed. So you can think of them as the vendor CDs or software bundles that you received for the new reporting tool you just purchased. Until someone installs it, the item will appear only in this list. Once the software is installed, however, a different form of it will appear in the Applications/Installed Software grouping.

The types of systems containing software products/technologies information include the following:

- Software Asset Library or Definitive Media Library (DML)

- Procurement Systems

- Approved Technology Inventories (Company-Approved Software)

Applications/Installed Software

As discussed, items in this grouping differ from the Software Products/Technologies in that they are the entities that are created on workstations, servers, handhelds, and so on, when the vendor CD or software bundle is used in an installation. The byproduct of the installation is this application/installed software entity. These items are the ones that users will call in for tickets on and run your business. They need to be carefully tracked and reported on with respect to the equipment they rely on.

These items will eventually act as the layer that helps you piece together your business services listing with the hardware that supports it. Most companies manage these relatively well because they are the projects that are funded annually for new development and maintenance. The problem that may arise is that there are usually poor enterprise controls around these systems, and they are typically managed at a departmental or unit level so you will need to pull together many different ones to get a complete picture of your environment. If your organization is more mature, you may be fortunate enough to have a relatively stable and comprehensive listing of all your organizations' installed applications.

The types of systems containing applications/installed software information are the following:

- Software Distribution Systems

- Version Control Systems

- In-House Built Application Management Systems

Facilities

This section is often overlooked because it is not an IT component like a server or a router. It is, however, the buildings where your servers and routers are running, so you really need to consider incorporating this information sooner rather than later. Depending on your office and data center locations, especially if you operate internationally in developing countries, the quality and reliability of the local utilities may not be what we have come to expect in the United States. The reason that this is so critical is because if you lose power to the building, all your IT components in that building will go offline. Battery backups and backup generators are great systems, but as the Northeast region of the United States experienced in August 2003, a region-wide blackout disrupted every sort of service possible that depended on electricity. Even organizations with backup systems that were located exclusively in the blackout area could not operate because the regional grid was down. Organizations that did have additional facilities in other regions scrambled to assess what systems were down and which they could recover elsewhere. This scenario plays into your Business Continuity and Disaster Recovery plans, but they are real situations that you need to consider. So, you need to think about what impact it might have on your business if you do not know what equipment is in which data center, localized technology center, or small satellite office.

There have been some very good tools released recently to help with Data Center Management activities that not only help lay out your equipment in your data center, but also integrate with some Change Management systems. This is important for the obvious reason, but also remember that smaller satellite offices are typically leased space in larger buildings that undergo their own maintenance projects. If you rely on equipment that resides outside your data centers, and you are not able to correlate building maintenance schedules with equipment running in those offices, you could be allowing vital systems to be abruptly taken offline without any notice to your users. If your company is looking to implement one of these solutions, you should get involved in the project and ensure they integrate it with the CMS so that you can obtain all of that value.

The types of systems containing facilities information include the following:

- Business Continuity

- Disaster Recovery

- Data Center Management

- Facilities Management

Leverage Incumbent Tools

There is no question that the complexity and magnitude of a CMS initiative can grow to unmanageable levels. There is also no question that this is why you should leverage any tools you already have in place in order to minimize the amount of new work you need to do to implement a CMS. The only reason you would be starting from ground zero is if you have no tools in place or you have no faith in the tools that are in place. Neither of these is likely because you are already operational and would have a hard time being so if this were the case.

We have already briefly touched on using existing tools in this chapter, but there are aspects about leveraging incumbent tools that need to be further discussed, such as the approach to and dangers of leveraging them. As with anything else, there are always advantages and disadvantages to doing something, and leveraging incumbent tools is no different. It could greatly accelerate your initiatives progress, but it could quickly send it down the wrong path before you realize it. So, use them liberally, but be sure you know everything about them before you do.

There are many ways that you can leverage these tools, but we're going to discuss them in terms of how you might actually use them. The four ways that we see you using them are Inventory, Discovery, Verification, and Audit. Although there are some differences between Verification and Audit, we discuss them together for our purpose because they tend to go hand in hand many times. Leveraging all four collectively should enable you to deliver a very stable and reliable CMS, as well as quickly identify areas of concern. However, it can present wrong data much faster and, if that data is used, could result in outages to your system.

There is a concept in the security profession called *security in layers* that you should understand because the similar concept applies here when leveraging incumbent tools and implementing your CMS. Essentially, it says that you should not rely on one single element for anything and should stack multiple checks and balances together to ensure the result you want. A metaphor commonly used is that of a combination lock. You must get all the numbers correct in the proper sequence in order for it to open. In the case of the CMS and incumbent tools, you can leverage the tools, but you need to put in place the necessary validation steps to ensure that the data from the tools is accurate. Because there will be minimal human intervention, you cannot rely on a person to detect an abnormality. You must have a second or third tool in place to be able to detect the inevitable variances that you will encounter. If you know that a tool is not very reliable and you still plan to use it, you need to put several quality assurance checks in place to elevate your error detection capability before the data reaches the CMS. Obviously, there is a threshold where it no longer makes sense to use an unreliable tool, but that threshold is something you need to decide on. It is one of the many risk/reward decisions you will have to make during this initiative.

Figure 5.13 demonstrates this concept by showing how you can achieve a much more secure mechanism when controls are aligned and coordinated. The figure shows three different scenarios to demonstrate that having controls in place alone is not enough. If they are in place but not aligned, it is still relatively simple to get past them. Ideally, you want all of your controls to be perfectly aligned and coordinated, forming a totally impenetrable barrier, but that is not typically realistic. The realistic model is the one where you do have controls in place, and you have gone through the effort to align and coordinate them. You recognize that there are gaps between them, but do not find it necessary or cost effective to eliminate. This does leave a path available for things to get through, but it is a risk you have chosen to accept.

Easy
Controls may be in place, but they are not aligned or coordinated.

(You can go straight across to the other side.)

Impossible
Ideal situation where controls are all aligned and coordinated.

(You cannot get through to the other side.)

Reality
Realistic situation where controls are somewhat aligned and coordinated.

(You can weave your way through the open spaces between the pieces to get to the other side, but it takes significant effort.)

FIGURE 5.13   Coordination and alignment of controls

You can view the four areas of incumbent tools as being layers of control by which the data will arrive in the CMS. You need to use them together as a complete system in order to achieve a higher level of data quality and comprehensiveness. Alone, each one may do its job very well, but they need to fill in the gaps left by the other tools in order to do a complete job for the CMS. Essentially what you are trying to do is use each tool for its strengths and balance its weaknesses with the strengths of the others. Once they are all pulled together and working as a collective unit, you can determine how comprehensive the data is and what level of data quality you are dealing with. At this point, you can define the manual processes that will be needed to supplement the tools you are leveraging in order to achieve your desired goals.

Inventory

When you look around your organization, you will surely find many "lists of things." You will also probably find that they typically stand on their own with little or no reference to other "lists of things" in your environment. So, they deliver the value that they were intended to deliver, but without having them associated to the other lists, your organization is not fully capitalizing on the value they can help to deliver.

Most of your inventory-related lists are manually generated and originate at a corporate level because of a need to count things. The systems that typically track these lists are your Procurement and Asset Management systems. They are financially driven and tend to do a good job in capturing the objects that are requested for purchasing. Unfortunately, they tend to stop there, and because the Asset Management process is not usually tied in with the Change Management process, any modifications to the equipment are usually lost. Some aspects of Asset Management also happen at the departmental level, but not for financial reasons. They tend to be because the department is responsible for a particular type of hardware and must maintain an inventory of those items. So, you can see that the full list that began at the corporate level is broken down into smaller lists that rarely ever get reconciled. The end result is that lists are created everywhere for different reasons, and if you ever tried pulling them all together, they would not look like the master list from where they were born.

Try to find the fewest number of sources that provide you with the highest amount of items you are seeking to include in your CMS. Also, evaluate the level of support you will get from the source owner because you will be going back to them during your Verification and Audit cycles with corrections that they need to make to their data. This is a key element that you need to factor into your decision to use the source. The reason is because if they are not willing or allowed to make modifications to data in their system, when you identify that something is wrong or missing, you have to maintain the correction on your end in the CMS. This essentially forces you to now maintain your own variation of the list, which defeats the purpose of using theirs. Sometimes you are better off leveraging a source that is not quite as complete or accurate, but has an owner who is excited about participating and helping. These sources will be easier to use and in the end be of a higher value to you and the organization.

Having an inventory of your items is only part of the effort because at this stage, "you don't know what you don't know." You have been able to cultivate a variety of sources and pull them together into collection of lists that you believe has every item you need in your CMS, but you don't know for sure because the lists were generated for specific reasons and not for a larger effort. What you need is to compensate for this potential weakness with a tool that has no association with the processes from where these lists originated. This compensation helps to ensure that the lists are complete and accurate. The technology that helps you do this is one that discovers items in your environment without you telling it that they exist.

Discovery

Discovery processes include leveraging technologies that can, with guidance and boundaries, identify IT components in your environment without a lot of manual intervention after it is kicked off. Discovery technologies have many purposes, and you will likely need to use different ones for different reasons across your organization. Some discovery tools perform inventory roles, whereas others are more centered on auditing functions. With regards to the CMS, there are two main reasons for using them. The first is to compensate for weaknesses in the data gathered from tools in your inventory efforts. The second is to obtain data that might not otherwise be gathered easily or in a timely manner. The discovery should help identify items that were not listed in your inventory lists or maybe were actually there but not named or labeled consistently. It will also help gather information that may exist on several pieces of equipment across your enterprise but is not possible to manually gather often enough to meet your requirements.

The issue of identifying items that were not listed in the inventory can happen for many reasons, but your main focus is to make sure that you detect when something is no longer in existence or when something new suddenly appears in your environment. You need to work with your inventory partners to ensure that any inconsistencies between your discovered lists and their manually generated ones are resolved according to whatever Service Level Agreement (SLA) or Operational Level Agreement (OLA) you established with them. Depending on your organization, you might want to seek out people in your IT Security organization to see what tools they use to detect unauthorized and/or unregistered equipment on your network. Some other good sources within your company to help with discovery are network administration tools, event monitoring tools, software distribution tools, and radio-frequency identification systems. There are more, but this should give you a sense of the wide variety that exists.

The other main element of discovery that is important for you to leverage is one that scans your environment regularly and has the ability to pull out details about the devices on your networks so that you can get a fresh set of data on a periodic basis. The frequency in which you get the refresh will depend on the types of items, environments they are operating under, volume of changes, and criticality of the systems they support. We discussed agent- versus non-agent-based tools previously, so you should already understand how to mix and match the two in order to get a complete picture of the environment.

There is an argument that can be made about using your discovery tool as your inventory generator. We agree that this is absolutely possible, and in some cases already being used by many companies. Again, your objective is to get good data that is stable and reliable, so why wouldn't you use it if it fits those criteria? A word of caution: Remember that there are no human eyes on the data it generates, so you need to employ additional checks and balances to make sure the data remains stable and reliable before entering the

CMS. This may come by way of comparing two different discovery tools to ensure both are consistently reporting the same data, or it may just require additional manual auditing of the data. In either case, the point is that you need to be extra careful with data that you are using if it does not pass through some form of human control.

Verification and Audit

The Verification and Audit processes and tools you have in place are fundamental to your ability in making sure that you do not miss anything. This is where you can build confidence in your utilization of the incumbent tools and identify any gaps you may have. Verification and Audit have somewhat of a different focus from each other, but they tend to work very closely together, so we felt that it would be clearer to discuss them together. Where appropriate, we note any significant difference between the two so that any potential confusion is minimized.

First, we need to get an understanding of where both Verification and Audit are each focused. Verification focuses on testing and scrutinizing the data after you have done an evaluation of it. Audit, on the other hand, is focused on the trustworthiness and legitimacy of the data. So, in other words, the Verification aspect is used as your due diligence before and during the process, whereas the Audit is used after Verification has been completed. We have grossly oversimplified the difference between the two, but hopefully it helps draw the distinction between them.

Your Verification tools will likely be used as an ongoing active element in your day-to-day operation of the CMS. They play a significant role when you are merging your data together from a variety of sources and reconciling the results. Business rules engines have performed this type of function for many years, but unfortunately, the technology from the current ITSM vendors have barely leveraged these capabilities and hence are still in their infancy in our opinion. They are still for the most part using a very binary approach that is not adaptive and essentially requires you to predefine the resolution for all conditions that could be met. This obviously is not an ideal model. Some technology vendors appear to be heading in the direction of implementing a more sophisticated rules engine. At the time this book was written, unfortunately, none have made enough progress to warrant being singled out.

The auditing technologies are a bit more straightforward and are likely to be in place already in your organization. You can leverage these tools to perform your spot checks of the data to ensure that your Inventory, Discovery, and Verification are all working according to specification. They help you better understand the weaknesses of your Verification rules, as well as gaps that surface in your inventory and discovery cycles. As with any Audit process, you need to leverage these tools more often as the trustworthiness and legitimacy of your data drops. It might drive you to reevaluate your data sources and manual processes if you see it happening more often. You should define the thresholds for each source and each process for which you trigger increased Audit activity, as well as the threshold once crossed; you eliminate the source from contributing to the CMS.

Collectively, Verification and Audit enable you to implement data quality measures throughout your entire CMS cycle. They help when integrating new sources, as well as help to identify sources that are not meeting your quality and completeness requirements. You will find that over time, these requirements change as you get more comfortable with the data sources and as they improve. Once the sources stabilize in their level of quality and you are running in a normal mode, you should revisit the thresholds and determine if you should elevate them to drive even higher levels of quality. This is ultimately up to you and your organization to decide. Essentially, you are defining where your "80/20 rule" threshold needs to be. An important aspect to remember is that your goal is to *deliver value to the end users*. So, even if the quality or completeness of the data is not where you want it to ultimately be, evaluate the value that the end users will get out of having access to the data at these suboptimal levels and make a determination as to whether you can release it to them or hold off until it improves.

Frequently Asked Questions

Question: Can a CMS solution be implemented without automatically discovered data?

Answer: Automatically discovered data is not a requirement for a CMS solution. It will, however, directly impact the depth and breadth of your solution. If you are not able to leverage tools to discover any of your data, you will need to do it manually; obviously, the cost of doing it manually will likely discourage you from implementing the same depth and breadth that you would with a tool.

Question: I have heard from some people that discovered data should never be used for your CMS. Is this true?

Answer: The only reason you should exclude data from your solution is because the quality and reliability do not meet your minimum criteria. There is absolutely no reason why you would exclude data from your solution solely based on the fact that it comes from an automated tool. If the data generated by the tool is not reliable, you are excluding it because of the reliability, not the mechanism by which it was generated.

Question: You cannot begin designing your CMS solution until you have defined all of your business services. Is this true?

Answer: In the ideal world, having all the business services defined and prioritized would be very beneficial because you would know exactly what data elements you would need to manage and which you could ignore. Unfortunately, if you were to wait for all of your business services to be defined, you would most likely never implement a CMS.

Question: Is there a scenario where you might consider implementing a CMS solution based on a technology-centric approach?

Answer: First, let's be clear that it is not an ideal approach if there are other options. However, if the situation you find yourself in is one that has no business services, IT services, or application models defined, you need to assess what value you might be able provide with a CMS solution that is based on a technology-centric approach. The value in your first phase might be to simply bring forward some of the low-level technology details that end users do not currently have access to. In parallel to that effort, you should promote and facilitate efforts to design the models and services that will ultimately drive the future phases of your CMS solution.

Summary

The strategy discussed in this chapter is somewhat generic, but we have found that one of the biggest challenges organizations encounter is simply getting started. There are so many different elements that need to be worked on that it can become overwhelming and bring the whole initiative to a grinding halt, waiting for something else to happen. After some initial design work, there will be many elements that you can work on in parallel; only when you get about two-thirds of the way through will you need to start bringing a lot of it back together. The reality is that a CMS initiative is not one that can be handled easily with a traditional Waterfall-style project methodology where you sequence though Requirements, Design, Implementation, Verification, and then Maintenance. An Agile or Spiral model of software development, both of which are iterative in nature, is much more conducive to the success of your initiative. Determine what foundation of design you absolutely need in order to get started on some of the different elements; then get started on those while you revise your design based on what you are learning. It requires a lot of coordination and communication, but in the end, you have a much more comprehensive CMS solution and one that can accommodate the growth of your ITIL adoption more easily.

CHAPTER 6

Integration—There's No Way Around It!

The issue of using "best of breed" products versus a single suite of tools from a single vendor directly impacts your CMS implementation, regardless of which you choose. If your company philosophy is to choose a "best of breed" approach, your integration efforts will likely be significantly higher than if you had chosen to use suites of tools from a reduced number of vendors. On the other hand, using suites of tools does not guarantee that the vendor integrated the individual components well and obviously the individual components are not likely to be the best products in their respective categories.

As the CMS grows, it will likely become central to most, if not all, of your operational processes. The scope of that role requires it to have tentacles throughout the environment in both IT and business, and there simply is no software vendor out there that has products for all your needs. Because of that, you have no choice but to integrate tools across your environment. If you are lucky, your company has already put some effort into a product and technology rationalization effort to reduce the quantity of similar products in use. There is no great magical solution or direction, however; it is simply going to take a significant amount of effort on your part to pull together all the pieces to meet your CMS requirements.

If you have a close working relationship with your vendors, you should include them in some of your discussion so that they better understand the client needs, and hopefully they will incorporate them into future releases of their products. It is not realistic to believe that vendors will build integrations with products from competing vendors, but it is fair to ask that they provide an open and nonproprietary interface for you to use when integrating products from competing vendors. Some vendors still believe that locking everything down under an umbrella of proprietary code and design is conducive to growing business, but it is not. Fewer companies are permitting this arrogant behavior on the part of their vendors.

Standards: Past, Present, and Future

Standards have a storied history in management software. Always promising, they often fell short because of lackluster adoption by vendors or disinterest among buyers. Simple Network Management Protocol (SNMP) is one notable exception, as it is now built into countless systems, especially network devices. XML is another successful standard, spawning hundreds of derivative standards.

The growth of XML was fueled by business applications and business process modeling, with management tools adopting XML a bit later. By this point of the book, it should be apparent that XML is the new basis of management standards. The beauty of XML is its flexibility, and this flexibility enables many extensions for management functions. The Configuration Management System (CMS) benefits through XML modeling of potentially any configuration items (CI) and the simplified linking of data relationships.

CIM and the DMTF

Several standards bodies exist for various software modeling and integration movements in the technology industry. The body most relevant to the CMS is the Distributed Management Task Force (DMTF), first introduced in Chapter 2, "What Is a CMDB?." The DMTF is relevant because two of its standards are integral to the CMS. The Common Information Model (CIM) and the CMDBf specification are the two main software pillars of the CMS, and the DMTF now holds jurisdiction over the development and evolution of both. The suite of DMTF standards is shown in Figure 6.1. The CMDBf work fits in as a management initiative at the top of the diagram.

How you store the data locally to each Management Data Repository (MDR) is irrelevant. The common access and interchange is what is truly important. However, one of many virtues to CIM is as a basis to represent common data. Although it has flaws, it is the best generally acceptable model available to anyone who wants to represent data to be used by another tool. The main problem is that it is an incomplete model of the objects you need to represent. Still, it is the best overall option, and you will find that many software vendors embellish upon this basis to make it more complete.

CIM is an ambitious effort. The DMTF web site contains 1270 XML files to describe CIM version 2.19 (released July 2008), the most recent specification as we are writing this book. It has evolved and grown through the work of many people for over a decade. It is daunting to try to comprehend all of its intricacies, so we turn to software tools to help us. We make no attempt to delve into the complexity of CIM. For those who want to learn deep details, we suggest visiting the DMTF web site's CIM pages.[1] Deep detail is not required to understand the CMS; however, you should understand CIM's role in the CMS.

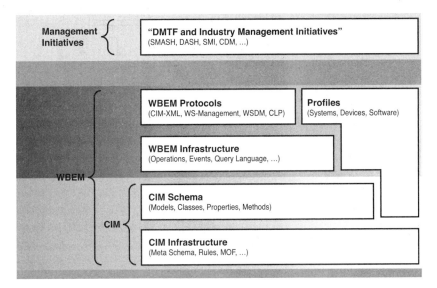

Copyright © 2008 Distributed Management Task Force, Inc.

Figure 6.1   DMTF standards

CIM is an object-oriented data modeling specification that forms a good foundation for the CMS. CIM metadata defines the objects that represent the CIs, and relationships are inherent in the model and its XML encoding. A portion of the CIM meta schema structure is shown in Figure 6.2.

The DMTF is working to more seamlessly merge CIM and the CMDBf specification. They are complementary standards, so this work is progressing. CIM defines the CIs, and CMDBf defines the access and interchange to construct higher-level abstractions that convey the meaningful information needed from the CMS. Both CIM and CMDBf are great innovations that you should leverage, but also recognize that neither is a perfect answer to your needs. Use them as a foundation and build upon them.

---

1. The DMTF web site for CIM details is found at http://www.dmtf.org/standards/cim/.

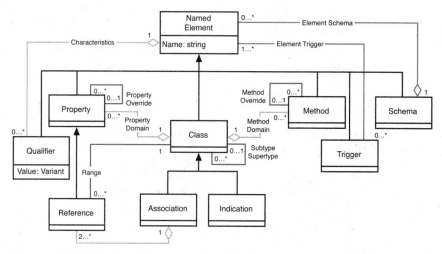

FIGURE 6.2   CIM meta schema structure

CMDB Federation Standard

ITIL v3 is undoubtedly the biggest development toward a superior vision of the CMS, but the CMDBf is a close second-place contender. Because the CI relationships are the most significant factor in CMS technology, any standard that supports relationships across the dispersed data repositories is indeed powerful. The CMDBf specification is that standard.

CMDBf holds more promise than many other preceding standards because vendors and users alike have a vested interest in its success. The real value lies not in the data, but in what you do with the data. Vendors currently focus heavily on their CMDB products as independent offerings, because the CMDB is a new, competitive market where each can innovate. These functions will eventually become commoditized and infused within other tools. The consumer tools (for example, Service Desk, capacity planning, Change Management workflow) are where value is delivered. Software vendors will choose to compete more on the consumer tools than on the CMS modules. Broad acceptance of CMS standards benefits their ability to focus their innovation on the consumer tools.

At the San Francisco itSMF U.S. conference in September 2008, CA and IBM demonstrated the first cross-vendor federation of their CMDB products.[2] The CMDBf specification was the foundation of this demo. It happened because two of the CMDBf authors, Marv Waschke of CA and Mark Johnson of IBM, along with others, decided it was important enough to put competitive differences aside and cooperate toward an actual working implementation. We can thank them for their courage to take a step uncommon among vendors who are normally vicious competitors. Such cooperation is rare, but this worked. It was not just a victory for these technologists proving the realization of their intellectual dreams. It was also a huge marketing coup for both CA and IBM because they were the first to do something that history will regard as a significant milestone. Everybody won!

Waschke and Johnson were successful because they took the initiative to make it happen and were granted the freedom to do it. One other major reason this CMDBf demonstration was so successful was because they were smart enough to leverage existing technologies as much as possible. The most notable of these technologies was the open source COSMOS code from the Eclipse foundation.[3] CA and IBM technologists simply attached CMDBf-compliant COSMOS front ends on their existing CMDB products to produce the demo. Both CA and IBM are actively involved in the Eclipse community.

The COSMOS code was built by the open source community specifically to address management software integration. Like CMDBf, it is a cooperative movement that spans the competitive boundaries between companies. It is more of an altruistic effort to spawn benefits to the entire IT community, vendors and users alike. Other vendors, and even adventurous end users, can streamline delivery of CMDBf-compliant software by following the lead of Waschke and Johnson.

---

2. On September 8, 2008, CA and IBM issued a press release titled "CA, IBM First to Demonstrate CMDB Federation, Interoperability," announcing the demonstration of their interoperability using the CMDBf specification and code from the Eclipse COSMOS project. The press release is available at http://www.ca.com/us/press/release.aspx?cid=184376.

3. The COSMOS (Community-driven Systems Management in Open Source) project was formed to build an open source set of software components that can be used to build common capabilities that can be shared across management software vendors. Among these capabilities is integration, which was the main goal of the CMDBf demo. More details can be found at http://www.eclipse.org/cosmos/.

CMDBf Architecture

As we showed in Chapter 4, "The Federated CMS Architecture," all environments are built using a series of consumer-provider relationships among the various CMS elements (mostly MDRs). CMDBf supports this structure explicitly. The high-level architecture for CMDBf is depicted in Figure 6.3. It shows how Data Consumer Interfaces (DCI) and Data Provider Interfaces (DPI) enable this chaining structure.

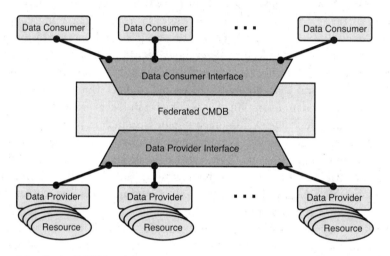

FIGURE 6.3   Basic CMDBf architecture

These interfaces are the real focus of CMDBf. The internals are not as important as the interchange between them, because this is the challenge addressed by CMDBf, and the focus of this chapter. The figure shows the DCI naturally communicating with data consumers, and the DPI likewise communicating with data providers.

The data providers are shown as those elements directly tied to their related resources. In the true spirit of federation, however, MDRs can be consumers *and* providers. Thus, MDRs need to link to each other using these relationships. Figure 6.4 shows how two adjacent tiers of the structure are linked. The DPIs below communicate with the DCIs above them. They speak the same language to enable efficient referential linking.

The upper level is sometimes called the *federating CMDB*, and the lower levels retain the identity of MDR. A federating CMDB implies that it is the part of the structure that is assembling (federating) the elements below it. Any level above the lowest is actually a federating CMDB. Do not confuse this with the term *federated CMDB*, which covers the complete CMS. Many people will confuse them, and this is one of many reasons the CMDB term is unfit to identify the CMS.

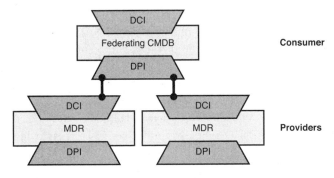

FIGURE 6.4   CMDBf consumer-provider relationships

Because an MDR can be both a consumer and provider, the linking can be connected in any way to accurately represent the CIs in precisely the way needed by the ultimate consumer tool (for instance, an application performance analysis tool). Figure 6.5 illustrates an example structure with multiple MDRs linked in a hierarchical chain.

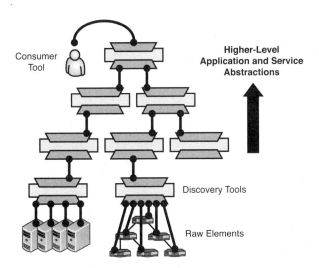

FIGURE 6.5   Service chaining in CMDBf

The lowest level of the chain involves discovery tools communicating directly with the raw managed elements (servers and network devices). The figure shows each discovery tool's DPI linked straight to the raw elements. This is a future prospect in the pure form of the CMDBf specification, when the raw systems themselves incorporate DCIs internally. (It is not yet possible to take the DCI to this level, so the DCIs must reside in external software MDRs.) This allows a fully federated structure down to the lowest possible level (analogous to the four basic nucleotides in DNA). Until this is a reality, different discovery technologies and methods will be needed, as we described in Chapter 4.

Likewise, the consumer tool will someday contain a CMDBf-compliant DPI so it can speak directly to the highest level of the CMS service chain. Just as in the DCI for the raw elements, proprietary methods will be used until this idealized DPI inclusion is a reality. In both cases of DCIs embedded in managed elements and DPIs embedded within consumer tools, the commercial products will be slow to incorporate these interfaces. Consumer tools will be first, including DPIs as early as late 2009. Embedded technologies in the managed elements will take longer (not common until 2011 or 2012).

CMDBf Basic Connections

Each MDR supports standard services that are used in the assembly and navigation of the CMS. The Data Consumer Interface (DCI) will likely support some form of query service and an optional registration service. The query service governs the raw exchange of data as determined by the CMDBf-compliant query issued by another MDR's Data Provider Interface (DPI). The registration service is a web service (similar to that introduced in Chapter 4), which enables service announcements and other "handshaking" among the MDRs. This handshaking keeps all the parts working in harmony.

On the DPI side of the MDR is a client that communicates with another MDR's query service and, if it exists, its registration service. Together, the two DCI services and the client are the basic magic of CMDBf MDRs. You can see this in Figure 6.6.

You can see that each MDR has its own local data store. In keeping with our theoretical presentation of federations, these local data stores can be in any form as long as the interfaces conform to the CMDBf specification. In most situations, this local data is combined with data queried from MDRs below this MDR. The local and remote data is then combined with some internal modeling technologies to make a sensible presentation of the assembly to whichever software (consumer tool or another MDR) needs this particular abstraction. This modeling capability is optional, but we highly recommend it to keep the abstractions sensible.

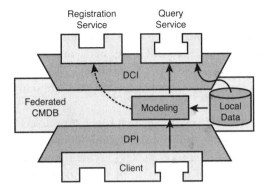

FIGURE 6.6   MDR internal structure

When the MDR uses the registration service, it is the abstraction that is advertised as available for use, not necessarily the raw local data. In most cases, the query service will also present the abstraction, but raw local data is also allowed.

When the MDRs are connected, the client must adhere to the specifications, initiating the conversation with the registration service and then exchanging the desired data (no more; no less) via the query service. This is shown in Figure 6.7.

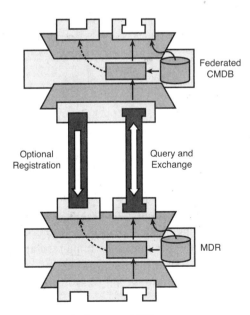

FIGURE 6.7   Communication paths between MDRs

CMDBf Push and Pull Modes

In CMDBf, the MDRs can work in push or pull mode, or both. The premise is simple for each. The consumer MDR either pulls data from the MDR below it, or the MDR below it pushes data to the higher MDR. Both modes will be encountered, and they interoperate as long as they are built according to the CMDBf specification.

You can see how each exchanges data in Figure 6.8. In push mode, the consumer negotiates with the appropriate provider so it knows where it will get the data it needs. It then receives data asynchronously when the provider has something meaningful to present. In pull mode, the consumer requests data, and the requested data is then sent from the provider to the consumer.

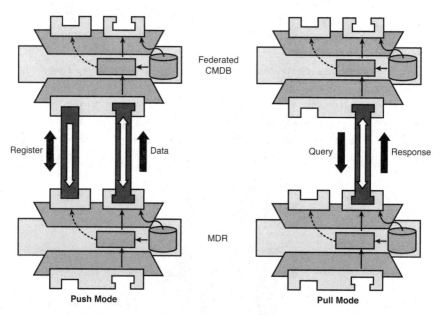

FIGURE 6.8   Push mode and pull mode exchanges in CMDBf

Table 6.1 lists the various requirements for the services in each mode. In the table, the difference between Implementation and Client is in reference to the requirements of each side of the transaction. In this case, the Client is the remote side of the transaction, whereas the Implementation is the local side. The consumer tool row specifies the requirements of an external consumer tool that will be using data from the CMS.

TABLE 6.1 Push and Pull Modes in the CMDBf Specification

Role	Mode	Query Service		Registration Service	
		Implementation	Client	Implementation	Client
Consumer	Push	REQUIRED	Optional	REQUIRED	N/A
	Pull	REQUIRED	REQUIRED	N/A	N/A
Provider	Push	Optional	N/A	N/A	REQUIRED
	Pull	REQUIRED	N/A	N/A	N/A
Consumer tool	Either	N/A	REQUIRED	N/A	N/A

Push mode is the more attractive mode, as this facilitates an asynchronous delivery of data when needed. We explain this accuracy issue in more detail in Chapter 7, "The Future of the CMS." Realistically, support of both modes is optimum, especially given the current state of actual CMS deployments and the near-term migration from CMDB to CMS. We accept that most of the earlier implementations will be pull mode. Pull mode is more analogous to the polling that is now common for remote data collection, so it is the more logical next step as these polling systems evolve.

A hybrid push-pull implementation is the recommendation of the CMDBf. The MDR pushes enough data to the registration service of the federating CMDB to prime the federating CMDB. This gives the federating CMDB enough knowledge about the MDR to correlate and reconcile the data with this and other MDRs. As the consumer tools navigate the CMS, the federating CMDB then pulls what it needs from the MDR. Such a hybrid maintains the purity of the data while also keeping the linkages of the various parts solidly connected.

SML: Another Standard for the CMS

The Service Modeling Language[4] (SML) is a language defined by the W3C for expressing complex service and system models and instances of the models. SML can express interrelated and constrained models more easily than XML Schema. Unlike CIM, SML has no content. It is only a language. It is complementary to the DMTF's CIM, but CIM is all content and incidentally uses a language. CIM tends to address the lower levels of the service chain and SML—along with other standards—focuses on the higher levels. CMDBf will

---

4. Full details about the Service Modeling Language (SML) can be found at the World Wide Web Consortium (W3C) site: http://www.w3.org/TR/sml/.

work with both CIM and SML, although some of this work is still in progress. It is too early to discuss the full details of SML and its role in the CMS, but we expect SML to be as integral to the CMS as CIM and CMDBf.

The Eclipse Foundation's COSMOS project (Community-driven Systems Management in Open Source) explicitly makes use of SML (Service Markup Language), WSDM (Web Services Distributed Management), JMX (Java Management eXtensions), and other modeling standards.[5] If COSMOS becomes integral to CMS implementations as we expect it will, you will see more use of SML at the higher abstraction layers. We recommend you keep abreast of developments with COSMOS, SML, and the entire CMS movement. Your ability to adapt to the continually changing world of the CMS will depend on you remaining current with the changing standards landscape.

Ownership of the Standards Evolution

At this point, it appears the DMTF has a firm grasp of the future direction of most of the work related to the CMS. This is good, as it is a fine organization with dedicated people committed to the needs of the market. Others will certainly contribute, especially where they reflect higher level application and business process inclusion. OASIS and the W3C both have management standards in place for web services and SOA, not just for the manag*ed* systems, but also for the manage*ment* systems. It is important that these efforts mesh well with the DMTF work. We believe they will indeed work together. It should not be difficult to make the technology work, as they have all converged on similar web services in their basic architectures.

Vendor Readiness

Vendors have not yet been effective at genuine multiparty integration. This will change with the arrival of better standards. Early CMDBf support is finally emerging. The CMDBf interoperability demo by CA and IBM is an important first step. The demo was simple in its scope, but the fact that it was done at all proved to be a turning point from the CMDB of the past.

---

5. We introduced WSDM (pronounced "wisdom") in Chapter 4, but until now, we have not mentioned JMX. JMX (Java Management eXtensions) was developed by Sun Microsystems to add management instrumentation to Java-based applications. This adds embedded intelligence to allow management tools to extract structural and behavioral data from these applications.

Despite this progressive first step, federation will be adopted slowly by most vendors. Vendors vary in the level of support they offer for the integration and federation technologies we recommend as the right path forward. Integrating tools usually require some form of adapter code. This code will either be provided as a fully productized adapter or it will require custom code that needs to be developed by a software vendor's professional services arm, an independent services firm, or as an effort internal to your own organization. There is no such thing as out-of-the-box integration, at least not yet. This is sometimes even the case across a single vendor's tool set, mainly because these tools tend to be assembled through acquisitions that remain incompletely assimilated organizations and product families.

As you assess a vendor's suitability for your CMS, try to gain some understanding of its vision and philosophy. Because the technology is changing so much, the vendor's institutional philosophy will probably be more important than the technology it now offers. No vendor is yet able to deliver the CMS you need, but some visionaries are innovating according to the various progressive developments we present throughout this book. Find these vendors, and your future CMS success will be much better. If your vendor is stuck in the CMDB of yore, you will both suffer. Note that the CMS involves many software components from several vendors. A single-vendor answer to all your CMS needs is unrealistic.

To be fair to all vendors, the CMS is not an easy development for them. We must be patient with them as they work through the natural challenges of changing marketing and strategy not to mention the heavy engineering resources needed. A robust CMS takes time; however, it is the vendors who bear the responsibility to produce the technologies you need. It is also their responsibility to earn your trust as a strategic partner in your quest for IT excellence. This extends beyond the technology into education and philosophical guidance. Their reward will be your business!

The CMS is still a relatively new concept for both vendors and users. Legacy CMDB philosophies carry heavy inertia. The transition to the more enlightened view of the CMS will suffer because of this inertia, but we can all accelerate industry progress toward this higher enlightenment. The main object of this book is to foster some progress toward this objective by shedding light on the issues and pragmatic solutions to move forward.

CMS Object Modeling

Object-Oriented Analysis and Design (OOA&D) has been around for many years; for those of us who got started learning OOA&D from Ivar Jacobson,

James Rumbaugh, Peter Coad, Edward Yourdon, and others, we continue to apply some of the same fundamental concepts today that we learned so many years ago. The CMS is no exception, and you should look to some of the same OOA&D fundamentals as a way to design and document your CMS requirements.

A large part of the problem with modeling a CMS is the ease in which you can get caught up in the weeds. Using traditional methods to do your requirements gathering and designs can work for you, but sometimes you will find yourself drilling down so deep into the details of an item, such as a router or server, you lose track of what the purpose really was for identifying that item as a CI. Maintaining an abstract view of the object and its relationships with the other items enables you to keep a better perspective on the whole of the CMS and not get tied up in the details of the item. In our opinion, object modeling is more of an art than a science, and it isn't something that you're going to just pick up for this initiative. It is, however, something that many people have done for years, so it shouldn't be hard to find someone in your organization who has the skills. Look to your data modelers or your metadata modeling folks for assistance with this effort. A good data modeler should be able to understand the object level of detail that you need for your CMS and help you model your CMS at the right level of detail. The object attributes you identify as required should not be dealt with at a source or technology level. They are just attributes of the object and independent of all technological aspects. The time will come when you match the object details with the technological sources that feed them.

We couldn't possibly teach you how to model a system in this book and do it justice, so we recommend that you educate yourself on the basics so that you fully understand what is going on. You should also understand why you need to model your CMS and how it benefits you. Because people are more apt to understand something when they see it in graphical terms; it is in your best interest to model your CMS that way. Modeling your CMS provides you and your technology partners with a relatively simple picture of how all the CIs come together to make up the CMS. The CIs relate to one another in a data structure that is so interconnected, it is nearly impossible to comprehend. When it is referenced, however, the structure resembles a tree.[6] It also serves as a good vehicle for people who need to understand what attributes exist in

---

6. A *tree* is one type of data structure used in computer science to represent relationships between objects. It is called a tree because it graphically resembles a tree when drawn. A good overview of this data structure can be found on Wikipedia at http://en.wikipedia.org/wiki/Tree_data_structure.

each item and the structure of the object tree. With this model, they know how to traverse the object tree to get the data they needed. The details of how exactly they traverse the tree are obviously product dependent.

Some of the existing CMS product suites have aspects of modeling in them to facilitate this effort, but you really shouldn't look to them as your primary modeling utility. We recommend that you use a quality modeling tool to help you with this because if you don't model your CMS properly, you will be working to undo the mistakes for a long time. The CMS model is not a static document; it is something that you will be working with regularly to modify as you integrate your data sources. As you learn more about the data sources, you need to check the model and make sure it still represents what you intended and that the data can be accessed by the users based on the relationships that might need to be in place. What this means is that you can't incorporate detailed information about an item without already having built the tree that those details are a part of. The user would not be able to get to the details if they can't find the tree.

Software Engineering and Development Skills

A CMS requires you to do some software development of your own. It is not something you can just buy off the shelf and install. You can buy many of the parts, but the assembly of these parts requires someone to link them. The emerging standards (for example, CMDBf) will help, but some manual coding will be needed through 2010, and probably some beyond that.

The implication to your organization is that you need to identify someone to actually write code to make these parts work together. These people may be internal staff or contracted help, but they must be technically qualified in the languages used. Skills in XML, Sun's Java, Microsoft's .NET, and maybe even some C++ will likely be required. Once established, this work will diminish, but some level of involvement will be permanent.

Software Engineering Versus Programming

The science of software engineering has really been lost in the last 10 or 15 years since resource gluts encouraged wasteful programming and companies started to look at outsourcing portions of their development organizations. The difference between software engineering and programming is so vast that it is a concern that more people don't fully understand the dichotomy. The many failed software efforts, both internal and outsourced, are evidence of this point. True engineering of any form follows proven processes of discipline that account for potential pitfalls and ensure a higher probability of success.

Software engineers don't simply write code; they design it for a purpose and then develop code to execute that purpose. Programmers take detailed specifications and write the code to meet that specification regardless of what it says. If the specification is missing an obvious element, the programmer will most likely not pick up on it and will code the specification as requested. The software engineer, on the other hand, would likely detect the potential issue and design the code to meet the intended specification, while accounting for gaps in the specification. This is not intended to disparage programmers, as they are vital in our efforts, but you need to understand that there is a significant difference between the two.

It is also important that you understand who on your team is a software engineer and who is a programmer. A great approach to creating an atmosphere where programmers and software engineers exist together is to have the software engineers infuse some of the development discipline into the programmers. Cross-pollination of skills is a productive tactic to raise the quality of software development efforts.

The effort to integrate products typically requires more software engineering skills than it does pure programming skills. Most products do not work well together easily (for example, incompatible interfaces and languages), so there won't likely be a clean and easy programming assignment that you can document and hand over to a programmer. If the integration is large enough that you need a team of technical people, you might be able to mix in both types of individuals and use them according to their ability. Do not expect a programmer to play the role of an engineer. If you do, you will likely have to revisit the code because it wasn't designed to meet future needs. Always remember that you design for the future but build for today.

Product Dependency

The products you have in-house and need to integrate determine the extent of integration you need, in addition to the technologies you need to use. Some vendors offer a robust set of Application Programming Interfaces (APIs), but others are still focused on protecting their product more than making you successful. The ideal would be to have an industry standard-based interface, such as Web Services or XML, but that is not always the case. You can often supplement API deficiencies if the sources are based on a relational database. If this is the case, you can design database views for your integration and do simple SQL queries to get your information. There are situations, however, when you might be forced to use a vendor-specific query language to get at the information in the vendor's tool if it is not willing to provide you with the database schema, a data model, or a mature set of APIs. In these cases, you could always reverse engineer the database to determine the schema, but it will take some effort to do so, and you will be vulnerable to any changes made by the vendor to the database in the future.

Outsourcing Potentials

Outsourcing the integration of your tools is a definite possibility under two conditions. First, if you are looking for programmers to take detailed specifications without the need to design or architect the integration, there is some benefit in outsourcing resources. The second situation where it might make sense is if the outsourcing provider has extensive knowledge about the internals of the two products you are trying to integrate and close relationships with both vendors. Only under these two conditions do we feel that outsourcing this work is a wise decision. If you are trying to integrate internal systems, outsourcing is unlikely to be a successful option from a financial perspective because your internal resources would likely still need to be heavily involved in the effort.

If you are trying to outsource the integration of two incompatible products, you are in the best situation if you can find a sourcing provider that has resources knowledgeable in both products. The sourcing provider will likely need to get additional technological details from the software vendors about the products, and that will be unlikely if the provider doesn't already have a strong relationship with the vendors. If the vendors provided an open interface that didn't require major amounts of resources, you would likely do the work internally rather than outsource it. When you look to outsource, it implies that it is a large effort.

In the case where you have already done all the research and developed detailed specifications for the vendor products you are trying to integrate, you could try to leverage external resources, but we recommend that they be onshore/onsite rather than offshore/overseas. In any sourcing model, clear terms and conditions, as well as explicit specifications, benefit you greatly. Product integrations rarely go smoothly or exactly as the specification details it. If the resources are working overseas in different time zones, the resolution of issues could take longer, and you will probably encounter delays with getting the integration complete.

The major issue with building an integration between two vendor products is not whether you decide to outsource it or not, but who will maintain the integration. You need to remember that all vendors will likely have a major and minor release each year for their product. Any of these releases could impact your integration and require you to revisit the integration every time. At the very least, you need to confirm that the integration still works every time you push out a release. With any luck, it won't require recoding the integration.

Frequently Asked Questions

Question: Why do I have to integrate with other systems?

Answer: It is very unlikely that your only source of information will be the CMS. At a minimum, you need to leverage any sort of inventory or procurement systems for the raw listing of items in your environment. Beyond that, integrating systems that maintain the services you offer or applications you support are vital to your success.

Question: Can I just do periodic manual bulk updates instead of integrating the systems?

Answer: Yes, this is an option if your business requirements can accommodate that. Your users need to wait a longer period of time before they see updates, but if your business requirements do not demand more frequent updates, and you have the resources available to do it manually, then yes, you can do periodic manual bulk updates. Bulk updates impose time constraints that may present serious challenges as the environment becomes more dynamic. Bulk updates are a reasonable start, but not a long-term solution.

Question: Does the integration have to provide real-time updates?

Answer: No, it does not, unless your business requirements demand that. You should research the frequency and quantity of updates that occur in the external sources to determine if real-time or near real-time would actually provide an added value. In some cases, you will find that the source from which you are trying to pull the information does not get updated in real time, so there would be no advantage to you to build a real-time integration.

Question: At what frequency should the integration run?

Answer: The frequency is driven by your business requirements, assuming that the technologies in place can accommodate the requirements. You should expect frequency to increase, as we explain in Chapter 7, "The Future of the CMS."

Question: Should we pull in all the information every time or only the records that changed?

Answer: Your network administrators strongly encourage you to only pull in the records that changed since the last pull. In some cases, the source systems may not have the capability to provide you with only the changed records, so you might need to pull all the records every time and then determine for yourself which ones changed. One thing to be aware of is that after all the changes are identified, you need to merge them with the records that already exist in the CMS, and this likely has a performance impact on your production system. You might, therefore, need to run these merging activities in the off-business hours. This limits how much time you have available to merge the data and how much data you can merge every night.

Summary

In an ideal world, the various tools involved in the CMS would all plug together seamlessly. This world will be reality, but not for many years. In the meantime, you need to be cognizant of the integration challenges and the available solutions. Integrating CMS components requires some work by somebody, whether those people are on your direct staff or supplied via a software vendor's professional services arm, a consulting firm, or an outsourced element of your operation.

Standards are coming together well. The CMDBf, CIM, and SML standards hold great promise for the CMS. It will take a few years for them to become universally applied, however. The biggest step forward among these standards is the CMDBf specification. You should familiarize yourself with this great innovation and pressure all vendors to adopt it. The future of your CMS will be brighter when it is widely available. This future is challenging, but also exciting, as we explain in the next chapter.

CHAPTER 7

The Future of the CMS

As this book is being written in late 2008, the industry movement around CMDB prepares for major changes. People recognize that the common wisdom of a single monolithic CMDB is wrong and a new model is needed. The CMS is now about a year and a half old, and its principles are slowly starting to take hold. The next several years will see major changes in CMS technologies, tools that use the CMS, and the vendors involved in the IT automation software business. We will also finally witness a gradual deemphasis on the term CMDB. By 2013, a very different CMS landscape will exist. This chapter predicts how that new world might look.

Dynamic Technologies and Services Fuel the CMS Imperative

The first thing that will happen in the CMS evolution is a rapid increase in sensitivity to the need for a CMS. Although some organizations have dabbled in the CMDB and a few of them are making great inroads, the transition to a CMS is more of a groundswell. Throughout this book, we mentioned many factors fueling this growing movement, but we believe it is prudent to expand on one of the most potent factors: the explosive growth of dynamic complexity.

A hallmark of a great organization of any kind is its capability to adapt to changing conditions. Nowhere is this more acute than in IT. We are in the business of business adaptation, so we bear a profound responsibility to be adaptive ourselves. Indeed, the technology developments for adaptation keep coming, seemingly at a blistering pace, but our ability to manage these developments always lags. The whole emphasis on process structure is intended to minimize this lag, and a good CMS is the foundation of this structure. You must ensure that the CMS is able to absorb these new developments and adapt to the changing requirements of the CMS use cases. This is the focus of this section.

Rather than talk in generalities about dynamic complexity, we explore a few notable developments that are tangible and probably already straining your organization's service development and delivery.

Virtualization

Virtualization is all the rage today, with most of the attention directed at virtual servers (for example, VMware, Microsoft HyperV, and Xen). The topic spans well beyond servers to storage, clients, and networks. Mainframe operations have used virtualization for decades. The introduction of virtualization brings two additional challenges to the CMS. First, it is another layer in the service chain, and second, there is the need for an accelerated speed of adaptation.

The additional layer is obvious to anyone who has implemented virtualization. A physical resource can host multiple virtual resources, and the CMS must capture the inherent relationships and configuration details associated with each. The basic virtualization concept is illustrated for server infrastructure in Figure 7.1 and for networks in Figure 7.2.

Virtual Servers

In the server example (see Figure 7.1), you can see a physical server that hosts four virtual machines (VMs). Note that the applications, whose functions are not relevant for this example, hosted on this physical resource are related directly to the VMs, not the physical device. This is an important facet of virtual servers that enables flexibility to move the applications around for optimum service delivery. What makes the service flexible, however, makes the CMS pursuit more difficult. The additional layer between the physical server and application, needs to be discovered with your technology solutions and represented appropriately in the CMS to form a complete picture of the overall service chain.

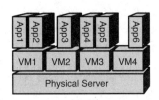

FIGURE 7.1   Virtual servers add an additional layer.

The physical server is represented as its own CI, with all the typical attributes and relationships we covered before. Each VM also has its own CI, with some strikingly similar attributes and relationships. The most important relationships are the mapping from the physical to virtual instances (P-to-V) and vice versa (V-to-P) because they determine the structural assembly of the overall service. If we return to our server example from Chapter 4, "The Federated CMS Architecture," and assume that the physical server is now hosting VMs, we can expand the CIs. Excerpts of the XML description may appear something like this:

```
1    <physical_server>
2    <hostname> DEN002B </hostname>
3    <manufacturer> Hewlett-Packard </manufacturer>
4    <model> HP ProLiant DL360 G5 </model>
5    <serial_number> PDQ1010202 </serial_number>
6    <physical_mem> 16000 <units> MB </units> </physical_mem>
7    <operating_sys> VMware ESX 3.5 </operating_sys>
8    <ip_address> 10.20.30.40 <version> 4 </version> </ip_address>
9    <hosts_vm> DEN032V </hosts_vm>
10   <hosts_vm> DEN033V </hosts_vm>
11   </physical_server>
12   <virtual_server>
13   <hostname> DEN032V </hostname>
14   <manufacturer> VMware </manufacturer>
15   <model> ESX 3.5 </model>
16   <serial_number> KD328345BN21 </serial_number>
17   <physical_mem> 2000 <units> MB </units> </physical_mem>
18   <operating_sys> Red Hat Ent. Linux 5 </operating_sys>
19   <ip_address> 10.20.30.41 <version> 4 </version> </ip_address>
20   <hosted_on> DEN002B </hosted_on>
21   </virtual_server>
22   <virtual_server>
23   <hostname> DEN033V </hostname>
24   <manufacturer> VMware </manufacturer>
25   <model> ESX 3.5 </model>
26   <serial_number> KD328345BN22 </serial_number>
27   <physical_mem> 4000 <units> MB </units> </physical_mem>
28   <operating_sys> Microsoft Windows Server 2003 </operating_sys>
29   <ip_address> 10.20.30.42 <version> 4 </version> </ip_address>
30   <hosted_on> DEN002B </hosted_on>
31   </virtual_server>
```

Several details are notable in this simplified conceptual excerpt. We changed the operating system on the physical server to VMware's ESX version 3.5 (line 7). This then becomes the server "model" for the VMs hosted on it (lines 14 and 15 and lines 24 and 25). We increased the physical memory (line 6) because virtual server infrastructure is memory intensive. Two new attributes were added to the physical server to indicate which VMs are hosted on this physical device (lines 9 and 10).

The new CIs (the virtual servers) look similar to the physical server, even with physical memory attributes. This similarity is important to the success of virtualization, as the VMs should appear no different than traditional servers from the perspective of the applications. The "physical" memory is, in fact, a virtualized segmentation of the actual memory, but the applications and the so-called *guest* operating systems that run on each VM see this memory as physical memory. Each VM has its own IP address, because to the world, they appear just as servers always have.

Each VM also has a hosted_on attribute (lines 20 and 30) to indicate which physical server hosts the VM. In combination with the hosts_vm attributes on the physical server (lines 9 and 10), we can map the relationships. Both upward (P-to-V) and downward (V-to-P) mappings are needed, just as in other relationships, because CMS consumer tools will navigate in either or both directions. Obviously, the P-to-V mapping should match the V-to-P mapping. If they do not, the infrastructure will not work, so the CMS must accurately portray the actual state where the VM software will ensure they do indeed match.

Virtual Networks

Networking has several virtualization possibilities. The two most common virtual networks are virtual private networks (VPN), as seen in Figure 7.2, and virtual local area networks (VLAN). In the VPN example, you can see the physical network topology where nodes are physically connected in a chain. The VPNs traverse this physical structure node by node, but offer what appears to be a clear, uninterrupted path from point A to point B. Effectively, this is a direct network connection.

This has been in place for years, especially in telecommunication service providers. That T1 line you purchased from AT&T in 1990 to connect two offices was actually a whole series of interconnected infrastructure inside AT&T's network. However, what you saw were points A and B apparently directly connected to one another.

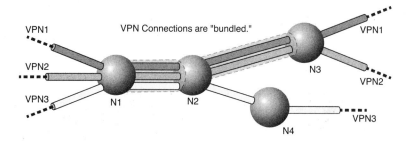

FIGURE 7.2   Virtual private networks spanning a physical network

The underlying CMS details are similar to those we showed for the servers. Each link in the network has an address on each end of the link, and the nodes (routers or switches) direct traffic according to the rules of network protocols. Each VPN also has an address on each end, different from those on the physical network.[1] When an application communicates between the two points on the VPN, it knows nothing about the physical infrastructure, only the VPN-level addresses. It basically sees a clear pipe through the complex underlying network structure.

Dynamic Change in Virtual Infrastructure

In addition to the extra dimensions introduced to the CMS, virtualization also shifts the frequency of change to a level never before seen.

This is the real challenge for the CMS, as structural extensions are relatively easy to keep up with when compared to the fluidity of a virtualized environment. One of the beautiful features of virtual infrastructure is its ability to adapt its use of physical resources as conditions change. If a VMware virtual server needs more resources available on another physical server, for example, the VMotion software can move the VM to the other physical server, usually with no noticeable impact on the applications and users dependent on that VM's hosted services. This movement is illustrated in Figure 7.3. Note how the applications App4 and App5 follow this migration. The movement should be transparent to the applications. They only know that they reside on

---

1. For simplicity, we ignore the possibility that Network Address Translation (NAT) can allow the same address to be used in different places.

VM3, regardless of what underlying physical infrastructure provides the actual resources for VM3.

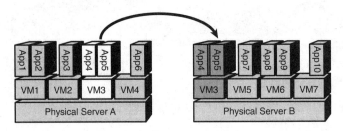

FIGURE 7.3   Virtual server movement

When this shift occurs, many changes are happening within and across the virtual and physical environments. These changes must be captured within the CMS to accurately reflect the real world. Here are just a few of the CMS changes that are required for the scenario in Figure 7.3:

- The hosts_vm attribute pointing to VM3 on physical server A must be cleared.

- A new hosts_vm attribute on physical server B must be set to point to VM3.

- The hosted_on attribute for VM3 must be changed from physical server A to physical server B.

- Storage resources for the VM are shifted to follow the VM. These changes need to be captured in the CMS.

- Network connectivity must change, because the VM is now somewhere else, theoretically even in another geographic locale. The normal network infrastructure must now redirect all traffic for VM3 from physical server A to physical server B. There is also virtual network infrastructure built into the virtual server hypervisor software that facilitates network "traffic" to and from the VMs. This also adapts. The CMS must capture all these changes to both the actual network (and its various virtual dimensions) and the virtual network in the hypervisors on both physical server A and physical server B.

As you can see, an extraordinary number of changes need to be made to raw data and service chain abstractions in the CMS. This is humanly impossible, so the automation tools help us ensure complete and accurate updates to the CMS and documentation of the changes for historical and/or research purposes.

The Perils of Polling and the Promise of Proactivity

Because virtualization squeezes change frequency to ever-tighter intervals, changes must be captured as quickly as possible. Ideally, the CMS will be a perfect reflection of the change, but some lag time is certain, especially given the available technologies. Most discovery tools gather their data through polling, with intervals typically 24 hours or more apart. As technologies and services become more dynamic, changes occur more frequently. A Publish/Subscribe (pub/sub) or Message Queue paradigm might no longer be a choice, but actually a necessity. Virtualization is one technology that is already proving its ability to adapt frequently enough that polling intervals are becoming a serious impediment to CMS accuracy, and for that matter, all management functions (see Figure 7.4).

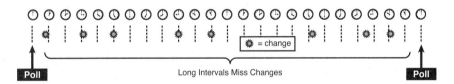

FIGURE 7.4   Polling misses changes.

When changes occur more frequently than every 48 hours, a polling interval less than 24 hours becomes statistically prone to errors.[2] You have to poll at twice the fastest rate of change to ensure accurate capture of the changes. As the polling interval shrinks, polling overhead grows exponentially (see Figure 7.5). You can keep shrinking the polling interval only so much before the polling overhead reaches a point of absurdity. This is simple mathematics at work, as we noted in the discovery section of Chapter 4. Even with a divide-and-conquer approach of federation, polling becomes untenable in dynamic environments, resulting in stale data. As we already showed, stale data is hazardous to the success of the IT effort. The ease of making changes

---

2. The Nyquist rate is a mathematical principle that states a sampling rate (what we are calling a polling rate) must be at least twice the rate of the information rate to be sampled (polled). It is typically applied to electrical engineering situations dealing with signal processing, but the double-frequency rate applies to many problems, including configuration data discovery. The "information rate" in the CMS example is the highest frequency of change. If changes can occur every two hours, the polling rate can be a maximum of only one hour. See http://mathworld.wolfram.com/NyquistFrequency.html for more details.

and the simplicity of making those changes with technologies like VMotion will make the volume of changes increase over time. Hence, we must accept that the interval between changes will drastically shrink as these Dynamic Change technologies become prevalent.

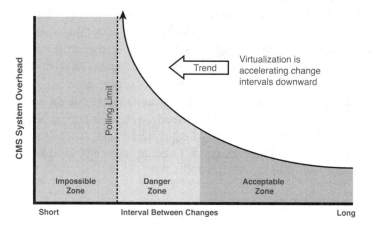

FIGURE 7.5   Dynamic environments will render polling ineffective.

The best approach for virtualized environments (and any dynamic situations) is to change the update mode from polling to event-triggered notification (see Figure 7.6). Instead of requesting periodic updates, rely instead on the systems themselves to inform you of any changes. When a change actually does occur, the virtualization technology tells us what changes have occurred.

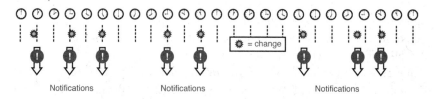

FIGURE 7.6   Real-time change notification

The overhead of polling can be substantially minimized with the addition of event-triggered notification. The notifications require a slight amount of overhead on the managed device to do the local processing, but it would be insignificant with modern hardware capabilities. The caution for overhead would be related to a so-called *flapper*, where state changes are fluctuating rapidly and possibly spewing a heavy stream of notifications. Good design of the local instrumentation on the management element can avoid this.

Before you discount this as science fiction, consider what happens within the basic operation of any virtualized technology. The fundamental operation requires tight coordination of many events and data exchanges. If we can only expose these events and data changes to the CMS, we have asynchronous updates to the CMS! Such capabilities are within reach, and vendors are already beginning to show progress.

You need to determine whether your environment demands real-time or near real-time notification, a decision that could have significant cost implications.[3] The difference between real-time and near real-time is the time it takes for processing the event and the transmission of the notification to its destination. We believe that in most cases, near real-time will be the most cost-effective option, but ultimately, your business requirements will define which is right for you.

The advent of web services and their integration into virtualization technologies are enabling tighter coordination beyond the boundaries of the core virtualization software. CMS tools can leverage these web services to receive data updates as they happen. We can avoid stale data by introducing real-time or near real-time updates to the CMS and document these changes along the way for historical and research purposes.

As comprehensive automation becomes more popular, configuration synchronization will become an integral function of these automation systems. Here is a simple example that is possible today with some custom coding to link the automation elements.

A virtualized server farm must adapt to support the changing demands for an application. The administrator executes an adaptation request for the farm to adapt itself to the capacity level requested. The automation system consults the CMS to determine where capacity exists and which components (hardware, software: virtual *and* physical) are related to the new and old scenario. This CMS information guides the automation to perform the necessary automation tasks on each of the components. The Change Management process is invoked to oversee the necessary changes, and the final step is to verify that the change has indeed taken place. This verification is a discovery

---

3. The cost of real-time insight grows exponentially as you approach a time interval of zero, similar to the effect shown in Figure 7.5. There is a point near zero, on the order of a few seconds, that is near real-time, where costs using event-triggered notifications are acceptable. Even with the dynamic technologies foreseeable through 2013, a few seconds is more than good enough for the CMS. Well beyond 2013, we will need innovative technologies to get us closer to zero!

step that checks to see if the actual state matches the desired state supposedly established by the automated change. If they match, the CMS is updated to reflect the modified environment and the adaptation is deemed successful. If they do not match, the state of the CMS and actual components reverts to the original state and relevant parties (the CMS knows who they are) are notified about the unsuccessful adaptation.

This automation example is attainable, but we will soon see automation also execute the adaptation request manually performed above by a human administrator role. Such incremental improvements to automation will continue to highlight the need for CMS consultation and updates to occur as required steps of the process. In doing so, the synchronization of the CMS becomes as close to real time as the automation allows. For all intents and purposes, this *is* real time.

SOA

Service-Oriented Architecture (SOA) is a broad term that encompasses many concepts of web services, software modeling, communications, and nearly every other facet of modern technology. It is quickly becoming the backbone mechanism of all forms of business execution and changes the flexibility of business services and applications. If VMware virtualizes servers and VPNs virtualize networks, SOA can be seen as virtualizing applications.

In SOA, components of applications and business services are scattered about the enterprise and even beyond traditional borders. The CMS must map these components just as it would any composite application. The main difference is that the relationships can shift frequently, and they are negotiated via service brokers. These service brokers are integral to the applications and services, so they must be represented as part of the SOA service chain.

You might find a quick definition of a service broker helpful at this point. A service broker is a function provided by a distributed software component that "announces" its available software services and then negotiates with other requesting components to provide these services. SOA, web services, and the CMS will use brokers to establish flexible connections across distributed software components. In the case of the CMS, a "service" is the data contained in the brokering Management Data Repository (MDR). If the MDR is a network MDR, other MDRs will know this network MDR holds the information about a particular router because the network MDR's service broker tells everyone about it. The various MDRs then "hook up" and complete those relevant links in the service chain.

You may notice that SOA bears some similarities to the CMS itself. This is because a CMS, done right, is an SOA-based service. Both follow the same principles of flexible component assembly using brokers to help orchestrate this assembly.

As you build your federated CMS with domain managers, the CMS functions for SOA will be embodied in their own domain manager, and will overlap greatly with other application and business process domain managers. At this level of the service chain, SOA is intertwined with the other domains because this is representative of how the higher-level services are actually built. Remember, the CMS is supposed to be a representation of reality. The software models should reflect this reality.

VoIP and IP Telephony

After over a decade of hype and hope, VoIP has finally caught on. More than just another network protocol, VoIP represents a movement toward more comprehensive IP telephony and unified communications. This movement finally takes the network, server, and application elements and produces a higher-level service. Other services do this as well, but IP telephony is the first major turnkey service where these pieces of technology are inextricably integrated. It will continue its growth through 2011 into a pervasive service across enterprises. A Forrester Research survey conducted in Q1 of 2008 indicates only 18% of North American and 17% of European enterprises do not have plans to deploy IP PBX technologies.[4]

The mandate of IP telephony is to finally break down the barriers across technology domains. For the service to work at all means the networking engineers, server administrators, and voice-based application experts must all cooperate. There is no "us and them" in VoIP or IP telephony. It is only *us*!

As such, VoIP-based services become a catalyst to replicate the cross-domain structure and realize the same operational benefits. The CMS is the central truth to enable effective cross-domain management. If it works for IP telephony, we can make it work for all services. This is the momentum sparked by VoIP. This is the CMDB imperative.

---

4. Forrester Research's *Enterprise and SMB Networks and Telecommunications Survey, North America and Europe, Q1 2008* surveyed 96 North American and 81 European enterprise decision makers. Forrester's definition of an enterprise is a company with annual revenues exceeding U.S. $1 billion.

Mobility

One of the great features of VoIP is the ability to "take the service with you" as you move about. Many other services capitalize on mobility too, but again, voice is leading the way. The first instantiation of this concept was the cellular telephone itself. Since its invention,[5] the natural plan was for the phone service to move with you wherever you go. When you are mobile, an extraordinary amount of information is always changing, coordinated across a vast array of network nodes and servers.

In the case of your mobile telephone, much of this complexity is the responsibility of your wireless service provider, all of whom have achieved remarkable results. In the case of VoIP and mobile computing, much of the responsibility will fall on those of us supporting the IT services. Like the dynamic challenges of virtualization, relationships and other attributes of mobile systems are constantly changing. In fact, the changes are happening at a much faster rate than even the most fluid virtual servers. We can learn how to build adaptive management for these other services by following best practices and technology innovations used in mobile systems.

In some regards, mobile management is still immature. Yes, we can track assets and how they connect (relate) to other elements of the environment, and we can even provision service details to ensure seamless functioning of the mobile systems. The weaknesses are in the CMS side of the story. Because it is difficult to capture the truth about mobile services, all functions and processes that derive the truth from the CMS are limited.

The truth is there. We just need to tap into the currently existing technologies that make mobility work in the first place. We will see rapid innovation for the CMS in mobile technologies, but we will use polling sparingly. Because the frequency of change is so high (tiny intervals), any CMS for mobility will be extremely fragile and, therefore, nearly useless. The event-triggered notification mode must be used—and it will.

Convergence

Along with VoIP and mobility comes the logical convergence of the various modes of information creation, consumption, processing, storage, presentation,

---

5. The actual birth of the mobile telephone system is disputed, although Motorola is generally considered the company that introduced the first mobile phone in 1973. You can read a good historical account at http://en.wikipedia.org/wiki/History_of_mobile_phones.

dispersion, and manipulation. Voice, video, data, and whatever other modes we can imagine are all coming together to enhance the end-user experience and increase everyone's productivity. We all have participated in teleconferences where the speaker's voice is augmented by slides presented to all participants simultaneously. This is the proverbial tip of the iceberg. We will soon see fully immersive virtual reality moving from the realm of academics and die-hard gamers into real business functions.

This convergence highlights all the previous points we made about mobility, VoIP, virtualization, and SOA. If we are to realize the dream of convergence, all management systems, including the CMS, must fit the requirements posed by these developments.

Embedded Intelligence

The intelligence embedded in infrastructure and applications is relatively weak today. Processing power and memory within hardware is engineered to support only the basic functions and little else. Also, embedded instrumentation usually only provides a limited subset of the needed information. To attain more sophisticated management capabilities such as active event-triggered change notifications, smarter instrumentation is needed. The development of the various embedded technologies will be a slow evolution, but necessity makes it inevitable.

Impediments to instrumentation evolution are cost, performance, and complexity, but all three will be overcome. On the cost issue, better intelligence needs additional software code and resources such as memory, which adds to the cost of the managed element. With such overwhelming emphasis on the lowest possible prices for these elements, the extra cost of intelligence has been opposed by buyers. With low demand, vendors have little incentive to expand the technologies. Even if both vendor and customer agree philosophically with the virtues of this intelligence, price wins the battle.

Performance limitations exist because the commonly used resources (for example, CPU, memory) are dedicated to the primary purpose of the managed element (for example, routing packets). The additional load of management functions is seen as pushing the resources beyond their limit. To alleviate this, preemption takes place upon resource conflicts. As they reach their limits, the management functions are either postponed or ignored. This is unfortunate because the management features are shut down just when they are needed most.

The solution is to add resources, sometimes dedicated, to cover the management overhead. This adds cost and complexity, but Moore's Law[6] is coming to our aid. As technology advances, costs come down and complexity becomes hidden within integrated technologies (for example, silicon, packaged software). This will drive costs down and provide ample resources to support management functions.

The fusion of more management intelligence and the basic operation of the system is guaranteed, for reasons similar to those we highlighted for real-time discovery. The bond between intelligent instrumentation and pure functionality is inextricable.

Extrapolating this intelligence even further into the future, we can expect the federation of the Management Data Repositories (MDRs) to extend right into the managed element itself. Evolving to more than just a raw data source, full MDR capabilities will become embedded, complete with federation, processing, and even some localized analysis. By 2013, this *hyperdistributed* management model will be in place for the CMS.[7]

Flexi-Sourcing

Our gloomy assessment of punitive outsourcing aside, targeted outsourcing and even full outsourcing are not necessarily bad from a corporate perspective. In fact, we will see much more emphasis on targeted outsourcing, as commodity functions are offloaded to providers who can (hopefully) perform these functions at a lower cost. We already see many situations where the call center function of the Service Desk is outsourced. Another very common implementation of targeted outsourcing is wide area network (WAN) services. It is now rare for an enterprise to install and manage its own WAN links. They will almost universally turn to a telecommunications provider (for example, AT&T, BT, and Verizon) for these services.

As more operational functions migrate to commodities, targeted outsourcing will increase. This is because it is a financially responsible move. Why

---

6. Moore's Law is the famous technology evolution prediction published in 1965 by Intel co-founder Gordon Moore. Moore stated that transistor density on integrated circuits would double about every two years. Remarkably, this law has held true for over 40 years! Some believe that Moore's Law is coming to an end, but only time will tell, and evidence from Intel, other semiconductor makers, and leading academics suggests the progression will continue through 2020. See more about Moore's Law at Intel's web site: http://www.intel.com/technology/mooreslaw/index.htm.

7. Glenn O'Donnell first proposed hyperdistribution of management technologies in his research paper, "Hyperdistributing Management Technology," published on February 26, 2003, by META Group, Inc. (acquired by Gartner in 2005).

grapple with managing a function that has limited business differentiation if someone else can do it cheaper with satisfactory results? It is better for the IT organization to focus on initiatives that differentiate the business.

With more functions outsourced, possibly to several different providers, data visibility and ownership can become blurred. This institutes a challenge for the CMS. If you outsource your server hosting to XYZ Services Corp., your access and visibility to those servers might be obscured. Some access to the servers is assured, to maintain the business purposes of that infrastructure, but you will also need to establish a remote connection for management purposes. Even if XYZ is performing all operational management of those servers, it is still wise for you to have CMS access for higher-level functions and processes (see Figure 7.7).

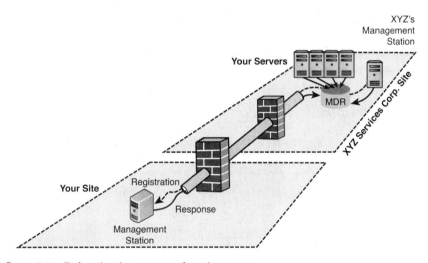

FIGURE 7.7   Federation in outsourced environments

The MDR should be shared by both you and XYZ. There is no technical reason to prevent this, but you must negotiate your rights to access this data when you first agree on the contract for outsourcing the hosting services.

The model where multiple services are outsourced, often to different providers, has come to be known as *flexi-sourcing* (a more *flexi*ble model to outsourcing). There are valid business reasons[8] to do this so flexi-sourcing

---

8. Commodity operations (for example, Service Desk, infrastructure monitoring) can be provided by other service vendors, often at lower cost and with better effectiveness. More IT organizations are outsourcing these functions so they can focus their efforts, money, and people on more strategic functions that provide better value to their end-user customers.

will become common practice. You will need to consider the impact on the CMS and other management functions and plan accordingly. Note the similarity between Figure 4.14 in Chapter 4 and Figure 7.7, where 7.7 is merely an extrapolation of 4.14 to account for the outsourced components. This similarity is central to the concept of flexi-sourcing. It matters little where the parts of the business technology lie or who manages them. The XYZ scenario will play out in more instances within your environment. Each instance needs proper negotiation to avoid extra unanticipated fees or restrictions.

In the end, regardless of what is outsourced and what is kept internal, a unified view of your entire service chain is essential for your CMS. Whether an MDR in the federated model is internal or residing in a Wipro data center in Bangalore, its inclusion in the overall CMS should be the same. Specific access technologies (for example, additional VPN tunnels across firewalls) and contract terms are the main differences. The use cases will differ depending on who consumes the CMS data and for what purpose, but this is very similar even in a fully internal situation. The structural CMS topology and navigation must be identical for *any* CMS implementation.

Cloud Computing (SaaS on Steroids)

Cloud computing is one of the newest concepts promising to radically alter how we provide IT services. It combines all the organizational implications of flexi-sourcing and all the fluidity of virtualization, mobility, SOA, and the other dynamic technologies. All of these influences are being assembled in hybrid IT services that are amorphous and rather ambiguous. The "cloud" is mysterious by intent. What the cloud is supposed to deliver (for example, business applications, dynamic infrastructure) is not.

Cloud computing is the next evolutionary stage of Software as a Service (SaaS). SaaS has gained popularity for its simplicity and the ability to hand off operational and even developmental responsibility to another party and then "rent" the business service rather than buy and run it on your own. The most famous example of SaaS is Salesforce.com. Salesforce offers hosted Customer Relationship Management (CRM), a business tool now considered a requirement for sales, marketing, support, and other core functions of any business. Previous CRM solutions (for example, Siebel) were purchased, tailored, and maintained in the common software sales model. Indeed, this model is still the most common CRM model. What Salesforce did was to take CRM to such a level of simplicity that it has become extremely attractive for smaller businesses not capable of the overhead of the standard software model. It has been so successful that much larger companies are now making the transition.

Cloud computing takes this model further. Rather than SaaS for a specific function like CRM, cloud computing promises Anything as a Service (AaaS). This is an audacious vision, but one that will gradually emerge first as other SaaS forms (for example, custom business applications) and infrastructure as a service (web hosting is a good example). The full vision is years away; however, you should begin thinking about the CMS considerations now. As your own organization drives toward the cloud, consider the following:

- Which MDRs will migrate outside your borders?

- How will you access this data?

- How will you use it?

- How granular should the data be?

- How will you maintain up-to-date accuracy?

- How will you address the need for increased Supplier Management?

- Will the CMS itself become a service?

The answers to these questions are not yet known, although we can speculate some likely scenarios. In some ways, the remote MDRs will resemble the flexi-sourcing model. In fact, both cloud computing and SaaS are forms of flexi-sourcing. If you agree with this view, you can see how the punitive outsourcing dynamic could play a role in cloud/SaaS, just as it does in flexi-sourcing. After all, if a business leader or IT leader chooses to exercise the punitive option, cloud/SaaS may fulfill the need as well as—or maybe better than—traditional outsourcing. Flexi-sourcing is *flexible* to account for novel sourcing models, including clouds and SaaS. Both are just additional approaches to sourcing the needed services.

A cloud service differs little from an outsourced service with regard to the CMS federation. However, the timely updates and data granularity will be bigger issues. Cloud computing is the ultimate vision of adaptive services, with changes occurring frequently, so these changes must be accurately tracked in as close to real time as is practical.

The most profound question of all is the final one. We believe the answer is, "Yes, a CMS will definitely be offered as a service, but in varying degrees." To fully understand this, we can return to the producer-consumer chain using Salesforce as a simplified example. Let's take the example where the VP of Sales for a hypothetical business called ABC Bicycles is the consumer of the Salesforce CRM service.

ABC's bicycle salespeople access the service directly. They only care about the customer information managed in the Salesforce application. They don't care about the servers or databases or whether it's written in Java, .Net, or COBOL. For these consumers, the CMS is hidden, which is expected. Their information of interest is the customer data. This is, in essence, their CMS view. The producer (Salesforce), on the other hand, is *very* concerned about the CMS. It is the basis for managing the delivered service.

What is the role of ABC's IT staff and what, if any, is their CMS involvement in this particular service? Here, we need to break down the service into the parts delivered by Salesforce and those delivered by ABC's IT staff. The application, the servers, part of the network, and the storage are the responsibility of Salesforce, as are the related CMS domain managers. The clients and a different part of the network are the responsibility of ABC, as these are related domain managers.

The highest level of service abstraction is the responsibility of *both* ABC and Salesforce; however, each is built somewhat differently and for different consumers with different needs. Table 7.1 shows some of the differences in this scenario:

TABLE **7.1**   Service Abstraction Differences for the ABC Bicycles Example

	ABC Bicycles	Salesforce
Consumer	Business service manager (internal ABC)	CRM service account manager (Salesforce)
Producer	ABC client and network infrastructure MDRs	Salesforce application, server, storage, and network MDRs
Construction	Assembly of local ABC elements, with Salesforce elements included as a "black box" application infrastructure element	Assembly of local Salesforce elements, with ABC elements included as a "black box" infrastructure element
Needs	Visibility into the service, but control only over those elements owned by ABC	Visibility into the service, but control only over those elements owned by Salesforce

Both views are incomplete, because they have no visibility into the other's domains. Each service abstraction therefore contains a "black box" representing the other's domains. The black boxes can portray only the input and output data and some high level connecting relationships, but the means of operation are not specified. Another element is equally missing from both: the Internet. The Internet is an almost-black box with most of the detail hidden from view. It is an important element, but one that remains a bit of a mystery.

Although a cloud computing or SaaS situation will have inherent gaps in the CMS, you still need to build as complete a view as possible. The cloud services will eventually expose more of the internal detail to fill these gaps, but such transparency is years away, maybe well over a decade.

Finally, there is the proposition of the CMS itself becoming a service (SaaS). This is a likely scenario, although like the CMS described throughout this book, the federated parts will be in multiple locations and in multiple forms. Some of these parts will be SaaS implementations, functioning as elements in the bigger CMS. It is unlikely that the full CMS will be in SaaS form, except in situations where the entire IT organization is outsourced. Even where all but the most strategic functions are outsourced, the highest levels of business service and business process abstractions will remain internal, and each lower MDR will reside elsewhere.

Each different part of the CMS interacts and federates in the very same way, whether it is a traditional software form or SaaS. In this respect, SaaS is irrelevant. It's all software, and SaaS only defines where that software resides and the economic model for purchasing it.

Summing Up the Dynamic Requirements of the CMS

Throughout the previous points about dynamic technologies, some common requirements keep surfacing, as follows:

- Real-time coordination challenges the status quo of polling-based discovery. Everything is happening faster. The hyperspeed at which changes will occur mandates the de-emphasis of polling.

- Cross-domain modeling links infrastructure into services.

- New CIs and new attributes for existing CIs will emerge.

- Tools are few, but will expand quickly through 2011. We expect vendors to address the tool shortage with aggressive product development through 2011.

- All is not quite as it seems. The CMS must expose the truth hidden beneath the layers of technologies that virtualize and adapt services.

- The normal 18- to 24-month lag time between adoption of a technology and management of that technology is unacceptable. Management will become integral to the technology itself.

Watch the developments around these dynamic systems because they will be the beacon to indicate where the whole CMS movement is going. CMS technologies and methods introduced in these domains will quickly spread to the more commonplace domains.

The Extra Dimension of Time

The CMS is by no means a static entity. Such a thing contradicts the very purpose of the CMS. Among the many dimensions to the CMS labyrinth is time. Your world changes and adapts. The CMS must reflect this, and the prior section on dynamic technologies strongly highlighted this truism. Figure 7.8 shows how the CMS incorporates "slices" of reality through time.

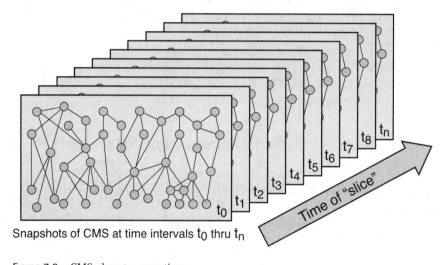

Snapshots of CMS at time intervals t_0 thru t_n

FIGURE 7.8   CMS changes over time.

A snapshot in time (the slice) freezes the state of the CMS at that point. It absolutely does *not* freeze the CMS. The CMS continues onward, morphing with the changing nature of the world. Just as a still photograph is a visualization of a moment in the continuum of the photographer's field of vision over time, a CMS snapshot is a moment in the continuum of the CMS over time.

The concept of a snapshot is extremely useful as we explore the use cases for the CMS. Each time we use the CMS, we are taking a snapshot. We take the CIs, relationships, and abstractions necessary for the purpose (no more, no less) and freeze them in the form of a snapshot at the moment of use. Five minutes later, we take another snapshot for a different purpose. It will likely involve a different mixture of CIs, relationships, and abstractions, but it will almost certainly involve a different state of them.

Figure 7.9 shows how these snapshots are extracted from the CMS. At the precise moment that the use case's consumer tool needs it, the "slice" is taken from the CMS, but we do not need every CI, every relationship, or every abstraction within the CMS. We only need those relevant to the use case. When the consumer tool requests its information, it will probably (not always) start at the highest layer of the service chain, and the CMS will navigate through the chain based on the desired abstraction model. This particular model is like a stencil, only revealing the desired view of the CMS and ignoring the rest. The resultant snapshot is precisely what the use case needs.

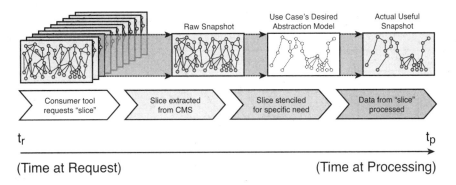

FIGURE 7.9   Carving the right snapshot from the CMS

Remember, while this snapshot is being extracted, stenciled, and processed, time keeps moving along. By the time the first step of this sequence is completed, reality has changed, and the CMS, if it is keeping pace, has also changed.

How does the CMS indeed keep pace? We covered the finer details of discovery, where some tools take periodic snapshots to feed into the CMS and others try their best to offer real-time visibility. Ideally, we want real-time visibility into everything, but this vision is nothing more than science fiction today and will remain so for years. Like everything in science fiction, however, we gradually take steps, some tiny, some profound, and we inch ever closer to science fact. This will be the case with the CMS.

We keep preaching about accuracy in the CMS, and time is one of the most influential aspects of accuracy. If we examine anything over time, tighter intervals between observations will bring us closer to perfect accuracy. It is not important to achieve perfection (it is futile to even try right now), but you undeniably want to approach perfection as closely as is practical and cost effective.

Figure 7.10 gives us a visualization to understand how the granularity of time intervals affects accuracy. Each path from point A to point B results in an identical end result. We move precisely the same Cartesian distance. If changes happen infrequently, the leftmost path (sampling interval) is suffi-cient. High accuracy is not needed. As our demands for more accuracy increase, we must shrink our sampling interval (in this case, move to the right). Each successive path doubles the sampling interval as we move to the right, giving us ever more accurate depictions of the true Cartesian path, a smooth 45° angle—the hypotenuse that completes the triangle with the first path of two lines.

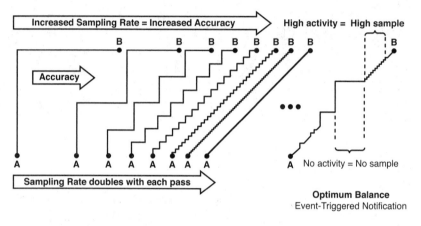

FIGURE 7.10   The effect of time granularity on accuracy

As we saw in Figure 7.5, there is a practical limit to the overhead of shrink-ing intervals. This applies to many topics, not just the polling that Figure 7.5 was targeting. Even if we have a discovery technology that is always watch-ing (not polling), tiny intervals are often wasteful. If an attribute does not change, peeking at it every five seconds to see its state is not only boring, but a waste of time and resources. The optimum balance between perfect accuracy and out-of-date samples is *event-triggered notification*. When the change occurs, tell me. If nothing changes, I will patiently wait while I perform other tasks.

This optimum balance is illustrated on the far right of Figure 7.10. To the human eye, this path appears chaotic and disjointed, but to the CMS, this is indeed perfection. It is an optimized balance of accuracy. Optimization is not an extreme position. It is a perfect balance between the yin and yang of the topic of interest. Event-triggered change notification is this balance for CMS with respect to time, and the capability to deliver this balance will be embed-ded within the discovery tools.

Each step in the evolution of discovery tools will take the form of a tech-nology development that gives us asynchronous event-triggered notification in our discovery. To use a tongue-in-cheek twist on a now famous statement, "Don't ask—tell!" If a CMS use case desires the state of an attribute at some point between its triggered notifications, it is unnecessary to request the state from the raw source. It only needs to observe the previous change. If nothing happened, why ask again? This is the equivalent of the children in the back seat of the car asking, "Are we there yet?" as the family travels down the highway. Object assembly over time leverages the state preservation. Each snapshot is a sample of the state of every CI, relationship, and abstraction at that point in time. Some of these will be recent, some in the distant past, but reality is constructed from these prior state changes. Things like your compliance needs and storage capacity will determine how much history you need to keep readily accessible and when you can archive old snapshots.

If you are a vendor developing or using CMS technologies, we implore you to build your tools according to these principles around state changes. You need not even take our word for it. The market will demand these technology capabilities. The requirements will become increasingly persuasive as time moves forward. The vendors who can meet these market demands will dominate the CMS and the power derived from it. If you are an end user of the CMS, all of this deep philosophy of state may be irrelevant, although you should be aware of the issues so you can impose informed requirements upon your vendors.

How You Will Effectively Use CMS Snapshots

There are different reasons you may choose to use snapshots, which we discuss later in the chapter, but in Chapter 9, "Leveraging The CMS," we dedicate an entire chapter to the consumption of the data in the CMS. Although we do not necessarily use the term "snapshots" throughout Chapter 9, it should be obvious to you that the snapshots are the means by which you will be able to leverage the data. Following are three categories of usage, whereas Chapter 9 takes the perspective of each process area.

Verification and Audit

Snapshots play a major role in your ability to confirm that modifications to your environment were executed as requested. By taking snapshots, you can capture the state of objects and their relationships both before and after modifications occur. As we know, there should be no modifications without an RFC. You can utilize the snapshot at the closure of an RFC to ensure that the software was deployed as per the details in the RFC. If the snapshot mirrors the request, you can verify that the change was properly executed. If it does not, you have the choice to revert back to a configuration defined by the previous snapshot or investigate an alternative solution. In either case, the hope is that you detect the inconsistency before an outage occurs.

Roll-Backs

Roll-backs are probably the easiest to understand because having a snapshot of the environment you just modified makes "undoing" the modification much simpler. Knowing exactly what versions of code were on each piece of equipment and being able to access that code via the Definitive Media Library (DML) greatly reduces your risk of causing an unrecoverable outage when deploying software. If you know exactly what the environment looked like and you have that code readily available, you can reapply it should you encounter difficulties with a deployment. Sometimes, errors in deployed code are not always detected right away and time might go by before an issue arises. During that time, changes to other pieces of equipment in your target collection may have taken place of which you might not be aware. Having the snapshots available enables you to research the differences between the snapshots over that period of time and make an informed decision on how exactly you will roll back the changes.

It goes without saying that roll-backs, although simple in theory, will always present some difficulties. The number of changes that occur before you determine the need to roll back, the interdependencies of your applications and services, and the infrastructure complexities that exist in your environment all will factor into how far back in time you can go with your roll-back. There is always a danger with any deployment, and a roll-back is just a different form of deployment. You must also remember that depending on the scale and function of the original deployment, there may be some incompatibilities with the new data and the old models. Again, consider it a deployment, and use those processes with the snapshots to ensure your success.

Simulations

Snapshots provide much more value to your enterprise than simply supporting the previous two uses. They enable you to perform simulations and analyze how certain software configurations may have withstood the demands of day-to-day operations versus other software configurations. Once the snapshot data is available to you, you can overlay Change, Incident, and Problem ticket information to determine if there are trends with certain configurations. You can leverage that data to help you perform "what-if" deployment scenarios, IT Security virus infection studies, assist in Disaster Recovery modeling, or for Business Continuity certification testing. Only a few uses were listed, but there are many more that you will find valuable to your organization. The key is to have the data available to you, and then the uses will be amazingly clear. It is likely that this "what-if" capability will be embedded within each CMS vendor's tool; however, as the CMDf adoption grows, it is possible that we might see independent vendors build simulation tools that are vendor agnostic so long as they comply with the CMDBf standard.

Reconciling Snapshots with Reality

Regardless of whether you use technologies for your discovery or you rely on manual intervention, you must perform some amount of reconciliation between your actual environment and the snapshots in your CMS. This is especially true when you first start out so that you can ensure the accuracy and completeness of the snapshots. Once you mature and have been able to demonstrate a high level of accuracy and completeness, you may be able to scale back on these efforts. They will most assuredly consume a significant amount of time and resources.

How you go about actually doing the reconciliations will vary widely from company to company depending on a multitude of factors. The complexity of your environment, deployed technologies, amounts of changes that occur, controls, and governance of your environments and regulatory implications all factor heavily into how you can or should do your snapshot reconciliations. One thing that will be consistent is that you need to perform it from both the Change Management process perspective as well as the change detection perspective.

The Change Management process perspective would demand that upon closure of any RFC, a snapshot be taken and compared to the RFC to ensure that the environment actually looks like it should as per the details in the RFC. The change detection perspective, however, is triggered when a modification in the environment triggers an event that notifies the CMS of a modification. The CMS then must compare that event trigger with its current snapshots and any RFCs that are in progress or recently closed to determine whether or not the modification to the environment was authorized.

The Feedback Loop of Change

Time is a vital concept for anything we do to the CMS and the environment it represents. Every meaningful action we take will involve some change. When we do this, we are essentially taking a snapshot that represents the time point marking the commencement of the action. We then make whatever modifications are relevant to that snapshot. Modification examples can be capacity adjustments, resource consolidation, performance optimization, or even wholesale replacement of some segment of the environment. The possibilities are nearly limitless, but the two common factors are that something is changing and that time keeps marching forward.

The modification produces yet another snapshot. It should not yet reflect reality because the modified snapshot must follow a Change Management process culminating in the execution of the changes reflected in the modified snapshot. The final task of the Change Management process is to merge the most recent snapshot with the modified snapshot to represent the modified CMS. We must take this additional snapshot out of the CMS because time has elapsed since our prior snapshot and the state has likely changed. The merged snapshot is then "inserted" into the ongoing continuum of time to represent the accurate state of the CMS (and the environment) at that precise moment.

Figure 7.11 shows this simplified change cycle as it applies to the CMS and the various snapshots. In actuality, the tools do not take a complete snapshot, but these visualizations are used to more clearly illustrate the concept. The actual best method to handle the "snapshots" is to merely modify only those CIs, attributes, and relationships that are changing.

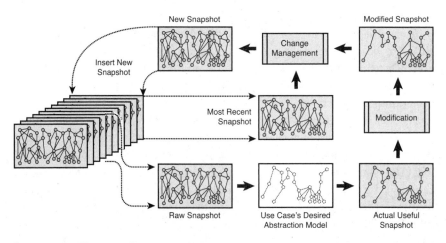

FIGURE 7.11   Changing CIs

In Figure 7.12, you can see how a snapshot is extracted from the raw data stream through time. This example highlights nine attributes and how those attributes change over time. Some change more frequently than others. At any slice of time, the state of the attributes can be determined by taking the attribute's setting at that time. In this example, the attributes are simple characters. Our snapshot is taken at time t_{26} and assembled by taking the most recent value for each attribute. The resulting snapshot is a set of characters

that spells "PEPPERONI" when arranged according to the sequential numbering of the attributes (the relationships!).

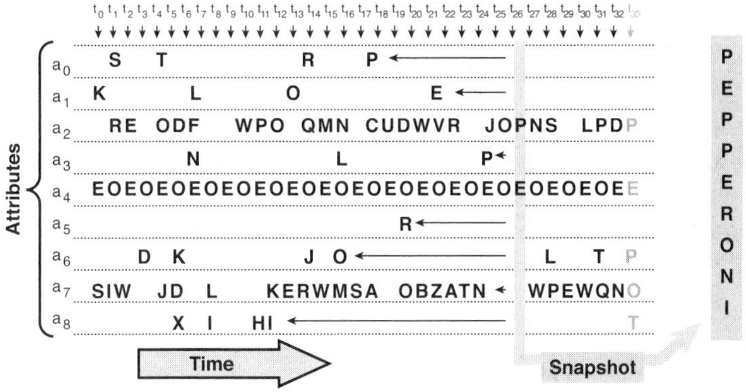

FIGURE 7.12   Assembling "snapshots" from most-recent data

If we modify this set of attributes to change "PEPPERONI" to "PEPPER-
POT," the final data merging will work as follows:

- Attributes a_6, a_7, and a_8 are updated as they reflect the modifications.

- Attributes a_0, a_1, a_3, and a_5 are unchanged, and the most recent snapshot at time t_{32} shows they have remained unchanged since time t_{26}.
  These need no updating at all.

- Attributes a_2 and a_4 are unchanged, but they have been updated in
  the CMS between time t_{26} and time t_{32}. The Change Management
  process must resolve this discrepancy and only approve the change if
  these two attributes should indeed be set to "P" and "E," respectively.
  For that matter, attributes a_6, a_7, and a_8 are subject to the same
  Change Management scrutiny.

- The final snapshot approved and executed via Change Management
  then becomes the new state of the CMS at time t_{33}.

It turns out that attribute a_4 actually need not be updated. The most recent
change to that attribute since the t_{26} snapshot is the setting we want to give
it anyway. Getting to this level of minutia is generally not worth the worry.
There is no real harm in updating the attribute to "E," even though it already
is set to that value. The update is less overhead than the decision processing
that compares the current value to the desired value.

The tools will handle these issues. Most people involved with the CMS need not be concerned with these automation tasks and can be oblivious to them. It certainly helps to understand what is happening under the covers of your CMS tools. If you plan to write custom CMS code, you need to know these details and how they may or may not work with the other tools in your CMS tools portfolio.

Every CI, every attribute, and every relationship of the CMS ideally has a timestamp assigned to it. The timestamps are used to keep the entire assembly of data accurate through time. If one were to examine the raw data, it would appear to be a mess, but by managing "snapshots" through time (as dictated by the timestamps), we get a clear image of the real state of the CMS and all of its contents *for that specific moment in time.*

ITIL v3 and the CMDB Shift

We are delighted with the changes brought about with ITIL version 3. Across the entire ITIL spectrum, ITIL v3 is a landmark step forward, but the implications to the CMDB discussion are among the most profound improvements. With the introduction of the CMS, the former notion of the CMDB has been shattered. This is a phenomenal development because it finally allows everyone to discard ill-defined beliefs about the CMDB and move toward a CMS that is actually useful and achievable.

The CMS accounts for the inclusion of many raw data providers in many forms, and it inherently uses federation to build the overall model of the business and technology environment from the nuts and bolts of infrastructure to business processes, and everything in between. In addition to the structural issues already described, the ITIL v3 CMS includes the task and process definitions to turn the CMS into a truly useful collection of information. After all, information is a worthless concept if there is no means to use it.

The Definitive Media Library (DML) is an integral part of the CMS in ITIL v3. The DML provides many of the ITIL processes informational support, but in particular, the Release and Deployment Management process leverages it the most. In ITIL v2, this entity was referred to as the Definitive Software Library (DSL), but it implied a much more narrow scope because of its name. It was renamed to a media library to encompass all elements that might be incorporated in a release. The vital connection with the CMS comes by virtue of the fact that changes made to the environment reference specific objects in the DML, and therefore the CMS has access to that historical information. If a change is made without reference to an entry in the DML, it is possible that the deployment was done using unauthorized versions of code, and it should be researched before an outage occurs. A benefit of having these references is also that roll-backs on failed deployments could be greatly simplified because the previous versions of code are readily available in the DML. Utilizing the historical data of previous deployments available in the CMS and access to the software in the DML allows Incident Management to identify the previously deployed version of software and remedy the situation by having that version applied.

The transition from CMDB to CMS will be slow, but it is already happening. Remnants of the monolithic CMDB are well entrenched and will persist, both in implementation as well as mindset. Migrating from the "CMDB" to the CMS will follow a logical progression of technology, awareness, and staffing. A few of these progression steps are shown in Figure 7.13.

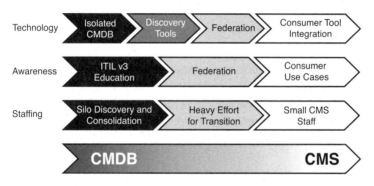

FIGURE 7.13   Transition steps from CMDB to CMS

Technology

Most CMDB products are currently isolated software entities, only including external data through copy integration (importing a copy). For example, an Asset Management system cannot be replaced by a CMS; however; there are many data elements within it that the CMS could leverage. If the CMS could just reach into the Asset system, use the data element it needs without making a local copy, and then go on with its other business, there would be very little concern with the Asset data being stale. We already showed how importing and copying are unsustainable over the long run. Still, this is the typical and, in many cases, the *only* starting point for CMS initiatives. These CMDBs will evolve into modeling tools that represent higher-level abstractions and which properly federate to their remote data, but other steps are required along this progression. The Asset Management tools represent another form of MDR, but Asset Management will also evolve to consume elements from the CMS.

The first step of automated discovery is already taking shape. Discovery tools are now covering nearly all corners of the infrastructure and have now moved into the application domain. We will continue to see discovery move up the service chain, and these tools will also migrate to better visions of accuracy. As the managed technologies become more intelligent, the discovery gets ever closer to the real-time perspective.

The technologies will gradually embrace federation, moving away from simple copy integration. The aggregation MDRs (those that build higher abstractions from elements below) will need to move first. Without a means to assemble the abstractions in a federated structure, federation capabilities in the lower MDRs will be less effective. Once you are finally able to assemble a lower level into abstractions at the next level up, federation will finally experience its inflection point. This will mark the time when federation becomes reality.

Finally, the consumer tools (for example, incident analysis, provisioning systems, Service Desk) will get much better at leveraging the CMS. Integration today is fragmented and nowhere near the federated model. When federation is realistic, the consumer tools can start making use of information provided by the CMS. These tools will ideally access the CMS using the same federation technologies used internally to link the CMS structure itself.

Awareness

The first step in heightened awareness is always education. The active stakeholders in the CMS should pursue ITIL education, and especially ITIL v3 education. The basic Foundations certification is not absolutely necessary, but we highly recommend it. Employers are more frequently seeking ITIL-certified staff and requiring such qualifications for the top ITIL-oriented jobs.[9] At a minimum, an understanding of the principles presented in Foundations training is indeed absolutely necessary. Additional higher levels of certification are recommended for the key players, but again, it is the philosophy and the details that matter most.

Hopefully, this book is also an aid to CMS awareness. This is certainly our intent, but we defer to our readers to make that call! The natural next step beyond ITIL is to truly understand federation. This is precisely why we stress

9. The IT career site Dice.com posted an interesting article on ITIL certification requirements: http://career-resources.dice.com/job-technology/jumpstart_your_career_with_ITIL_certification.shtml.

it so much that we dedicate an entire chapter, plus segments of others, to this topic. The CMDBf work is a major development that expands on ITIL v3. It will no doubt prove to be a pivotal moment in the CMS evolution, and it will be the basis for widespread technology solutions. You can help accelerate this trend. Learn as much as you can about true federation and the CMDBf specification. Then, lobby your vendors to adopt the standard for federating their tools. Vendors will respond to market demand, and *you* are the market!

With strong awareness of federation among the key people and good federation emerging in the tools, you can begin building real value with the use cases. This is the final awareness stage in the transition from the CMDB to the CMS. At this point, the structure of the CMS is in place, and you are now getting real value from the CMS investment. From this point forward, the CMS and the consumer use case tools will reinforce one another, further building value.

Staff

Staffing for the transition will initially focus on technology domain (silo) discovery and consolidation. Much of this can be done with existing staff, but some augmentation is warranted to overcome the initial "bump" in workload. This augmentation should increase through the federation development, where professional services will be the best means for increased staffing. As the CMS reaches the point where the consumer use cases are starting to demonstrate real value, the augmented staff can wind down and the original staff can begin to focus on more core elements of their jobs rather than being overwhelmed with research to make simple decisions. We hope that in the future individuals are spending the majority of their time applying valuable knowledge and experience to deciding whether to permit a change rather than sifting through year-old architecture diagrams and making numerous calls to find out what the environment looks like.

Regardless of the phase of the CMDB-to-CMS transition, strong leadership is the most important staff issue. Strong leaders must be involved leaders, not simply those who pass down edicts and leave their staff to fend off the masses that are fighting to maintain the status quo. They need to be physically present at some of the major meetings. They must be able to speak intelligently about the topics and be capable of understanding the rationale behind the decisions being made at lower levels. No one expects them to be knowledgeable about the details and lead a process facilitation session; however, if nobody ever sees them actively participating, they will surmise that the initiative is not high on the priority list. *ITIL is much more of a cultural shift than it is a technology movement.* Everyone involved in IT Service

Management—or should we say, everyone who hopes to be employed by a company moving toward an IT Service Management model—has no choice but to accept that life in IT will never be the same again.

We have written in other chapters about how there will be resistance to this transformation, but there is no other way for IT departments to survive the continuous pressures from their business partners to be more efficient and transparent. The future IT staff will be more nimble and will operate with a very clear bottom-line mentality. Much less time will be spent doing hours of research to resolve an outage, and more time will be spent identifying trends to prevent them. In theory, the efficiencies gained will allow companies to reduce head count. However, it may turn out that the time saved through the efficiencies may be directed at activities that are not currently performed because there is no time to do them. This is a reason why we worry about companies that embark on ITIL initiatives with the primary purpose to "save money." Although efficiencies can be quantified and dollar values placed on them, it is much more likely that the efficiencies are in the form of "soft dollars" calculated only by internal chargeback mechanisms between departments. Unless you have a sophisticated internal financial system between you and your business partners, it will be hard for you to quantify and qualify the efficiencies in real dollars your company can place on its financial bottom line. You may want to employ the services of Six Sigma experts to help you measure and quantify the value of your ITSM initiative.

The Service Catalog and the CMS

Any business must clearly articulate the products and services it offers to its customers. In a restaurant, it is the menu. The menu precisely defines the food items and (sometimes) the prices for these items. When you visit your local pizza shop, it is unlikely that Moo Goo Gai Pan is on the menu, but you can get a slice of pepperoni pizza. In IT, the menu of services is the *Service Catalog.* Let us start out with the fact that there could be more than one Service Catalog. There could be a Service Catalog that the IT organization offers to its business partners, and one that the business owners use to define and model their business. We are not implying that there should be multiple Service Catalogs at any one level, but there could be different ones between the different levels of operation such as Customer–to–Business and Business-to-IT. If you outsource any portion of your IT operation, you may have yet another Catalog, originated by the external provider, between yourself and them. The same holds true if your business leverages third-party specialists to execute some of your business. At each of these levels, you need to clearly define what is available, the costs associated with delivering or consuming the service, and how the service relates to the next level above or below it. This is where the CMS comes into play. Remember that internal IT organizations are also businesses, or should we say, they need to be managed as such.

The IT Service Catalog is the list of business services offered by the IT organization. If a service is in the Catalog, IT can deliver it along with SLAs and the associated SLO metrics. Anything not in the Catalog is not a valid service offering. It will either be delivered at extra cost or not at all. If the consumer desires a service that is not in the Catalog, the terms, requirements, expectations, and deliverables should be negotiated jointly between the consumer and the producer. Once both parties agree, it is added to the Catalog, and it becomes an official service.

IT provides its business partners with technology solutions that enable them to run their business, so you need to think of yourself as a Profit & Loss (P&L)-driven organization in the IT Service Provider business—the key word is "service." Your organization will provide services such as Application Hosting, Disaster Recovery, Messaging, Collaboration, Business Continuity, Application Development, and so on. These are the types of IT Services that you include in your IT Service Catalog. After determining your cost to deliver each of them, you can provide your business partner the "menu" of services to choose from when you enter into your next budgeting cycle. Remember that not everyone likes or needs the same things, so you have to offer different levels of these services such as 24 x 7 x 365 versus standard weekday business hours, sometimes referred to as Gold, Silver, and Bronze levels of service.

Services in the Catalog must have a tangible producer and a tangible consumer, and all direct relevance to this service is only between these two. Most times, the services are business services that are consumed by business customers and produced by IT. For example, the technology elements of hiring a new employee (for example, provision of a PC, set up email, and establish login credentials for critical business applications) form a business service. Data center internetworking is not a business service, but it is a service produced and consumed by different parties than a business service. In this case, both parties are IT, and one or both of them may be outsourced via the flexisourcing model.

The business services are a bit more straightforward and could align directly with the products offered by the company if you are in a services-oriented industry, such as banking, but they could possibly align to product manufacturing processes as well. Banking transactions such as Open Account, Deposit, and Withdrawal are simple examples of what the Business Service Catalog might look like for a services-oriented business. The granularity at which you define your Catalog depends on different factors, such as how you charge for your product/service, your ability to manage your business at that level, and the value you will reap by managing your Business Service Catalog at that level.

The Service Catalog is a requirement of strong service management. Its popularity among vendors is a welcome leading indicator about the state of IT service management. You can always get a feel for the future by observing the themes being touted by management software vendors. The big theme at the September 2008 IT Service Management Forum conference in San Francisco seemed to be the Service Catalog, followed closely by the CMDB. The pairing of these two at the top of market awareness is telling. It tells us first that they are both in demand and both in need of clarification. As you dig deeper into the two, you learn something even more intriguing—they are different views of the same thing—the CMS!

Yes, the Service Catalog is an MDR that fits well into the CMS. In fact, ITIL v3 agrees. In the hierarchy of the CMS, the Service Catalog represents an MDR near the top of the service chain. For business services, the service abstractions represented in the Service Catalog are just below the business process level. It may be the highest level of the service chain directly provided by IT, since the business process level is usually an abstraction that uses the business services that IT provides. This marks the handoff between IT and business.

The Service Catalog also includes technology services that remain internal (such as our networking example). These services also have consumers and providers, but neither is a business user. Remember, a service need not be relevant to the business user, but it must certainly be relevant to someone. All of these services, business and otherwise, are maintained in the Service Catalog, and everything encompassing those services is unraveled and assembled below those points. The CMS service chain is well suited to this need.

As we write this, the Service Catalog and the CMS are two distinct entities in the market. Vendors are positioning CMDB or Service Catalogs, but few are linking the two into the same CMS structure. This will change rapidly, as the vendors and their customers alike conclude that the Service Catalog is actually a part of the CMS.

The CMS model helps to bridge the boundary between the services delivered by the business (Business Service Catalog) and the enabling services provided by the IT organization (IT Service Catalog) that allow corporations to operate. In Chapter 5, "CMS Deployment Strategy," we discussed business service models and IT service models, but we did not address the role of the CMS. Figure 7.14 builds on Figure 5.8 from Chapter 5 to show how a subset of the technology components in the environment work together to form three IT Services that then collectively help deliver one business service. The figure is not complete by any means and does imply that the other business services modeled do not require IT services. Figure 7.14 simply presents a model that has four business service Catalog entries and three IT Service Catalog entries that are mapped via the CMS relationships.

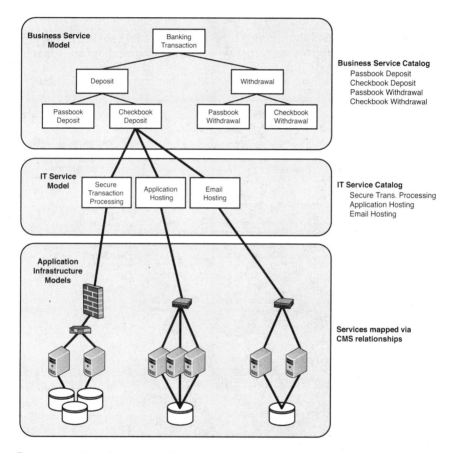

FIGURE 7.14   Sample entries in Business Service Catalog and IT Service Catalog

As you can see from Figure 7.14, the CMS must have the ability to stitch together IT components into a variety of shapes that could be pulled together to form an IT Service. If the CMS is not designed to have this ability, or if you follow the lead of the vendors and build your Service Catalog independent of the CMS, you will not be able to traverse the CMS hierarchy to determine what impact IT components have on the business. If we once again use Figure 5.8 from Chapter 5 that we built our Services Catalog with in Figure 7.14, but remove the CMS influence that provided the IT service model and business service model, we would have no idea which IT components enabled the various business transactions (see Figure 7.15). Even if you define a Service Catalog but build it independently from the CMS as the vendors are currently promoting, there is no real way to easily understand how the IT components contribute to the Service in the Catalogs. To be fair, vendors are now beginning to see the relationship between the Service Catalog and the CMS and will hopefully adapt their future product direction and functionality to address this. As you pursue the union of the two, be sure your vendors are committed to this same union.

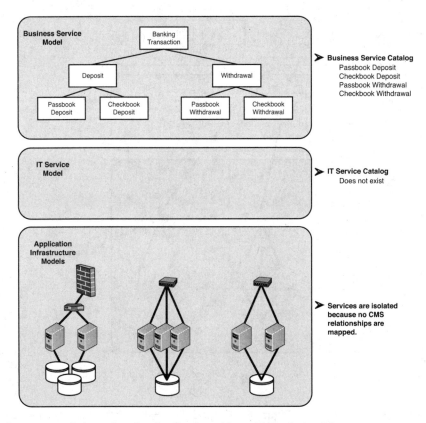

FIGURE 7.15   Independent Service Catalog with no CMS relationship

The bottom line is that the CMS must have knowledge of everything that happens through the IT components and how they contribute to the products your company is trying to deliver. Only with a tightly integrated CMS and Service Catalog can you achieve this. The Service Catalog, IT or Business, does not have to be extensive to start out. You can start small and then expand, but you must, without question, design the capability into your CMS from day one.

Object Modeling Technologies Need to Mature

Part of the difficulty in designing and implementing a CMS, we believe, is that people run into a problem conceptualizing and visualizing what the CMS really is. Those who most quickly grasp the concept of a CMS tend to be those who have spent some amount of time in their careers doing object, data, or metadata modeling. This is because the CMS is a virtual entity that needs to be graphically displayed with characteristics and relationships very much the same way an object model exists, and without good tools to do this, most individuals are left without much support.

Object modeling tools have come a long way but there is an inherent challenge with object modeling that tools have not been able to fully resolve. When designing an object model, it is always a challenge to find the proper level of abstraction that maintains a certain level of simplicity while still going deep enough into the details to address whatever system requirements you are trying to model. It is not a trivial dilemma to resolve, but the vendors need to find a way to allow the products to adapt to this seemingly mutually exclusive situation. Tools that provide advanced visualization and manipulation of the models will help tremendously, but such capabilities are rare in the current modeling tools.

A way to potentially address this situation would have the current modeling tools allow for more dynamic manipulation of the models so the user could, in essence, "step back" from the model to visualize it from the 20,000-foot level. The user would then drill down into certain parts to isolate the proper level of detail and lock in that level before focusing on the next area. Current tools do not make this easy, and it is almost impossible for anyone other than a very skilled modeler. Again, we are not implying that this is a simple hurdle for vendors to overcome, but it is, without question, a necessary one.

Another aspect of the tools that needs to be addressed is their ability to easily interface with other sources and external systems. In many cases, the current modeling tools are just that, only modeling tools, and they are unable to help you take the step from a paper model to an implementable technology. What this means is that even when someone designs a strong model, they are left with a massive challenge to translate that model into a technology that can be implemented. Part of the challenge is that the developers are not typically familiar with object or metadata models so it requires tremendous amounts of time on your part or the modeler's part to now educate the developers on the story that the model is telling them. We say "story" because that is sort of what a model does—it tells a story.

A well-designed object or metadata model tells the reader a story about the characters it contains, their interrelationships, and how they go about interacting with each other. It demonstrates what sort of behaviors are allowed, prohibited, or possibly encouraged depending on a particular condition between the characters or objects. One of the beauties of a well-designed model is that anyone, from a business owner to a technical programmer, can pick up the model and, with very little instruction beyond what the symbols mean, read the model and fully understand the system's intentions.

Most object modeling tools cannot easily facilitate that today, but they must do so in the future. If you are fortunate enough to have a modeler available to you that has both strong visualization and interpretation skills, you will be ahead of the game. Unfortunately, for most organizations, it will be the developers who will carry most of the burden. If you are a vendor or if you are a CMS user developing your own code as part of the CMS tool set, you must study these issues and develop the models and tools accordingly.

CMS: The Lifeblood of Every IT and Business Service Function

Everything we have in today's world is a product of the information our ancestors passed down for hundreds of years through songs, chants, stories, images, documents, and so on to educate the following generations on their history and how to do things. The quality of these teachings probably even determined whether civilizations prospered or collapsed. These teachings contained information that had been aggregated and refined over generations, with each storyteller adding their element of experience in order to help those they were teaching. Knowledge itself is built upon prior knowledge, reassembled to form new concepts, ideas, and solutions.

The CMS can be viewed as a form of storyteller if it is designed and used properly. It can aggregate information from across the enterprise and transform it into an image that you can use to protect service integrity. It should be used to help predict the future of components based on how they behaved in the past. The CMS enables you to avoid meaningless outages caused by repeated incidents. It may even save your IT organization from being out-sourced to a solution provider if the driving force to do so is the fact that the provider has a clear services model and offers your business a transparent cost-per-service menu.

The threats are real, but the CMS is a key to protecting your future relevance. The financial bottom line drives decisions, and if you are an internal organization that does not manage itself like an external organization, you are at risk of being downsized or outsourced. Business leaders are being pressured to increase revenues and customer satisfaction, while also reducing costs. When a significant amount of their budget is spent on IT with minimal, if any, transparency around how it contributes to the bottom line, they will be looking to other solution providers that promise better.

The CMS is the vehicle that you can use to help drive and enable your business. It gives you the insight into what exactly is going on in your infrastructure, and because of its wealth of data, it enables you to identify trends in equipment related to your business cycle, season, region, and so on that you otherwise would have never been able to detect. This massive convergence point of data brings together every aspect of your company that when pieced together in a certain manner, brings clarity and simplicity to the otherwise chaotic world of IT. In theory, if you achieve the goal of delivering a comprehensive CMS, and you have a skilled and efficient IT organization, you could easily compete head-to-head with an external vendor that is trying to convince your senior management that they should outsource you and not only win the battle, but demonstrate your superiority.

The old saying of "you're only as strong as your weakest link" is especially true when talking about the CMS and the services it provides. Currently, most businesses work extremely hard to keep all their business applications up and running, but how many really know all the pieces of equipment that contribute to their stability? How about the business services that they contribute to? We can assure you that most do not, especially when referring to the business services. It is not because they don't want to; it is because they cannot realistically do it in real time, and especially not for every application in their organization. The job is too daunting and not cost effective without a robust CMS.

The future CMS has all the pieces in it. It has the ability to aggregate data from a variety of sources such as software distribution, Asset Management, and Identity Management; assess the pieces; and then knit them together into an understandable and actionable image. Having the business services defined in very granular detail that matches the level of detail developed in the XML schemas and SOA-based applications empowers the CMS to take that next step forward from being an IT Service Management tool to a Business

Service Management tool. That is where we have to go. That is where the technology must go.

Our experience is that many IT departments still think of themselves as technology shops, but they need to start thinking of themselves as businesses that deliver IT services. To do that, we need to put in place systems that track our products (IT services), so that we know the exact costs to deliver them and how we can reduce those costs while also improving their quality. We need to also change the incentives so that they do not encourage the very behaviors we don't want. For example, if we reward the network, server, and storage departments based on their discrete objectives, it is likely that each could meet their "uptime" objective, but yet collectively miss the overall business SLA. Most of us have heard the objectives by senior management that they want their organization to achieve five nines of availability. This means that they want the systems to be 99.999% available over the course of the year, which equates to approximately five minutes of downtime. If in the previous example, each of the three domains achieved this five-minute target, but none of it overlapped with each other, would that not equate to 15 minutes of downtime to the business over the course of the year, three times longer than what their SLA states is allowed? The business does not care if a server is down or if it was the network or if it was storage issues—all they know is that their business service was down for more time than it should have been.

Is IT any different than any other business? No, but for some reason, most IT organizations have spent more time talking about "running like a business" rather than actually trying to do it.

How can you possibly run like a business and deliver a product when you don't know what goes into that product? If you do not know with 100% accuracy every server, router, SAN, DB, and network connection that participates or could impact the delivery of your Checkbook Deposit Banking Transaction, how can you run your business? Fortunately for IT departments, they have not been asked for the ingredients to their product, until recently that is. Unfortunately, few have recipes for their products, but the CMS can help to provide those recipes. Not only can it provide the recipes; it can also help identify where certain additional ingredients are needed and where others might be extraneous. It will help you create your first IT menu.

In the future, we expect that the CMS will be able to tell a story like no other technology we've seen before (see Figure 7.16). It will be able to take its wealth of information and tell a salesperson the story of why he is not able to use the Lead-Tracking System and what alternatives he can use. At the same time, the CMS will be telling the Service Desk worker a story about how the change request just executed by the server administration team corrupted the DNS table that is vital to the Lead-Tracking System. Finally, the CMS is also telling the operations and business continuity teams that the DNS Server with serial number SN123xyz located in the Den1ver Data Center was corrupted by the actions to execute Change Ticket number CHG0879. Upon resolution of the situation, the CMS can then tell the business partner the story about how well his money was used that day and whether his SLAs were met. Think of it as the United Nations for IT. It should have all the data available to it in order to translate what is happening in the environment and pass on that information in as many languages as necessary based on the people impacted.

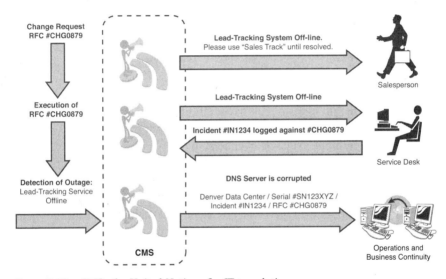

FIGURE 7.16   CMS...the United Nations for IT translations

The future CMS will have the ability to concurrently tell different populations the same story in languages that each group can understand instead of in only one language that most groups don't. More importantly, the CMS will be able to directly tie the impacts of low-level technology pieces to business services that have direct financial consequences attached to them. For far too many years, IT has spoken in technology terms to their business partners, and the reverse is also true with neither IT nor business typically having a clear understanding of the implications. The CMS will be that translator and intermediate storyteller that helps each side truly understand things in their language. Before that can be done, however, the CMS must have the data available so it can speak at all these business and technical levels—one of your largest challenges.

Frequently Asked Questions

Question: Do I need multiple copies of the CMS for different purposes?

Answer: What appears to be multiple copies is merely different views of the same CMS, composed of different CIs and different service abstraction chains at different points in time. We referred to these as CMS snapshots. Different user roles will likely utilize different snapshots.

Question: My company has used virtualization successfully for a long time; why do I need to integrate my virtualization tools with Change Management?

Answer: Regardless of how successful you may be with virtualization, you still need to document the historical changes that your environment is going through. There are always situations where you will need to look back into the history of why a CI might be in its current configuration, and without the change tickets, you may not have a clear understanding. The key to the integration is to establish the linkage as a background communication where the change ticket is automatically generated and processed without human interaction so that it does not burden the Help Desk personnel, but you still have an audit trail if you should need it.

Question: We use a standard drawing package to design our models; why would we need a modeling tool instead?

Answer: Drawing packages do a good job in helping you to draw out a model you want, but they do nothing to help you figure out what model you want. They also are not very flexible when it comes to collapsing layers of objects or depicting the relationships between objects. These tools are a great place to start, but if you plan to do much more than a rough draft of a CMS model, you really should look at getting a more sophisticated modeling tool.

Summary

Although the CMS is already a prominent topic in IT Service Management, this is just the beginning of a long and exciting journey. The CMS is changing radically, and so is its impact on your organization. The technologies comprising the CMS will be developing quickly over the next few years, but more importantly, the technology and business drivers that require the CMS are also evolving. These latter developments threaten to shatter IT as we have known it. They are great innovations for business and keep technologists employed and excited. The problem is that traditional IT operations will collapse under the pressure these innovations will impose.

New approaches to IT Service Management are needed to instill and maintain service stability and service quality. More automation must replace the tedious, error-prone, and wasteful aspects of IT management. A strong CMS that can reliably supply trustworthy information about the environment is the only way to deal with the onslaught that will make today's complexity appear primitive in comparison. The CMS needs to incorporate a strong sense of the passage of time so we can understand the changing world and be able to play a role in this change. We cannot allow our CMS effort to become a victim of change. We must make the CMS an integral factor in the very notion of change. This is not just possible—it is inevitable.

Because our entire landscape will continue to change at an ever-increasing pace, our efforts to manage it need to continually change as well. The next chapter addresses how we should employ proven methods for quality improvement to ensure that we can achieve the continual service improvement that has worked wonders for manufacturing operations for decades.

CHAPTER 8

Continual Improvement for the CMS

The Configuration Management System (CMS) is not a destination, but a journey. Everything outlined so far is good advice, most of which is proven by experience through countless mistakes and victories. As a whole, however, it portrays an ideal state, a CMS nirvana if you will. Everyone embarking upon this particular journey is going to be nowhere near this nirvana at first. It will take solid planning, commitment to the mission, and methodical execution to move toward nirvana. Indeed, nirvana will never be attained, as its definition will keep changing with business conditions. This does not mean that you should give up and not strive for attaining it, however. What you will attain this year might have been last year's nirvana, and what you achieve next year might be this year's. The point is that you have to keep striving for the goal out in the distance. It forces you to work harder and achieve more.

We all start from the beginning and build upon the CMS in small increments. There can be no big bang approach to the CMS. Anyone who attempts a big bang will fail because it is too ambitious. Your accomplishments are many to be had, with each of them more satisfying than the last, and they will come with your incremental successes if you stick to the vision. In this chapter, we offer pragmatic guidance for this evolutionary approach to the CMS, and how continual improvement practices can be leveraged to take your initial CMS "seed" and nurture it into a more robust and useful implementation.

Metrics for the CMS

Success at anything can be known only if there is a set of measurements that tell us what constitutes *success*. We must identify and track many metrics to understand how well we have done and how well we plan to do. This is part of the never-ending pursuit we call *Continual Service Improvement*. Throughout this chapter, we show how these metrics are established, captured, assessed, and leveraged to optimize the CMS. If you have no exact measurements established, use what you have in order to demonstrate some progress until you can establish more significant and reliable metrics.

To begin this chapter, we offer a few key CMS metrics that you can use to form a foundation for your CMS effort. We hope you expand upon these because there are more that apply to every CMS, and it is likely that your enterprise or your industry has others that should be added. Do not overextend the scope of the metrics, however. More metrics will equate to more overhead in capturing them and doing something about them. As in all things, you should balance comprehensive coverage with simplicity and overhead.

Table 8.1 shows a few metrics that are directly relevant to the CMS. Use these as operational guidance to direct the evolution of the CMS. They do not, however, offer much direct insight to the real benefits of the CMS. In reality, the CMS alone does not provide any significant value, but what the CMS enables is extraordinary in its value. This list is not comprehensive. It is meant to get you thinking about what types of metrics make sense for you to use in your organization. Determining the right metrics is often the hardest part of quality measurement.

TABLE 8.1   CMS Metrics

Metric	Goal	What to Expect
Configuration items (CI) under management control	No hard value, but it will start large and become huge as the CMS matures.	The number of CIs will prove to be an efficiency metric because you use this raw value to calculate others, such as CIs per IT administrator and cost per CI. Discovery tools cause this value to explode because it captures the complexity with more accuracy. If you think you have 500 servers, and discovery tells you there are 800, 800 is the real number you will use.
Percent of CIs populated automatically	As high as possible.	Without discovery, this number will be low. Even Change Management alone cannot assure a high degree of CI accuracy. You need to augment it with discovery. Seek a rising trend rather than some fixed value as your goal because the ideal of 100% is impossible.

Metric	Goal	What to Expect
Number of Management Data Repositories (MDR)	The number will start low, but not at one, because many of these exist and just need to be located.	Build an ideal portfolio of MDRs when defining the CMS architecture. The usual suspects (servers, network, and so on) are included, but geography and business unit structure might dictate other divisions. The number of MDRs in your architecture should be the goal, so drive toward filling the voids in this architecture. Note that the architecture must remain flexible to changing needs, and thus the MDR portfolio will also be flexible.
Number of federated abstractions for applications and services	Start low and seek rapid increase. The number will then level off as the CMS matures.	You cannot achieve a high value at the onset of your CMS. After you deploy application discovery and dependency mapping tools, you will have the abstractions, but federating to the lower-level MDRs cannot occur easily until your vendors adopt and implement standards—hopefully the CMDB Federation Working Group (CMDBf).

The metrics in Table 8.2 indicate broader value. They are derivatives of the CMS because the CMS affects these, usually amplifying the CMS improvements (for instance, small CMS improvements yield big improvements elsewhere). Again, this list is not even near complete and is just a means to help you get started.

TABLE 8.2   CMS Effect on Operational Metrics

Metric	The CMS Role	Expected Results
MTTR (Mean Time To Resolution)	Provide accurate information that was previously missing, incomplete, or inaccurate.	Because MTTR is heavily influenced by prolonged root-cause identification, accurate information will guide toward faster root-cause and therefore will reduce MTTR, maybe dramatically.
Change-related incidents (percent of total incidents)	Provide accurate information to guide configuration changes accurately.	Approximately 80% of all service-impacting incidents are the result of some sort of faulty change.[1] With the right information, most of these changes can be either avoided or executed with much better accuracy.

(continues)

---

1. It is widely known among experienced operations professionals that a high number of incidents are caused by faulty configuration changes. The precise percentage is the subject of dispute, but most research suggests that the typical IT organization experiences between 70% and 90% of incidents resulting from these changes. We use the 80% value as the generally agreed-upon figure; however, regardless of which number you use within the given range, it is unacceptably high.

TABLE 8.2   CMS Effect on Operational Metrics (continued)

Metric	The CMS Role	Expected Results
First-call incident resolution (percent of total incidents)	Provide accurate information to the Service Desk.	The Service Desk is better able to resolve incoming incidents when they have the right information. Thus, fewer incidents need to be escalated to higher-level (and more expensive) staff. Also, automation technologies that assist the Service Desk can be enhanced or developed.
Change Management execution time	Provide accurate information to accelerate change assessments and approvals.	Quicker change execution is extremely helpful to service adaptation. This is becoming ever more critical as technologies and services get more dynamic. The CMS can speed these changes, since decision makers (and automation tools) can act with better insight.
Asset utilization	Provide accurate information on all assets in place.	The goal of most Asset Management initiatives is to optimize asset utilization. You cannot reach this goal without knowing the assets are in place. Such information is seldom known with good accuracy, but a good CMS should make it obvious.

Metrics are the instrumentation of quality. Establish what they are, how you measure them, and what values you set for short-term, and maybe long-term, goals.

Whatever you measure, measure it early. **Benchmarks are essential because they establish a starting point.** You cannot measure progress unless you know how far you have gone. What the numbers tell you in the beginning might not be pleasant, but you need to know! Don't be worried about your starting point, and be sure to not inflate the numbers if they are worse than you expected because these are the metrics by which you will be measured. If you inflate them out of fear of exposing deficiencies, you will have to not only make improvements, but they will have to be significant enough to surpass the artificial metrics you started with.

The Cyclic Nature of Improvement

Continual improvement is a key behavioral principle of discipline. It is one of the great improvements made in ITIL v3 and has been popularized through proven success in Six Sigma initiatives and quality initiatives spawned by the legendary W. Edwards Deming.[2] Continual improvement is a cycle, whereby you keep reassessing the results of actions and keep tweaking actions over time. Figure 8.1 shows Dr. Deming's Plan-Do-Check-Act cycle that is now a foundation of nearly every quality improvement initiative. It has become a staple of manufacturing and should become just as pervasive in IT.

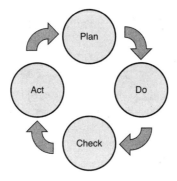

FIGURE 8.1   The Deming Plan-Do-Check-Act continual improvement cycle

To summarize the cycle:

1. You *plan* on how you will improve something, including the explicit objectives you hope to achieve.

2. You *do* what you planned to do.

3. You *check* on your progress by monitoring and evaluating your success against the objectives established in the plan phase.

4. You *act* upon the results of the check phase. In this phase, you tweak the process itself, if necessary, and you make sure improvement is complete before you initiate the next execution of the cycle.

ITIL v3 expands on the Deming cycle with the seven-step cycle shown in Figure 8.2.[3] As you can see, the cycle fits the Deming cycle well because ITIL v3 was heavily influenced by Dr. Deming's teachings.

---

2. Many references to Dr. W. Edwards Deming's work are available from his nonprofit organization, The W. Edwards Deming Institute®. The institute's web site is http://deming.org.

3. The seven-step improvement process is introduced beginning on page 43 in the official ITIL v3 publication *Continual Service Improvement*.

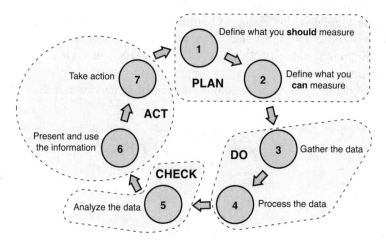

FIGURE 8.2   The ITIL v3 continual improvement cycle

For the CMS, we can examine the following actions that are taken in each of the seven steps of the ITIL cycle:

1. During each rotation through the cycle, you might be able to expand the set of metrics you should measure. Ideally, you define every possible metric up front, but it is unrealistic to assume that you know all of these metrics beforehand. Besides, changing conditions over time will impact this set of ideal measurements.

2. Technology limitations, funding, and maturity phases constrain the set of metrics that will be possible. Do not dwell on a comprehensive set of measurements at first, but you should determine a few metrics that can act as a benchmark for improvement. Table 8.1 shows a good starting point of metrics directly related to progress with the CMS, and Table 8.2 can also help greatly. These are not necessarily CMS metrics, but they measure the impact of the CMS on higher-level value to the organization.

   Each time you pass through the cycle, try to expand the set of metrics you can measure. Every metric you are capable of measuring is potentially a powerful weapon against the challenges of proving the value of the CMS effort. In all cases, these metrics should come from the set of potential metrics defined in step one.

3. With the CMS, you gather the data in this stage. If step two dictated that the goal was to discover a domain with a new discovery tool,

step 3 is where the tool is actually implemented and its execution commences. This is the active phase of the cycle, where theory is put into practice.

4. As the second step of the "do" phase, the CMS data is processed, maybe filtered, and possibly assembled into its higher-level abstractions. Whereas step 3 was just the start of the collection, this step actually does something with the data.

5. Now, we assess the success of the first four steps to see if they met the objectives established in step one. This is not analyzing the CMS data itself; rather, it is assessing the process of enriching the CMS. If our objective was to discover a domain, how comprehensive is the coverage of this domain? Have we captured what we desired? How rapidly were we able to complete these first steps? You should have developed these kinds of questions in step one, but now you have the ability to ask them and analyze the improvement.

6. After our progress is known, we must then disseminate it to the stakeholders and determine the appropriate action to be taken in step seven.

7. Finally, we make the actual corrections to the process, so we execute the next instance of the cycle more effectively. This leads us back to step one, as we commence the execution of the next instance of the cycle.

Our experience tells us that when you follow a continually executing process like this, you will certainly notice improvements.

It is a bit like a fitness program. When a person in poor physical condition first starts a structured program of exercise and diet, the progress in the initial cycles is impressive. After the person achieves a good state of physical fitness, incremental progress diminishes. What also happens in these situations is that the fitness program becomes a part of the healthy person's everyday lifestyle. The pain experienced in those early days of the program is gone, replaced by the stamina, strength, and happiness of good health. Your doctor might measure it in terms of lowered blood pressure, lowered cholesterol, or a better heart rate.

The CMS fits this metaphor perfectly. Each rotation through the cycle leads to the ever-increasing health of the CMS. It is painful at first, but progress develops quickly. After several iterations of the cycle, it becomes a lifestyle, more a matter of routine operation than a burden.

Begin with Small Steps and Build Out

The initial implementation of the CMS will be an incomplete coverage of the desired environment. This is natural, as you cannot capture everything at once. This first small step is used to prove the concept. Here is when you work out the kinks of the system, from architecture and design to deployment, population, maintenance, and use of the data. It takes many iterations of the process to approach completion of the CMS, but make sure these initial stages are approached with care. Mistakes will happen in these early efforts. Correct them in the beginning or you will suffer later, as the implications (both good and bad) are amplified over time. The suffering will come, for example, in the form of having to overhaul your complete CMS model to accommodate new CIs or new relationships between CIs.

Figure 8.3 graphically conveys how the CMS evolves from its incubation through the many iterations (only a few are shown for brevity). You can see significant missing details in the Mona Lisa on the left. This represents the limited scope of the first CMS proof of concept. As you expand coverage of new domains and go deeper with CMS detail in the domains already covered, the picture becomes clearer.

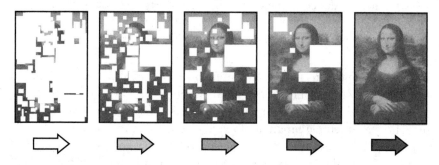

FIGURE 8.3   Iterative refinement of the CMS

The ultimate complete image on the right side of Figure 8.3 might never be totally achieved, but you should get close. As with digital photographs, the clarity of the CMS depends on the resolution to which you have defined the data and accurately captured it. From a high level, you should see the full image, and it should make sense. As you zoom in on the details, some might be missing what is the equivalent of the pixelized image. This is fine for the earlier stages and maybe even in a mature state. The precise detail you need is dictated by the use cases. Some need coarse detail and some need much finer resolution. Sometimes, this is dictated by domains and the ease at which you can autodiscover these details. As an example, the network is easy to discover and thus the detail can be finer. Conversely, business processes are difficult, and maybe impossible, to discover. Detail here is coarser.

Domain coverage should be restricted in the proof of concept, because it will be easier to firm up the whole process with a smaller set of data. Do not forget, however, that a smaller sampling size can lead to a larger variance in results; find the right balance for your company that is large enough to give you some assurance of accuracy, while still small enough to manage in a proof of concept. When you have successfully proven the CMS with this initial state, you will be well prepared to expand upon it.

Assemble the Extended Team with Strong Leadership

Strong leadership is mandatory for the CMS. After you decide to move forward with the CMS, identify the right person to lead the effort. Here are some traits to consider when identifying this person:

- This person does not need to be your brightest technical person. This is a job steeped in some heavy technology, but the "rocket scientists" should be involved in the direct development and implementation, not the leadership. This person should be a strong leader with good managerial skills, in addition to having strong technical skills. The leader should know enough technology to understand the strategy and progress steps.

- The real skills for the leader should be managerial. This means the person must be a great diplomat and organizer. Diplomacy is required to inspire the team and to negotiate the personal and organizational conflicts that always arise. In a federated structure, some parties resist the central elements of the CMS. An adept diplomat needs to balance a strong-armed mandate for central structure with the sensible embrace of those who represent the federated entities.

- You might have to decide if an IT background or business background is preferred. There are two schools of thought with regards to whether it is easier to train a technologist to become a business manager or a business manager to understand technology at a high level. The answer is ideally to find someone who is already skilled at both. You have to carefully assess all the individuals available to you when forming your team. If the team is very strong on the technology side, and you feel that you can supplement a business manager's lack of technology background, you might give more weight to business experience than IT experience. Someone who can manage but does not understand how to build the CMS will not be a good manager for this project, so that person needs to get up to speed very quickly; your technical team will have to provide a lot of support early on until this individual gets up to speed. If, however, your available resources are strong developers who are not very skilled in architecture or software engineering, you might have to go with a strong technologist and train him on the business management aspects of running the project. You should also provide an administrative type of individual who can perform the more routine tasks of collecting and tracking status.

The end goal of the CMS is to serve business needs and to integrate tightly with the business itself. It is important to have someone from the business side of your enterprise supporting the technologist to ensure that the business perspective is factored into the effort. Our experience is that it seems easier to instill the high-level technology knowledge into someone from the business side than it is to retrofit a technologist to understand the business processes intimately. Of course, there are always exceptions to this, and if you can find a technologist who has first-hand business experience, you have found your ideal leader.

- The bottom line for the CMS leader is an attitude and aptitude to "get things done" under difficult circumstances. This person must have the vision to guide the direction of the team and the desire to tackle problems that most of us would rather avoid. He or she must be organized, have the ability to manage a team of varying opinions, continuously motivate, manage a budget, communicate both up and down the ladder, sell the vision, and build excitement across the organization. This is an exciting, yet challenging job. It takes a special person to love this line of work, but those who do are guaranteed to succeed and position themselves among the real heroes of IT (and the business).

The rest of the CMS team includes a core of people closely aligned with the leader in the organization and maybe reporting to the leader in a typical direct-report organizational structure. Many on the extended team represent the various parties with a vested interest in the CMS. These include other IT groups (for example, data center infrastructure, network, applications, and enterprise architecture) and affiliated business entities (for example, human resources and business unit liaisons).

The leader needs to direct the work among this team, even across traditional organizational boundaries. This can be a challenge, so senior management support is warranted. Because the CMS and ITIL are defined with a Continual Service Improvement component, the leader must be able to sustain the energy and vision over the long run and not just during the traditional start-end cycle of a typical project.

Implement Discovery Sooner Rather Than Later

Many elements of the CMS, especially around federation, will not be available as you are getting your CMS effort off the ground. Still, there are parts of the overall system that can be deployed today. Most notable among these is discovery.

Discovery tools—such as those used for networking or server monitoring, automated software and license provisioning, or agent-based software distribution tools that monitor detailed configurations of workstations or servers—are needed regardless of the state of your CMS evolution. They are needed now, and they will be necessary ten years into the future. They will also evolve, and the future versions will be different in their mechanisms and federation. The basic capability and the value of this capability will remain largely unchanged, however.

By deploying discovery early, you start with an accurate view of the discovered domains. Start with the easy work. The network is a great first step because the embedded instrumentation readily exists and discovery is mature. Additional infrastructure domains should follow.

The application domain yields the biggest move forward for discovery. The visibility you gain will be priceless. This is the step where the "nuts and bolts" of the infrastructure views are finally assembled into something more meaningful. It will be much closer to the actual business service views that are so central to the entire business service management ideal.

Although this application visibility is enticing, we caution against jumping into the application domain prematurely. The infrastructure domains are the foundation upon which the application views are built. Establish these first, and then enrich them with the application discovery. *Isolated pockets of the truth are far superior to a comprehensive view of ambiguity!* With isolated pockets of truth, you at least have a set of data that you know for a fact is accurate and reliable for others to take action with. If, on the other hand, you have a broad array of data but cannot assure anyone which elements are reliable and which are not, you cannot expect them to go forward and use it as actionable data. It is too risky.

Bringing together these various domains into a unified and federated structure is certainly desirable, but you need not make these formal connections up front. In fact, it will be difficult and unwise to attempt such tight assembly before the technologies are ready to enable it. The assemblies are fragile without the right federation. This should wait until simpler federation is supported by the various vendors. You will have your hands full with discovery in the first six to twelve months of your CMS deployment. Stick to the plan, and do not become distracted by your desire to link the parts together. This will come when the time is right.

Making the Business Case for the Expanded CMS

By starting small, you can build a powerful demonstration of the ultimate potential of the CMS. The full CMS requires significant investments of time, people, capital expense, and possibly third-party services. You need to make a strong case for expanding the CMS beyond the incubation pilot.

Establish the metrics that indicate a successful pilot. These metrics should reflect the operational benefits gained from the CMS. It will be hard to identify direct ROI from the pilot or the ongoing CMS as it matures. *The fact is, the CMS alone is a cost to the business. The benefits are manifest in the use cases, not in the CMS itself.*

Follow some of the common operational metrics to determine the value of the CMS. A few of these are shown earlier in Table 8.2. Note that the CMS role for each of these begins with "Provide accurate information..." to intentionally point out that the CMS is the enabling technology that does indeed provide the information required to improve each of the metrics. Any attempts to improve the organization's performance are only possible with this insight. Without it, execution is more guesswork than discipline, and this flawed execution contributes to a perpetuation of the stereotypical sloppy IT operation.

As you demonstrate improvement on the metrics, you have an objective case proving the benefits of the CMS. When you request additional funding to expand the CMS pilot, you are much more likely to secure this funding if you can prove that it will bring such benefits. Each of these metrics translates into financial impact. If you can prove a $2 return for every $1 invested, no CFO would deny such investment. Metrics of the type in Table 8.2 are those most relevant to the financial analysis because they are more easily translated into costs and revenue.

It would be foolish to become complacent about financial benefits after the pilot phase, so turn this exercise into an ongoing facet of the overall disciplined operation. Indeed, continual improvement is a relentless quest for optimization. Track your metrics forever and take special note of CMS improvements along the way. If you can correlate positive inflections in metrics with CMS improvements, you are continually proving the value of the CMS and justifying continual investment in its refinement.

Statistical Quality Control

Statistical quality control is used in all forms of manufacturing to ensure consistent product specifications that result in exceptional customer experience. This is the essence of quality and another body of work pioneered by Dr. Deming and his predecessor, Walter Shewhart.[4] Inconsistencies in IT can be overcome by following their statistical quality control principles.

We must adopt practices from manufacturing that have proven to transform products from substandard into reliability characterized by precision. The Japanese learned from Dr. Deming and made quality the cornerstone of its industry following World War II. Just look back at the Japanese automobile industry for a remarkable transformation that raised the bar for other automakers around the world. We can thank Dr. Deming for the incredible quality of today's cars and trucks. Clearly, IT can benefit greatly from his work!

Quality Controls Assessment

What Deming brought to business in Japan and beyond was a structured set of principles for rigorously managing quality processes. Among his most notable fields of innovation is statistical process control, where metrics are continually measured, analyzed against acceptable constraints, and reassessed for their relevance to overall quality. ITIL and Six Sigma are heavily influenced by the Deming style of quality management.

---

4. Walter Shewhart is considered to be the father of statistical quality control. His work at Bell Labs in the 1920s and 1930s with W. Edwards Deming is the foundation of the work that statisticians, including Deming, have refined ever since. Six Sigma's and ITIL's Continual Service Improvement are manifestations of this work. A brief biography of Dr. Shewhart and his work is available at the American Society for Quality site: http://www.asq.org/about-asq/who-we-are/bio_shewhart.html.

A simple, but powerful, tool in statistical process control is the control chart. We illustrate a sample control chart in Figure 8.4. It plots a metric against some desired constraints that indicate the quality of the product or service being measured.

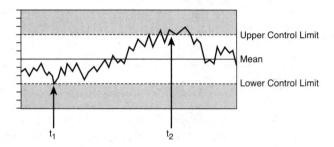

FIGURE 8.4   A sample control chart

The units on the Y-axis are irrelevant, but three levels are important to note. The *mean* is the ideal specification we want to achieve. This could be the nominal outside diameter of an axle shaft for a car or it could be the cache utilization for an Apache web server. The point is not the metric, but what we determine to be the optimum level. Almost nothing perfectly meets this ideal, nor should it necessarily be flawless. Optimization is not an extreme; it is a balancing point. Sometimes, "good enough" is good enough for the purpose, and maybe even within an optimum range of values. You must remember that the allowable tolerances between companies or industries can vary, so what is "good enough" for a recycling plant might not be "good enough" for a surgical metals fabricator.

This range is where the controls come into play. On the upper and lower sides of the mean lie two additional levels of relevance to the quality discussion. These are the control limits. They indicate thresholds to watch. If the measured value crosses these limits, we should take measures to bring the measurement back under *control*.

In Figure 8.4, you can see that our measurement starts off on the low end of the acceptable range, touching the lower control limit on one occasion at time t_1, but not crossing it. A good quality manager would find this acceptable, but uncomfortable, and would attempt to bring conditions up closer to the mean. By the middle, you can see it is rising, briefly straddling the mean as we want, but then it continues climbing and exceeds the upper control limit a few times near time t_2. This is an unacceptable situation that must be addressed. By the end, the measurements are right where we want them.

We already generate reams of "quality control charts," although many are more aesthetic than functional (for instance, many infrastructure performance charts). Each CMS metric, both the direct metrics in Table 8.1 and the indirect metrics in Table 8.2, should be tracked in a control chart. In the old days of manufacturing, control charts were created and maintained manually, but instrumentation in both manufacturing and IT now make this highly automated. Many of the same technologies used for the aforementioned aesthetic reporting can be used for automated plotting, reporting, and analysis of CMS quality metrics. We see many of them being reused by vendors for CMS purposes. It makes perfect sense.

Tracking CMS Progress

A good CMS plan accounts for realistic progress. Sometimes, the CMS evolves rapidly, and other times it will slow down. Figure 8.5 shows such a hypothetical plan designed to evolve over time. We also show how the progress can be tracked to determine how well it is matching the original plan. The metrics tell us how well we are doing. We show two overlaid curves to see how good execution and poor execution affect the tracking according to plan.

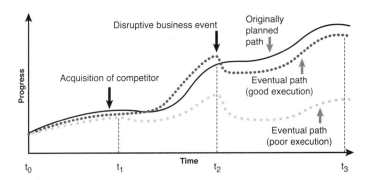

FIGURE 8.5   Adapting to shifting conditions

A number of events occur throughout the evolution of the CMS. You need to anticipate these events as well as can be expected and to be flexible enough to adapt as needed. The original plan should actually contain contingencies for the potential scenarios and how the organization will react to them.

In our example, the first event we experience is when we acquire a competitor at time t_1. Up to this point, both the good and poor groups have been tracking a bit behind plan. Note what happens right afterward, however. Both suffer a slight setback because all acquisitions are disruptive, but the good team recovers much more quickly. Because they thought ahead for such a situation, they were actually able to leverage people and technologies from the acquired company to accelerate progress and even surpass their original plan. Conversely, the poor team lost what momentum it had and could not quite recover.

Ideally, we never want to take a step backward, but it happens, and we must be able to adapt. A contemporary example of a disruptive event is the credit crisis that began in 2008 and still continues to plague financial services firms and the overall economy today. A significant disruptive event occurs at time t_2, and both teams are knocked backward with a hard jolt. The good team recovers and tracks the original plan, albeit behind the plan. By the time they reach time t_3, they are behind. However, given the significance of the t_2 event, the performance is admirable.

The beleaguered poor team continues to decline after the t_2 event. The obvious chaos triggered by the event has damaged morale in both teams, but the poor team has weak contingency plans or none at all. The result is a compounding deterioration that is difficult to stop. Eventually our hapless poor team recovers, but it is slow and probably the result of extraordinary effort and some painful changes. By the time they reach t_3, they are far behind.

If t_3 represents today, this poor team is wounded, but not necessarily doomed. If we look at the dynamics of the IT and business imperatives we outlined in Chapter 1, "The Need for Process Discipline," it paints a gloomier future for those who fail to execute. Suppose our starting point of t_0 is today. An event like that at t_2 will probably prove to be fatal to the organization. Business leaders are increasingly intolerant of poor execution and will turn to punitive outsourcing if the enterprise even survives such a shocking blow. Excellence begets excellence. Mediocrity begets demise.

Maintain Data and Information Accuracy

CMS accuracy is of paramount importance. Any thoughts of continual improvement have to address accuracy. If you build a CMS and its accuracy deteriorates, it is not much of an improvement.

Feedback

Every adaptive system in nature and in engineering implements feedback. Feedback is a means to automatically control the behavior of a system. Undesired feedback causes the irritating squeal in a public address system, and an inverted form of the same feedback eliminates the squeal. It keeps natural ecosystems in balance and plays a pivotal role in process discipline and continual improvement.

A simple model for process feedback is shown on the left side of Figure 8.6. The metrics tell the system whether to apply positive or negative feedback and in which amounts. If the metrics indicate that the results are running too low, we apply an appropriate amount of positive feedback (for instance, turn up the volume). If the metrics tell the system that the results are too high, the applied feedback is negative (for instance, turn down the volume). On the right side of Figure 8.6, we show our control chart, where the feedback is applied, and the resultant effects. In the case of the positive feedback, too much was applied, and the negative feedback was needed to correct this overrun.

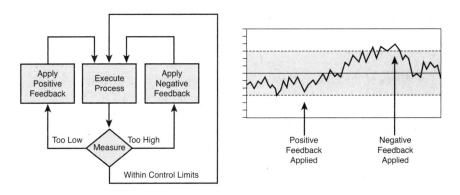

FIGURE **8.6**   Process feedback and the results

The analysis and application of feedback is ongoing. This keeps all systems that use feedback in check, including the CMS. Feedback in the CMS comes in a few different forms, as follows:

- Change management integration helps keep the information accurate. As changes are made, the change management process mandates the corrections to be made to the CMS.

- Discovery is always needed to keep the CMS accurate. This is one of the best feedback mechanisms available for the CMS, as it ensures a truer representation of reality.

- Derivative process analysis offers guidance on the suitability of the CMS. You might need to enrich the information with more detail or learn that you are offering more detail than is needed. You might find that the update intervals are too long, rendering the CMS contents stale. This guides you to seek methods to make the data more accurate, probably via newer methods and technologies that can produce finer data granularity.

- The direct CMS quality metrics, such as those in Table 8.1, indicate when the CMS needs correction. Beware of placing too much trust in these metrics alone, however. The CMS must be understood in the context of the derivative metrics from Table 8.2, because the CMS cannot be viewed in a vacuum.

- Budget considerations play into every quality initiative. As a common joke goes, you can have any two of the triad of high quality, high speed, and low cost, but the third is impossible. You can't have the best of all three: high accuracy, low cost, and rapid development. There must be a balance across them. There is a lot of truth to this, and it applies to the CMS as well. All the desires for high accuracy and rapid deployment must be balanced with a need to keep costs under control.

- Users of the CMS will tell you what they need and what they do not need. These are not the actual consumer tools of the CMS, of course, but the people who use those consumer tools and those responsible for their maintenance. Maintain close contact with this important constituency because the CMS provides value only if it gives the right people the right empowerment to do their jobs. Find out who the users of the CMS are servicing; these are the ones who will experience the benefits.

If you incorporate feedback into the development, deployment, and ongoing maintenance of the CMS, it will act as a means of self-regulation that ensures high quality in the CMS and the processes it serves.

Verification

Even after you have a highly automated system in place, complete with Change Management integration and discovery, you will want to periodically verify the CMS contents against reality. To build and maintain trust in the CMS, you need to repeatedly verify the validity of the CMS.

Verification requires manual examination; however, tools help. If you are trying to confirm an MDR for the network, SNMP browsers give you the true settings, as long as you give them the right access directives (the object ID, in SNMP language).

Evolve Based on Customer Requirements

The CMS will evolve, but you can evolve it only according to the needs of the customers. The "customers" in this situation are both human and technological. Certainly, other people in the organization are customers, but consider the needs of derivative processes and the technology solutions used to automate the execution of those processes.

You establish requirements in the beginning and supply the information needed to fulfill those requirements. The ongoing reassessments you do in the improvement cycle guide you through the changes dictated by the evolving requirements. You might begin by developing the level of detail needed for incident analysis, but then enrich the CMS later as you tackle the needs of a capacity planning integration.

Leverage Maturity Models

This book and many other information sources offer details about the ideal CMS. The ideal version of anything is usually impossible, and the perfect CMS is also impossible. What you strive to do is approach the ideal as closely as you can. The other truth is that we all start from the same point—a relative point that is nowhere near this goal of "as good as possible." Then again, if you think about a state that is "as good as possible," you begin to understand that this state itself will evolve. On day one, "as good as possible" is not good at all. As you build upon the CMS, "as good as possible" gets better. Thus, the state is dynamic. It changes over time, and it is useful to formulate a means to identify the various states of maturity as you progress forward.

The concept of a maturity model was popularized by the Capability Maturity Model (CMM)[5] that defines stages of sophistication for software development. This has now been replaced by CMMI (CMM Integration), which focuses on process improvement. In both models, five stages of maturity are defined. They are numbered from 1 (low maturity) to 5 (high maturity), and there is also an implicit stage zero that indicates a state of no formal process culture whatsoever, but it is not part of the formal numbering scheme.

---

5. The Capability Maturity Model (CMM) was defined by the Software Engineering Institute (SEI) at Carnegie-Mellon University. It is now a standard mechanism for determining the level of maturity in software development organizations. The five steps of the model have been duplicated in nearly every other attempt to develop maturity models, including the SEI's related CMMI (Capability Maturity Model Integration) effort for process improvement.

We use the five stages of CMMI to portray a maturity model for the CMS. This model is shown in its simple form in Figure 8.7.

5 Optimizing	• Most discovery data is unified into a federated model • Broad process integration is accelerating execution
4 Quantitative	• Most discovery data is unified into a federated model • Early process integration is happening
3 Defined	• Heavy use of discovery, but data unification is weak • CMS has replaced CMDB in team strategy
2 Managed	• Initial CMDB team is assembled and getting started • Focusing mainly on discovery
1 Initial	• Simple CMDB is assembled, but data is stale • Limited or no formal discovery is in use
0 Incomplete	• Knowledge of IT almost entirely in human minds • Verifying configuration is heavily manual

FIGURE 8.7   A simple CMS maturity model

In more detail, the stages of the CMS maturity model follow:

Stage 0. Incomplete. This state is the most chaotic and disorganized state of configuration information. The limited configuration that does exist is most prominently captured in the minds of those managing the environment. Verification of configuration information involves manual viewing of the CI. There is no real notion of a CI at all in this stage, as configuration management is a foreign concept to organizations in this state.

Stage 1. Initial. At this stage, at least a few people in the organization understand the importance of configuration information and are trying to do something about it. They are the nascent force of discipline. They may even purchase a CMDB product and attempt to install it and begin populating it. Discovery is usually not a consideration here, as the CMDB is populated and maintained manually, and discovery tools are not yet on the horizon. Some limited effort to extract configuration data from management tools may be in place, but the integration into the CMDB is not automated.

Stage 2. Managed. The CMDB is now becoming a more formal effort. An actual team is identified—maybe not a full organizational entity, but even a loose federation of involved parties is a good start. Most of the work is targeted at deployment and organization of discovery tools. At this stage, ITIL is also a more formal effort.

Stage 3. **Defined.** Here, we finally see a true organizational focus on both ITIL and the CMDB. Enlightenment has evolved to a point where the CMDB is now viewed more as a CMS. This signals the inflection where the IT organization is on the path to excellence. The CMS technology is heavily leveraging discovery. The information is still fragmented, but its accuracy is good.

Stage 4. **Quantitative.** In stage four, the CMS is taking shape. MDRs are well defined, and federation is beginning to link them into a unified structure. Early efforts to leverage the CMS for derivative process automation are in place. Most notably, the Change Management process is tightly integrated, ensuring that all changed elements are updated in the CMS as the changes are made.

Stage 5. **Optimizing.** The highest level of maturity is a point where the federated CMS is well defined and well organized. More notably, the integration with other processes is robust. They are benefiting greatly from the information provided by the federated CMS, enabling high degrees of automation and high degrees of maturity in these other processes.

The maturity model will evolve as well. After the CMS becomes commonplace and discovery technologies become standard operational practice, the definitions of high maturity will become more sophisticated.

Refinement Will Never End

The nirvana state of the CMS is a moving target. As new managed technologies and new management technologies appear, the CMS will need to adapt. Any continual improvement effort is just that: continual. This means that you never stop trying to optimize the CMS. The improvement cycle of Figure 8.2 is exercised over and over again...forever.

Frequently Asked Questions

Question: We prefer the Six Sigma or CMMI concepts of continual improvement. Why should we follow your advice about ITIL's version?

Answer: It does not matter *which* philosophy you follow, because they are all similar and indeed are all derivatives of Dr. Deming's work. We emphasize the ITIL model because of the close relationship between ITIL and the CMS. It also borrows extensively from Six Sigma and CMMI. The exact model is not the issue, but pick one and adhere to it with relentless passion.

Question: Can't we just relax and celebrate our achievements? Why should we be so serious about continual improvement after we attain a high level of maturity?

Answer: We beg you to savor the victories as you travel through the CMS journey. This is not an easy pursuit and each milestone should be celebrated because you deserve it. This does not mean you can become complacent, however. Complacency only drags you back down to the doldrums of wasteful operations and poor service quality. If you truly have risen to a high maturity level, continual improvement will be so engrained in your organizational philosophy and your own individual lifestyle that it will come as naturally as breathing. Excellence breeds excellence. By the very definition of excellence, if you stop the pursuit, you are not excellent!

Question: We are outsourcing our IT operations, so shouldn't the outsourcer be concerned about continual improvement instead of us?

Answer: No. Both parties are always responsible for quality. Each party takes ownership of the domain of its coverage. In this example, the outsourcer must ensure strong improvement of its coverage of the infrastructure. The internal organization will likely retain strategic control, so the higher-level abstractions are managed internally. Continual improvement knows no boundaries. All who desire excellence will practice continual improvement.

Summary

Continual improvement of the CMS mirrors continual improvement of any endeavor. The teachings of Dr. W. Edwards Deming were used to revolutionize manufacturing. They are equally valuable for IT processes and the CMS. Every successful quality improvement program exhibits strong resemblance to the Deming methods.

Any quality improvement program is based upon the right metrics and continual tracking of these metrics to keep them under control. You need to identify and measure the metrics relevant to CMS quality. Measure early to establish a benchmark. This gives you a reference point to accurately measure progress made in the future.

Start the CMS with a small scope to work out any process and technology flaws early and to develop a low-risk proof point for CMS success. This early victory helps justify additional investment in the CMS. Subsequent steps should be incremental and careful. If you feel that you are attempting too much, you probably are.

Maturity models are valuable tools for continual improvement. We presented a foundation for a CMS maturity model, and you can use it to help assess where you lie in the model and how to move into the next stage.

Finally, quality improvement is a never-ending pursuit. The other IT functions and processes that depend on the CMS require solid accuracy. Their quality is only possible with a high-quality CMS. We next examine some of these other processes that depend on the CMS in Chapter 9, "Leveraging the CMS."

CHAPTER 9

Leveraging the CMS

This chapter is probably one of the most interesting for us to write because it is the only one that speaks exclusively to the purpose and value in what you are trying to accomplish. In the previous chapters, we discussed the origins and future of the Configuration Management System (CMS), as well as how to go about designing and building it. In this chapter, we focus on many of the different ways you can use what you have built. You might not be currently able to do some of the points we discuss because of your company's current state of IT, and others might never become relevant depending on whether your business requirements warrant them. All of them, however, should help you appreciate the capability that will be available should you need to pursue it.

The usages of the CMS are limited only by your own vision and design. This chapter should help you expand that vision and enrich your design. When you come to fully appreciate the CMS's capabilities, that is the point at which your imagination begins to take over and you start asking yourself the multitude of questions: "If I could associate historical patterns of defects to particular technologies or architectures, could I employ a modified architecture/technology to prevent them?" "If I were able to detect a known trend in an item's behavior that results in an outage 30 minutes later, could I alert my business partners and inform them that we foresee the possibility of a service interruption in the next half hour, but are already working to prevent the potential service interruption?" These are just two questions that we believe you can answer after your matured CMS is in place.

This chapter is segmented into four principal areas: foundational elements, supplemental information, CMS-triggered activity, and user-triggered activity. Within each of these areas, we discuss many of the scenarios from the perspectives of different processes. In some cases, we explicitly refer to a process, whereas in others we might simply infer their inclusion. As you know, ITIL v3 is designed around the lifecycle, whereas ITIL v2 was designed around the processes. This should not lead you to conclude that just because we infer a process or leave it out all together that it does not play a role in this discussion. We cannot cover all the processes in each area and scenario, but hope that you can take the concepts and usage potentials that we do discuss and use them to formulate your own questions. This initial platform of knowledge that we hope to provide for you will be the basis for many of your visionary decisions and future CMS success stories.

We do not spend too much time on foundational elements because they have been addressed several times throughout the book when discussing what you should include in your CMS and how you should design or model it. Refer back to Chapter 2, "What Is a CMDB?," Chapter 3, "Planning for the CMS," and Chapter 5, "CMS Deployment Strategy," as just a few examples of where else we have discussed foundational elements. We do spend some time on the topic of supplemental information, but because it is also an inbound source and again has been covered in some depth, we have chosen to focus on the outbound data. We briefly review the reasons for including both foundational elements and supplemental information, but then spend the majority of the chapter discussing the consumption of the CMS data.

Inbound CMS Data

For the CMS to function and do its job, it needs data. This data must be then pieced together in a predefined structure before being disseminated out to the masses. There is some commonality across organizations and industries as to what some of the primary data elements are, such as assets (servers, routers etc.) and applications. Beyond these commonalities, organizations may view certain data as less foundational and more supplemental. Supplemental data is more supportive or ancillary in nature, whereas foundational is vital and an absolute necessity. These are decisions that you must make with your business partners when deciding what your services will look like. If you are fortunate enough to have a defined Service Catalog, we would recommend that you include the services as part of your foundational elements. If you don't, you should be looking to add them as quickly as possible with some of your supplemental information. There is no "one-size-fits-all" here; it is all about what you have available and how much of it you can get under the rigor of Change and Configuration Management control.

Think of the inbound data as working together to form a tree (see Figure 9.1). The foundational elements, especially those in your IT inventory, are your tree trunk and roots, whereas the remainder of the foundational elements are what form the upper parts of the trunk and major branches. The supplemental information could then be considered the minor branches and leaves. As your CMS maturity develops over time, you may decide that some of your supplemental information has become so critical to your operation that it can no longer be viewed as supplemental but now is foundational. This is very much the same way in which a tree grows—smaller branches grow and become major limbs, from which new branches can then begin to grow. The CMS evolves with your company and needs to bend and sway to accommodate the changing environment in your company. If your CMS is well rooted and your major components are strong, you and your CMS will survive most storms. If you don't establish strong roots with your IT inventory and services, your growth will be limited and unstable, and it will likely topple over when it encounters its first challenging storm.

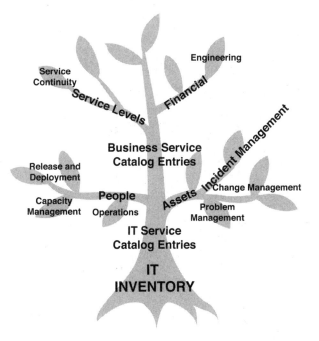

FIGURE 9.1   A well-rooted CMS

Foundational Elements

Foundational elements are those primary inputs that you must include to move forward. We have chosen to maintain a simplified view of what these primary inputs are by referring to them collectively as the inventory of items that will be aggregated and pieced together to deliver value. Think of these inputs as principal elements, and only when they are combined and linked together with other items do they start to deliver some value. In Figure 9.2, the primary inputs are made up of raw data about assets, IT financials, Service Catalog entries, IT inventories, people, and service levels.

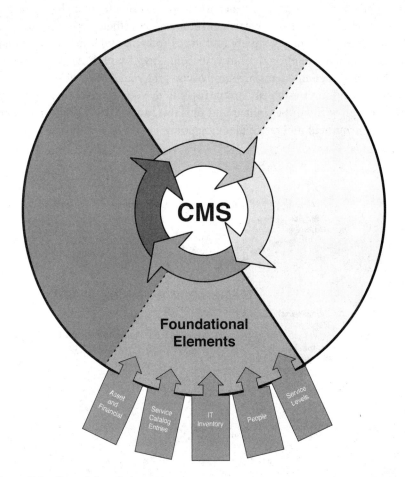

FIGURE 9.2   Foundational elements

We could get into a long philosophical discussion about what should and should not be foundational. We could debate the inclusion of financials, Service Catalog entries, and service levels as foundational elements, for example, but it would be pointless. Our belief is that each company will have its own slight twist to what it considers a foundational element. If you decide that something is not foundational, it just means that it moves into the "supplemental information" grouping. The reason for us including the five items we did in Figure 9.2 was to present a more advanced view of foundational data, but you can shift some of your inputs between foundational and supplemental depending on your business requirements.

We feel that if you, for example, have the capability to include financial data about the IT inventory items as one of your primary inputs, you can more quickly begin to associate costs to your services. This in turn will enable you to deliver bottom-line value to your business partners more quickly. If you cannot include this as a foundational element, focus on the ones you can that will deliver the most value the fastest. The key here is that the CMS exists to support the processes and the requirements they provide. The elements and attributes that it contains are necessary to enable the processes that interface with Service Asset and Configuration Management (SACM) and need to be managed with additional control and rigor.

IT inventory is exactly that—a list or catalog of all your IT devices, both hardware and software, that help you run your IT organization. This includes your servers, laptops, desktops, handhelds, workstations, routers, switches, appliances, firewalls, networks, storage units, and so on. Basically, these are the building blocks of your IT systems that you need to model each entry in your IT Service Catalog, as we discussed in Chapter 5. If the services you are first trying to deliver do not involve external users, firewalls may not be of importance to you, versus an organization that primarily deals with only external customers. You need to decide based on your needs what the most critical inventory items for your organization are. Refer back to Chapter 5 if you are unsure and need to refresh your memory on how to make these decisions. You should also do some research on the components in the Service Catalog, such as Service Package, Service Level Package (SLP), Core Service, and Core Service Package (CSP), described in the ITIL v3 Service Strategies book from the OGC.

Asset and financial information provides a tremendous amount of value if you can include it as one of your foundational elements. Even if you don't have your services in place, the ability to attach financial characteristics to your IT devices is a big step forward in your capability to deliver a service-based CMS. At this stage, the financial details may be discrete and localized to each device, but as you start to group your devices together and form cost models, you instantly have the ability to total up the costs of the services in the Service Catalog; this includes the detail of the decomposition, such as applications, hardware, and software to deliver a Total Cost Of Service (TCOS). The asset component of the foundational elements can then add ownership, licensing, and lifecycle characteristics, all of which provide yet more depth to the eventual service that will use it, as well as enabling better management of assets in terms of depreciation, leases, and so on.

The human or "people" aspect of foundational elements, which could be dealt with in terms of roles rather than specific people, is somewhat of a gray area because you don't place people under the control of your IT Change Management processes. This data should already be under the rigor of HR change controls. What you do place under that control is the data about people that could cause you a service outage. It may be critical to your organization, for example, that the management level of an employee be updated on a nightly basis because only certain levels can approve regulatory mandated events. If this data was not available in the CMS, the Change Management approval cycle might not be aware that an individual can no longer authorize an event. This might allow the event to go forward and be executed even though it does not have an authorized approval.

Service Levels and Service Catalog entries go hand in hand in that you cannot have Service Level Agreements in place without some sort of defined services. If you think back to Chapter 5 and Chapter 7, "The Future of the CMS," we discussed the concept of services existing at both the IT and business levels. In both of these, service levels must be defined and agreed upon by the provider and consumer. There are obvious predecessor/successor relationships involved in implementing your foundational elements, especially when it comes to operating in a *services* model, but also remember that some things can be defined and designed in parallel even if you cannot implement it that way. For example, you can define both your IT and Business Service Catalog and the Service Level Agreements you would like to implement before actually populating the CMS. You are limited to some extent in defining the IT services when you try to detail all the components that help to deliver it, but that is not the case with your business services. The implementation, however, needs to wait until you get some foundational pieces in place to deliver those services packaged in the way you have defined them. Be pragmatic and take the necessary amount of time to do it accurately. You can't take too long because the environment changes while you're designing it, but also don't rush into it and do it wrong. This is not something that can be easily undone without some negative impacts after it has been deployed. So, ease yourself into it at a good pace that you are comfortable with and that demonstrates good progress to your business partners.

In short, you do not have to wait to define your services before doing anything else. It is acceptable to decompose your applications in the CMS without the services being defined because Change, Incident, and Problem Management can still benefit from knowing what is affected from an IT perspective.

Supplemental Information

Supplemental information on its own doesn't provide a tremendous amount of value because there is no real context to it. It is sort of like Christmas ornaments without the Christmas tree. You may be able to appreciate the detail and intricacy of the ornament, but without the backdrop of the Christmas tree and all the other ornaments, it is just a lone decoration that suits no purpose. Placed on the tree, however, with all the other ornaments, lights, and garland, it becomes an integral part of a complex image. The IT environments we work in today are similar in that they too are complex and made up of many discrete elements, but the CMS helps to piece together those elements to present one organized picture of the environment.

Figure 9.3 illustrates some of the areas in the IT environment that could provide supplemental information for your CMS. Eight items are listed in Figure 9.3, but that does not mean that those are the only eight areas that could provide supplemental information nor does it mirror exactly the thirteen topics listed below. For example, Facilities is not listed on the diagram or below, but it is an important area of data and can for some companies even possibly be considered foundational. With the Green movement upon us and green service management efforts sure to follow, facilities will become ever more integral in our processes. We simply could not list every area and do them all justice, so some were intentionally left out. Again, your business requirements and industry regulations drive many of the decisions you need to make for your company, and those may be different than what a company in a different industry does. If you do what delivers value to your business partner, you have made the right choice. Following, we have listed a variety of areas, including those in Figure 9.3, which we feel could provide supplemental information and what that information might be. Where applicable, we have referenced the OGC ITIL v3 book and section in which the particular subject matter resides. Our intention is to provide you with our view of some of the types of information you can garner from these areas, but we do suggest that you reference the OGC manuals for a more in-depth understanding of the topic if you are unfamiliar with it. In the "CMS-Triggered Activity" and "User-Triggered Activity" sections of this chapter, we discuss in more detail how you might use the information from these areas.

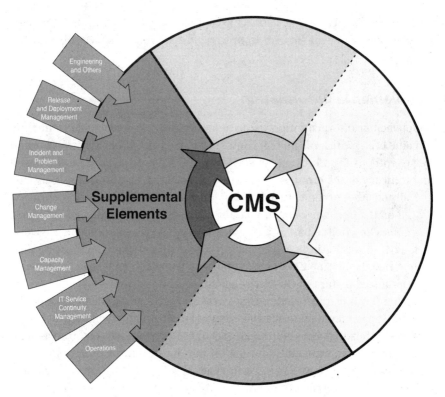

FIGURE 9.3   Supplemental information

Access Management: Incorporating this type of information in your CMS enables you to have a better view on which users are accessing what systems. For the Service Desk personnel, this enables them to quickly determine whether the system the caller is trying to access has the proper permissions or if they need to request them. After it is available, it is possible to deliver outbound communications to the "registered" users of the system if the system is down or experiencing difficulties with instructions on alternatives or updates as to when the system might be brought back online. Currently, it is difficult, if not impossible, for a company to identify the exact user population of a system and therefore must rely on a broadcast approach to all users rather than a targeted message to the known users. Following are three bulleted items that identify the location in the OGC ITIL book where the topic can be found, a brief statement describing the topic, and types of data that would be generated by the topic that could contribute to the overall CMS capability:

- **OGC Manual Reference:** Service Operations 4.5

- **Description:** Addresses the privileges that users have to services and systems

- **Types of Relevant Data:** Systems users have rights to, roles users might have in the system, and timeframes that user is authorized to access system

Availability Management: Availability information can help provide Incident and Problem Management personnel insight into the reliability of a system, as well as the agreed-upon needs of the business. This information is also beneficial to Change Management personnel when evaluating impact of pending change requests:

- **OGC Manual Reference:** Service Design 4.4.

- **Description:** Provides a central point of information for all service and resource availability needs, as well as metrics related to availability targets. Availability Management is also charged with improving the availability of the infrastructure for the purpose of delivering the services in a cost-effective manner.

- **Types of Relevant Data:** Metrics related to all aspects of availability, such as Mean Time Between Failure (MTBF), Mean Time Between Service Interruption (MTBSI), Mean Time To Resolution (MTTR), Mean Time to Restore Service (MTRS), and uptime/downtime for components, services, and the infrastructure throughout its entire lifecycle.

Change Management: Including the change history, impact analysis information, success/failure of changes, and pending changes provides insight into what may have occurred over time or what is occurring related to that service or its components:

- **OGC Manual Reference:** Service Transition 4.2

- **Description:** Efficient and systematic management of changes to items in the corporate environment

- **Types of Relevant Data:** Change history, effectiveness of previous changes, results of change reviews, pending change details, frequency, and motive of changes

Capacity Management: Supplementing the foundational information in the CMS with capacity-related data enables implementers and planners to have better sight on the current and future capabilities/limitations of the infrastructure. It also provides the Service Desk personal insight into potential reasons for performance-related issues that are being reported:

- **OGC Manual Reference:** Service Design 4.3.

- **Description:** Again as a process that encompasses the full lifecycle of an item or service, Capacity Management is involved from design through retirement. It is charged with ensuring that the infrastructure has the necessary capability, at an acceptable cost, to meet the needs of the organization.

- **Types of Relevant Data:** Overall capacity in environment (used and available), utilization patterns, capacity-related performance metrics, current and future demands, and forecast projections.

Event Management: Event Management provides raw data at a very discrete level, which if interpreted properly, can predict upcoming changes in the infrastructure that could prevent you from meeting your Service Level Agreements (SLAs). This raw data must be clearly identified and associated with the potentially impacted CIs and arranged so that false warnings and alerts are kept to a minimum. Much of your ability to become a proactive participant in minimizing service interruptions comes from your ability to translate these "events" into meaningful "heads-up" warnings and ultimately provide recommended actions to take:

- **OGC Manual Reference:** Service Operations 4.1.

- **Description:** The detection of an abnormal occurrence to an infrastructure item that in some way is related to services being delivered to your business partners. This abnormality could be the change in status of an item or the passing of a predefined threshold on a server, for example. The sensitivity and scope of these occurrences must be predefined and built into your monitoring tools and control systems.

- **Types of Relevant Data:** CI to event correlation data, control action recommendations, and ongoing active CI status data.

Incident Management: What the Incident Management data provides to the CMS is a tremendous wealth of knowledge about how the CIs and services have functioned over time, their impact on each other, and historical information about the effects of changes to the CIs and services. Over time, patterns emerge with services or technologies, providing you with the opportunity to develop incident models to address these repetitive situations:

- **OGC Manual Reference:** Service Operations 4.2.

- **Description:** A process that addresses all outages of services and/or questions related to the services as quickly as possible. An incident is a disruption in the normal functioning of a service or an all-out failure of it. A service does not have to be out in order for an incident to be generated. It is important to remember that incidents are not service requests, even though many times both are handled by the Service Desk. Service requests are part of the Request Fulfillment efforts.

- **Types of Relevant Data:** Incident models, historical metrics, RFC associations, categorization (both open and closed), prioritization, and responsible support groups.

Information Security Management: Information security has become a much more significant element in IT over the past 15 years with the explosion of the Internet and networking capabilities. The availability, confidentiality, and integrity of information have all come into question now that IT processes and services are spread across states and continents. An added difficulty comes into play because policies across country boundaries are different and, in some cases, in opposition of each other. The ability to maintain an Information Security Management System (ISMS) and link it with the services defined in the CMS could enable consumers of the CMS information to act more responsibly when handling sensitive information. The ISMS in conjunction with the CMS could provide a more rigorous security compliance structure that in some industries is vital:

- **OGC Manual Reference:** Service Design 4.6

- **Description:** The corporate alignment of IT and business policies related to information security to meet regulatory, corporate, and industry governance requirements

- **Types of Relevant Data:** Security policy details, governance requirements, data handling standards, and enforcement procedures

IT Service Continuity Management: Continuity Management has always been an important aspect of running a business, but only in the last 15 to 20 years has the IT element become vital to its success. The overall Business Continuity Plans can no longer succeed without equally detailed and comprehensive IT Service Continuity Plans. The reliance on reliable networks, the ever-growing globalization of companies, and concerns about cyberterrorism have brought the topic of IT Service Continuity to the forefront for many. Organizations need to understand exactly what components they need to have ready in the event of a disaster. They must know how those components are assembled so as to deliver the core services that the organization finds vital to its operation during a crisis scenario. In these situations, there is no time to investigate and research, there is only time to execute; the IT Service Continuity Management responsibilities address those needs:

- **OGC Manual Reference:** Service Design 4.5

- **Description:** Support the goals of Business Continuity Management by providing the technology components and corresponding plans necessary to resume business operations at previously agreed-upon levels and within agreed-upon timeframes

- **Types of Relevant Data:** Continuity plans, detailed external disaster site provider contracts, continuity and recovery metrics, and impact assessment results of changes to infrastructure

Knowledge Management: Much like the CMS as a whole, Knowledge Management (KM) helps to translate data into information. It does this outright by providing information such as stakeholders, performance expectations, and timeframes where applicable. One of the key elements to Knowledge Management being successful is the clarity and accessibility of the information. As we know, a large percentage of the time it takes to resolve an incident is spent researching the information versus making the decision on what to do. The combination of KM and CMS information, and tools that make accessing and mining it simple, could possibly be one of the most valuable elements of a CMS solution. The OGC Service Transition Manual offers a great description of the Data-to-Information-to-Knowledge-to-Wisdom structure[1]—a concept we speak to throughout the book when we refer to the need for data to be transformed into information. A difficulty in identifying

---

1. Office of Government Commerce (OGC). 2007. *Service Transition, ITIL Version 3.* Ogdensburg: Renouf Publishing Co. Ltd.

the exact information to associate with or include in the CMS is that the information is knowledge, and it is not easily captured or represented in a simple value. A lot of this information is knowledge buried deep in people's heads and not always easy to retrieve—the keepers of this knowledge either feel it provides them with some level of job security, or it is knowledge they feel is part of their everyday operation, and they don't think of it as an element of information that needs to be documented or communicated. Many times, this is referred to as "tribal knowledge" or unwritten knowledge that is not well known by others in the organization. In some cases, you will be allowed to retrieve it, but tread lightly around this topic when gathering the information because some people will not be receptive to your inquiries:

- **OGC Manual Reference:** Service Transition 4.7

- **Description:** The process by which the appropriate people are provided access to information that improves the quality of their decision making, while also making the decision process faster and more accurate

- **Types of Relevant Data:** Policies, learned solutions, firsthand experiences/accounts of scenarios, and tribal knowledge

Problem Management: Problem Management plays an important part in the maturity path of an organization's Service Management ambitions. It is the process that has as its main focus the prevention of incidents, especially those that have been previously diagnosed. Problem Management has a two-pronged approach: One is reactive, and the other is proactive.

The reactive component of Problem Management is what organizations are most accustomed to implementing. This is where the process is enacted as a result of an incident(s). The root cause of incidents and their resolution is incredibly valuable because many outages are a result of incidents that have been experienced before. Unfortunately, without a mature process in place, the root cause is rarely diagnosed, and hence no resolution is ever documented, leaving the outage and incident to repeat over and over.

The proactive component, which is actually a part of Continual Service Improvement, is charged with trend analysis of incidents and problems so as to implement solutions that could prevent outages in the future. The results of this analysis could lead to recommendations that influence engineering designs, product purchases, or a variety of other infrastructure decisions that may impact service levels negatively if not addressed:

- **OGC Manual Reference:** Service Operation 4.4 / Service Improvement 5.6.4.

- **Description:** As a component of Service Operation: The process responsible for managing problems through their full lifecycle. ITIL defines a problem as the cause for one or more incidents.[2]

  As a component of Service Improvement: Identification and removal of errors that impact service.

- **Types of Relevant Data:** Problem models, known error records, linkage between incident and problem records, root cause analysis details, and problem categorizations and prioritizations.

Release and Deployment Management: Release and Deployment Management is the vehicle that IT uses to move products (hardware and software) to the production environment and updates the CMS along the way as to the status of the package components. It has tremendous responsibility to build, test, and deploy the completed unit of work in a way that not only suits the intended purpose, but also does not negatively impact any other service already deployed. As part of this journey to production, many things are learned, such as glitches in the hardware/software that can be temporarily worked around, performance bottlenecks that need to be addressed in future releases, or functionality that does not fully comply with company standards. Many more could arise as well, but the important thing is that these things need to be either addressed prior to deployment or documented and made available in the knowledge base so that they can be addressed in future releases or targeted during service interruptions:

- **OGC Manual Reference:** Service Transition 4.4

- **Description:** The formal process by which packages of work units that fulfill stakeholder requirements make their way to production

- **Types of Relevant Data:** Release package details (IDs, dates, content), release and deployment models, standards and policy compliance details, RFC relationship(s), testing results, signoffs, release and build documentation, release package baselines, known errors, and workarounds

---

2. Office of Government Commerce (OGC). 2007. *Service Transition, ITIL Version 3.* Ogdensburg: Renouf Publishing Co. Ltd.

Service Asset and Configuration Management: We must start out this discussion about Service Asset and Configuration Management (SACM) by thanking a former colleague, Craig Norgard, for his tremendous insight and guidance in this area that, frankly, few others we have spoken with have been able to match. In ITIL v3, Service Asset and Configuration Management is about managing the information about assets/CIs and not about managing the assets themselves. In fact, it does not speak to managing assets at all, which leads us to assume that some other IT Asset Management (ITAM) process is actually responsible for managing depreciation, leases, licenses, total cost of ownership, and retirement with information from the CMS.

This is different than in ITIL v2, where Configuration Management, a primary process of Service Support, plays a significant role in Software Asset Management (SAM). Under ITIL v2, Configuration Management manages not only the assets and their associated lifecycles, but also the links and relationships between the assets. It also includes the management of relationships between these assets and other Service Management-related issues such as incidents, problems, changes, services, and SLAs.

Without asset information, the CMS cannot function, but what is important about Service Asset and Configuration Management, as opposed to just the inventory list, is the management process around the inventory; that is what SACM delivers. It validates the data while delivering a level of data integrity that is necessary for the CIs and their versions, baselines, relationships, and so on. A large portion of this data is what we discussed earlier in this chapter under "Foundational Elements." We chose to leave this topic in the "Supplemental Information" section not only to reinforce its importance, but to point out that some of the data generated by these management processes need to be fed back into the CMS as *add-ons* to the core information:

- **OGC Manual Reference:** Service Transition 4.3

- **Description:** A management process of service assets necessary to support all other Service Management processes

- **Types of Relevant Data:** Asset inventories, corresponding lifecycle status, data validation, and integrity metrics

SOA, SaaS, and Other Enterprise Initiatives: ITIL v3 is all about service, so we cannot ignore the role that Service-Oriented Architectures (SOA) and Software-as-a-Service (SaaS) contribute to the CMS. Both of these topics will greatly enhance the capability of the CMS but also drastically increase the complexity to maintain the CMS once included. The reason is because both SOA and SaaS force you to take that next step down the granularity scale with your CMS. Each of these concepts is intended to encapsulate how the functionality being delivered is put together. This is a great concept from an end-user and overall organization perspective, but it makes supporting and chasing down the cause of incidents more difficult because the operations personnel may not have access or knowledge of the internal workings of a SaaS solution. From the CMS perspective, you need to find out how you will identify and control these elements, or if you even can, before deciding whether to include it or have it associated with the CMS as ancillary data.

Outbound CMS Data

The purpose of the CMS is obviously not just to aggregate data for the sake of it—the intention is to aggregate it, add value with supplemental information, and then offer it back to consumers who can garner benefit from it. Following are two sections that address two principal ways that this occurs: CMS-triggered activity and user-triggered activity.

CMS-Triggered Activity

Activity triggered by the CMS, or more specifically, by conditions and patterns of data within it, comes mainly in the form of reports, alerts, and event notifications. Figure 9.4 shows some of these CMS-triggered activities, but again these are meant to demonstrate what sort of activities you could leverage and are not intended to be a complete set. We have discussed in a variety of chapters, especially Chapter 7, the capabilities that a CMS needs to have for all of us in the IT industry to realize the vision that ITIL provides. This is mainly because we continue to get buried deeper and deeper by the volumes of data being generated every day. Both software and hardware vendors are maturing their products so that they can provide up-to-the-second and sometimes even real-time diagnostic data for our operations departments to act upon. The difficulty is that the volumes of this data have become unmanageable without strong tools to aggregate it and then transpose that aggregated raw data into a meaningful message. One of the main things that we all want from the CMS is for it to pull it all together and tell us what it means so we can act on it, in terms our business partners can understand.

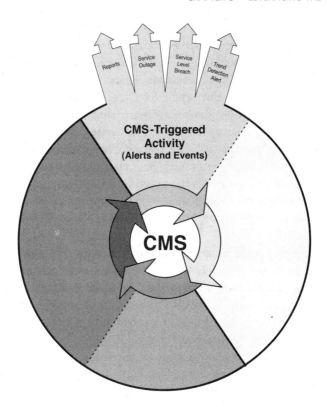

FIGURE 9.4   CMS-Triggered Activity

Reports

We have all been doing reports since the first mainframes were deployed. What the CMS provides is added value to the reports by making us aware of the associations to services and applications that we might not have otherwise known. This could help to provide better data to prioritize workloads or provide a better accounting of costs associated with outages and/or changes. The reports we are discussing in this section are different than those discussed in the "User-Triggered Activity" section that follows in that these are triggered by certain predefined conditions, such as a threshold being approached or periodically based on a date and time.

Some examples of the threshold type of reports that you might want to generate are capacity encroachment, asset failure, and license usage. For example, the capacity encroachment report might be triggered when your data center has only 25 empty server slots available. The report might contain the location of the available slots, the installs scheduled for the upcoming month, and how many slots would still be available if all the installs were completed. Upon receiving this report, you may choose to order additional racks or maybe research how many servers are being retired in the same timeframe, freeing up additional space. What is important to remember is that this may be a report requested by your Capacity or Availability Management organizations; it is not necessarily a report that the Configuration Management team creates for its own purposes. Configuration Management has the responsibility of making sure that the information about assets and CIs is available to the processes, but not to manage the capacity or availability itself.

Asset failure or license usage reports might be requested by your Supplier Management processes within ITAM so that those individuals can work with the vendors on warranties or costs of the used licenses. Engineering and site support groups may also be interested in these sort of reports so that they can ensure they have the proper levels of overstock in-house to accommodate failures or recommend a replacement product if the failure rate gets too high.

From a Configuration Management perspective, the reports you would expect—that is, verification, discrepancies, audit, and so on—would already be defined and in place. These would address verification and audit findings of modifications to the environment and the associated Requests For Change (RFCs). You would want to have reports that automatically trigger on a periodic basis, maybe nightly after batch processes complete or maintenance windows close, to identify what modifications occurred and if all of them had corresponding RFCs. The reverse report should also run to identify instances where RFCs were closed but no corresponding change occurred. It is important to execute both reports because they will tell you different stories about what is happening in the environment. Ideally, the combination of both reports will identify the CI that was modified but had no RFC and the RFC that was closed but had no corresponding modification in the environment. Again, the ideal situation will leave you with equal discrepancies on each report that match one-to-one with each other.

Alerts and Events

An alert is actually a type of an event that is a form of warning that a threshold has been reached, something has changed, or a failure has occurred. Alerts could have a relationship to reports in that they could be the first step in a series of actions where, for example, a recipient is alerted of a capacity threshold being reached or maybe a service level that was just passed. This sets off the Event Management processes that need to be executed to get the service back within the agreed-upon limits, or possibly it is just a notification to the service owner, informing them that the service level is not being met, but you are aware of it and already working to remedy the situation. Depending on the type of event, Event Management may trigger an incident, problem, or change, or it may just communicate some general information such as "backup job has completed."

One place where a proactive stance can be taken is in the area of trend analysis. Note that trend analysis can happen in many disciplines throughout your organization and across the entire lifecycle of a device. Some of this obviously occurs as part of Problem Management's normal cycle but is not limited exclusively to Problem Management. We believe that after you have aggregated the information with your CMS, you have a tremendous opportunity to mine the data and detect trends that, if not addressed, could cause service interruptions. Hardware and software devices do not typically work in a random manner. It may appear to be that way sometimes, but that is because we are not always able to visually detect the pattern, whereas a system such as the CMS should be able to. We look forward to the day when IT departments can notify their business partners of approaching outages before they occur. Even more ideal will be when you can demonstrate to them outages that never occurred because you detected a trend and applied a fix before any business customer was ever affected.

Notifications of events might be automatically distributed to recipients based on predefined triggers or because of relationships that exist. For example, if there was a network failure at a primary data center, it is possible that because of load balancing, the secondary data center might experience network delays. Instead of receiving multiple incident calls about slow performance that consume your Service Desk personnel's time, you could automatically trigger a notification out to the appropriate personnel, informing them that they may experience some network delays. This demonstrates your maturity in managing the environment, reduces call traffic (which costs you money), and frees up your resources to handle other issues that may still be pending. Ideally, if you had the capability to isolate a specific subnet that was impacted, you could target your event notification instead of sending out a site-wide event notice.

The preferred model for notification would be a publish/subscribe (pub/sub) model, where the interested parties would take on the responsibility to subscribe to events they would want to be notified about. This not only takes the burden off a specific group to maintain the distribution lists, but it reduces the likelihood that anyone or any group will be inundated with alerts and events that they are not interested in. There is some risk, of course, that an individual may not recognize that they should be interested in certain things. You need to work out the best ways to mitigate this risk, but one of them is to make sure you have very detailed documentation of all your CIs, IT, and business services and make it all readily available to anyone who might be interested.

If you can integrate a pub/sub model with a mature business rules engine and provide that as a combined toolset to the recipients of these alerts and events, you will have provided an unbelievable amount of value to your service delivery and operations departments. Be sure to note that your CMS can only handle so many instructions while still meeting its service level requirements. Be cautious to not overload it with events and alerts to the point that it cannot perform its day-to-day operational duties. You should run stress and performance testing exercises against your CMS platform to determine the "break-point" of your system prior to deployment. Be sure you document not only the break-point but also the scaling capability, so you know how you will handle the situation when you start approaching the break-point, such as increasing memory, hard drive space, CPU allocation, and so on.

User-Triggered Activity

This section describes how each of the listed areas could leverage or consume information contained in or associated with the CMS. As we described in the "Supplemental Information" section earlier in the chapter, the list described below and Figure 9.5 do not match exactly in content. They are meant as catalysts for you to think about what you need to leverage in your specific situation. The utilization of the information would come from user-initiated requests or activities in a more *reactive manner* versus the previous section, "CMS-Triggered Activity," where the utilization was in a *proactive manner*. As discussed previously, the information might in some cases be under the controls of Change and Configuration Management, but there may also be data associated with the CIs that is not under the full rigor of these controls but yet available that could provide value. You need to be careful in how you might use this information and ensure that its consumers are aware of what is and what is not being actively audited and verified by the ITIL processes. The following list is only a sampling of the uses of the data and should not be viewed as an all-encompassing list. The purpose is to enhance your vision of how data in the CMS or associated with the CMS could be used and provide a basis upon which you can build your own vision of usage:

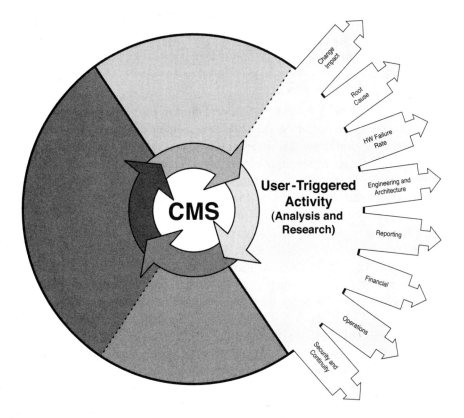

FIGURE 9.5   User-Triggered Activity

Access Management

When trying to grant user access to systems and services, it sometimes can be beneficial to know what others also have. If you are fortunate to have a system that already provides this capability, you are further along than many. For most of you, however, it can simplify things greatly when you can model someone's access (such as a new employee) similar to an existing employee or peer. For example: "Sally, the new employee, is replacing Tom and needs the identical access to systems that he currently has." The ability to quickly determine what systems they have access to and what privileges they have could save you a significant amount of time.

Another usage is in the support of audits or licensing. Many times, either auditors or software vendors question how many people have access to systems or how many licenses are being used. Having all the access rights associated to your services in the CMS could enable you to reduce license requirements or support your audit efforts.

Availability Management

The two most obvious uses of CMS information to the Availability Management personnel are ensuring that the agreed-upon availability targets are being met by monitoring incidents and limiting changes that could negatively impact those targets. Availability Management needs to consume a lot of information on historical operations of systems to set targets with the business partners that are achievable. If this information is not readily available, the targets may not be reasonable and could cause the business partners to have false expectations of what IT can deliver.

Because Availability Management encompasses the whole lifecycle, you can factor in current performance metrics of existing technologies and architectures and provide those metrics to the designers of new systems, so they can possibly adjust the design and architecture to achieve higher-availability targets.

All this information provides the business analysts with a tremendous amount of historical data to present to their business partners when discussing new systems and services. It provides everyone during those discussions with a true metrics-based view of what is currently going on in the IT environment, where these are limitations and where opportunities exist. An added benefit is that you can leverage metrics from other services and systems in your environment to demonstrate alternatives to what is being done with that business partner and work together to achieve more cost-effective availability targets.

Change Management

The ability for Change Management to perform an impact assessment is vital to its successful operation. In most cases, however, most of the information is not available for them to do a thorough job. The CMS provides that information so that the Request For Change (RFC) can be truly assessed. You can see all the services directly associated with the CI being modified, assess the availability metrics of the CI, and determine whether similar RFCs have been successful in the past or what incident(s) may have occurred with similar RFCs. What is also valuable is the ability to notify owners of downstream services that an RFC is being scheduled, and it may have an impact on their service.

Sometimes RFCs appear to impact only a single service, but because of their relationships to other devices or the usage of shared equipment, the RFC could impact many services. If, for example, a server was being taken offline for an operating system upgrade, you might think that only the services supported by that server were being impacted. If one of those services, however, provided a data file to another service, it is possible that the other service could also be negatively impacted. Without a CMS in place, it is difficult to tell if there are any downstream services and nearly impossible to assess whether they would be negatively impacted. The ability to perform a comprehensive due diligence effort is severely hampered and, at times, is not much more than a fast glance at an architecture diagram that has not been updated in years, along with a quick prayer that nothing breaks as a result of the RFC. We are not trivializing the work people do today, but we recognize that without information, they are simply limited in what is possible to do.

When Post Implementation Reviews (PIR) are conducted for unsuccessful RFCs, the ability to look back on the impact assessment, remediation plan, and RFC details so as to determine what data might have been missing is critical to the Continual Service Improvement (CSI) cycle of the CMS. It is also a means of feedback for the CMS owners. Incidents that occurred during the execution of the RFC should be associated with it, as well as the solution to the incident so that it can be prevented in the future.

Most of the benefit to Change Management falls under the generic umbrella of impact assessment, but this is a huge umbrella that has many moving parts. This should not be surprising because Change Management is such a major component of the overall ITIL lifecycle. Ensuring that the Change Management personnel have every possible piece of information about the environment and services easily accessible to them during the lifecycle of an RFC is essential to the IT organization maturing and becoming a service-based organization.

Capacity Management

The overall capacity of an organization is likely to already be known by whichever department runs Capacity Management on a day-to-day basis, but what is probably not known is the utilization of the capacity, especially on a service-by-service basis. Typically, the amount allocated to an application, system, or even service is not exactly what it needs because there are assumptions to account for peaks and valleys in the business cycle. For organizations to ensure that the service is not impacted, the capacity allotted must be significant enough to handle the peak, even if it is being wasted during the off-peak periods. A thorough understanding of all the business cycle demands is essential to allocate the capacity amount properly.

If, for example, you were able to aggregate data about each service's consumption of capacity across its full business cycle from the CMS, you could drastically reduce your overall capacity needs by allocating only the needed amount at those particular periods in the business cycle that it needed. This is especially the case with the new virtualization technologies now available that enable you to more dynamically allocate and reclaim capacity.

The ability to look back historically on your business cycles, technology architectures, software implementations, and database designs could all help you to better understand where capacity is being underutilized and thereby wasting money. The knowledge you garner from having this information also helps you to better and more quickly respond to new demands from your business because you understand their business cycles. If you can foresee upcoming demand based on the normal business cycle and new demand from RFCs, you could assemble that information, purchase capacity from your vendor in bulk quantities to reduce cost, and ultimately supply your business partners with the exact capacity they need (as they need it and at a lower overall cost to the organization). ITIL v3 speaks to this concept when it discusses the coupling of the Service Catalog with Patterns of Business Activity and User Profiles, as well as in the Demand Management sections of the manuals.

Event Management

Event Management relies on the CMS because it needs some of the logical interpretations that the CMS provides for it to translate a basic monitoring alert into a more meaningful occurrence of a possible incident that could lead to a service outage. There are occasions where your monitoring tools may be detecting natural and customary alerts, but because of their alignment, the timing in your business cycle, and other activity in the environment, it may actually warrant an incident to be generated and sent to the appropriate support group in advance of the service ever being impacted. We recognize that this is the ideal scenario where everything happens automatically, but in some regard, aspects of this are possible today. For example, if your business cycle was clearly defined and available to your monitoring group, they could modify their alerts and triggers to detect abnormal spikes or dips in system traffic that are not in line with the normal business cycle. Think of how some network security tools operate. They monitor network traffic and detect abnormal patterns which could be a sign of external attacks. If the traffic spike was typical of that network segment (for example, a service provider doing a nightly upload of their data), the network security tool would not flag it as malicious. The same logic needs to be applied in the CMS and our service management systems.

Let's use a manufacturing and production process example to demonstrate how the same scenario could impact an IT environment. Take a highly automated manufacturing plant that produces electronic widgets and, under normal circumstances, outputs 20,000 units of the widget each week, with a peak production demand of 50,000 units. This peak must be delivered by December 1 every year to its client to meet the holiday demand. Many components are used to build the electronic widget, and the consumption of those components is known and planned for in advance. If there were a disruption in the supply line of those components at the manufacturing plant of the component in October, it is possible that there could be a shortage of those components to meet the December 1 delivery date. The timing of the supply-line disruption is what makes the situation a potential danger. If that same disruption occurred in February instead of October, it is likely that there would be no event. Every business has its own cycles; you need to determine which of your services are sensitive to those cycles.

Incident Management

Because Incident Management's primary responsibility is to restore a service to its normal operation as quickly as possible, it is crucial that these individuals have all the information related to the CI readily available to them the moment the incident is recorded. They need to quickly determine which services are directly impacted and which services might be impacted if restoration does not occur fast enough. The CMS, with all of its interrelationships between CIs and services, provides this insight. The ability to quickly determine if an RFC might be the cause of the incident can provide fast access to a back-out or remediation plan to help quickly restore the service to it previous state and minimize the impact to the business user.

Incident Management is one of the most visible processes to the end users and therefore has the opportunity to demonstrate the most value of your effort. This value comes from the speed in which you can restore a service. It can also come from the ability to take a proactive stance on notifying the business partner of what service levels are being met, where they are not being met, and what the causes might be. With the information, your business partners can then take that information and work with the designers and architects of the systems or the operations personnel to try to address the situations before discussing the possibility of changing the established Service Level Agreements.

Information Security Management

The most obvious utilization of CMS data by the Information Security Management (ISM) processes is that of accessed and manipulated data. ISM personnel can aggregate data that is associated with potentially sensitive CIs and determine if it is in violation of polices. They can research how the data might have been accessed or manipulated and review the governance policies that were in place to decide if the policies need to be modified to prevent future access. Many times, unauthorized access to data occurs not because someone was intentionally trying to bypass policy, but simply because it was available and the individual did not know he shouldn't. If ISM personnel can identify these situations and proactively deliver awareness campaigns and modify the control mechanisms to prevent future access, the corporation will be that much more secure. Security must always be practiced in layers and with never-ending vigilance. There is no one solution that can ensure 100% security, nor would it be cost effective. Your business partners must work closely with you to determine what levels of control are necessary and cost effective, while enabling the organization to operate efficiently and within the required compliance boundaries.

IT Service Continuity Management

The CMS provides IT Service Continuity personnel a foundation of data to work with that is invaluable. With the lines between business and IT becoming grayer every day, a knowledge tool such as the CMS bridges the chasm between the two. Without the CMS, tremendous effort must be invested all year, every year, to try and just keep up with the changes to the IT infrastructure, business demands, and making sure that you can meet the continuity requirements. A mature CMS inherently provides most of your foundational data and structure for any continuity scenario. Not only does the CMS provide that information in the event you actually need it during a disaster, but it can proactively notify you of modifications to the infrastructure that invalidate previous continuity plans. Leverage the trend analysis, alerts, and events to your advantage and stay ahead of the changes rather than scrambling to figure out why things aren't working during a live disaster situation.

Knowledge Management

"Knowledge is king." The Knowledge Management process has the responsibility of making knowledge available as its sole purpose. It does rely, however, on high-quality and complete data for it to deliver on its goal. The Knowledge Management System (KMS) and CMS share and leverage many of the same raw data elements in order to provide the end users with a valuable toolset. Knowledge Management takes what the CMS has available and then wraps it with a layer of experiences, known solutions/errors, and resolved scenarios to offer an added value to the CMS that could be tremendously valuable if merged together properly.

Problem Management

For Problem Management, both reactive and proactive, to be efficient, it needs to have available to it data that spans the entire infrastructure in both the vertical (depth) and horizontal (breadth) perspectives. It needs to accumulate data from a variety of areas so as to fully understand where the root cause of an issue may reside.

From the reactive perspective, it needs to quickly assimilate the incidents that are being created, scan those for previously detected trends or errors, and offer back to the personnel any potential workarounds and spawn RFCs as needed.

From the proactive perspective, it needs to sift through more in-depth detail to identify trends that may not have been previously detected under the reactive model during an outage.

We walk through a proactive Problem Management scenario to help describe how it could benefit your organization. Let's say that your application developers have been using a three-year-old version (v4.1) of Acme Corporations data access software and have refused to upgrade to the latest version (v7.0). After performing some trend analysis on recent incidents and problems, you determined that the common thread through a recent wave of outages is that they are all using Acme Corporations v4.1 software. Upon further investigation, you find that a critical service to your organization was recently released, and it is utilizing v4.1 of the software, but it has not encountered any outages yet because the initial release was a limited rollout to only pilot users. The plan, however, according to the Change Schedule, is to roll out the critical service to the full client base at the beginning of the next month. Because proactive Problem Management detected this situation, you have the opportunity to inform the application team about the proven limitation in the 4.1 version and recommend to them that they upgrade the data access software to v7.0 before the release to prevent outages to a critical service. If this scenario were about hardware instead of software, it is possible that you could go back to your vendor and demand a better-quality product, lower pricing, or a higher level of warranty, or maybe it would be the basis for changing vendors.

Under both modes, data from the CMS is vital to the Problem Management process because it would otherwise not have the data available to perform the in-depth investigation that is required to perform root cause and trend analysis.

Release and Deployment Management

Release and Deployment Management must have access to all of the CIs, their relationships, known errors, workarounds, and so on for it to perform its function. Without this information, it simply cannot ensure that there will be minimal unpredicted impact on services or that issues identified during other releases are prevented from recurring. Also vital to its success is the knowledge of what else may be occurring in the environment during the planned release window. There are many occasions where components are shared by multiple services, and to minimize service impact, it might be advantageous to adjust release schedules so that both packages are released at the same time. Every element of data about any component within the release package needs to be available for Release and Deployment Management to fulfill its purpose successfully.

Service Asset and Configuration Management

The SACM processes can function only if a CMS is in place, but we must recognize that some of the ongoing activities need access to data, such as RFCs, trend analysis results, and impact assessment results—similar to Release and Deployment Management, Knowledge Management, and others. SACM is unique in that it provides both foundational elements and supplemental information, but then it benefits from the other supplemental information being available for it to support the other Service Management processes.

Service Catalog Management

The CMS and the Service Catalog have a tight relationship. For the CMS to present the information in terms of services, it must have those services defined and available. In defining those services, the CMS provides a wealth of information to help define them accurately and comprehensively. Also important to note is that the service definitions are placed under the controls of Change Management. Without the CMS, these services would need to be defined from scratch without any technological support to validate the contents and components of a service. The decomposition of the services is defined in the CMS, and this in turn is the basis for the technology aspects of the service-based cost models for the IT Financial Management process. Many times, the effort to modify "charge back" processes that companies have in place is bigger than the effort to address the operational process changes. This is because the process enables and drives certain cultural behaviors and how teams report their work. If you change this dynamic, you are also changing the control and power that these teams currently have. Those of us who want transparency in business are not typically the ones hiding inefficient processes.

Service Level Management

The leverage that Service Level Management gains from the CMS is that it has available to it the factual metrics of how services are operating. Access to data about how one service compared against another or how similar services that use different technologies compared against each other is immensely valuable when negotiating new agreements. Like any other contract or negotiation, you need to have as many facts available to you so that you can make informed decisions. The CMS is the source to provide that information. Be careful that you know what exactly the metrics mean and how they were collected before using them. There have been several articles written over the years, mainly about the sales profession, that address the concept of behaviors being driven by what is being measured leading to the wrong results. Let's take two pharmaceutical sales representatives who have call quotas of 15 doctors per day. One representative averages 16 calls per day but misses his sales quota by 9%, whereas the other representative averages only 12 calls per day but hits 104% of his sales quota. Anyone looking at this would recognize that the individual who achieved a 104% sales mark was most successful; however, it is possible that he was penalized for not achieving the 15 calls-per-day quota. Be careful that you completely understand the statistics you're measuring and what sort of behavior it will drive.

SOA, SaaS, and Other Enterprise Initiatives

There are many uses for CMS data after it becomes available. We have discussed several previously in this chapter that are directly associated with the ITIL processes; however, we must not forget other initiatives, such as SOA and SaaS, which stand to benefit tremendously from having the CMS data already available, validated, and under the rigors of Change controls. SaaS in particular is gaining a lot of momentum as we head toward the end of 2008 because organizations are demanding faster implementations at lower costs. By leveraging the CMS, some ITIL process efficiencies could help with the speed to market, but more directly impactful is the cost savings that could be garnered from a streamlined, highly effective, and efficient operations area that has access to the data contained in the CMS. After you have implemented the CMS, you should be able to measure the cost saving by comparing the baselines of when you started to where you are and then translate those metrics into real dollars that were not spent supporting an application or service.

The Complete Circle

We have described section by section the four major components that make up the CMS wheel. We began however with the visualization of a tree and how it needs a solid rooting in order for it to be able to grow and remain healthy. The CMS requires that same stable foundation as does the tree. Figure 9.6 illustrates all four sections on one circular wheel. The inbound and outbound modules illustrated are to help you visualize the sorts of data that are needed for that section, but you need to make the final decision on which of these modules or those discussed in the text but not drawn in Figure 9.6 are most important to your organization. Use the knowledge you have about your organization and industry and make educated decisions on what is important to you and don't forget that Continual Service Improvement is what will make you revisit the wheel to decide what is next.

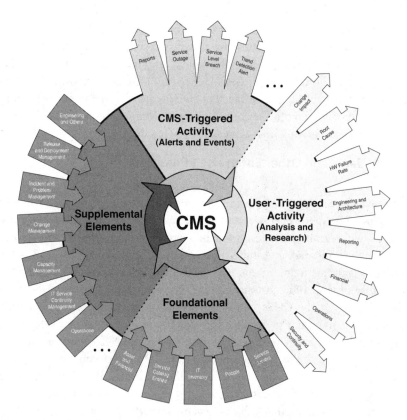

FIGURE 9.6   Complete inbound and outbound cycle of the CMS

Frequently Asked Questions

Question: Can I use the CMS for initiatives other than those that are ITIL related?

Answer: Absolutely. You should use it for any initiative where the CMS will help your organization gain value. You should be monitoring the performance of it and be sure that you don't impact the primary users. If you can ensure that the primary purpose of the CMS will not be negatively impacted and your organization can benefit from using the CMS for initiatives that are not ITIL related, you should consider it because it will deliver value.

Question: I don't have a formal asset system in place; can I use the CMS for that?

Answer: You need to understand that Asset Management has its own needs and objectives—needs and objectives that the CMS will not inherently possess. It can share data with the CMS, but we do not feel that they should be viewed as something that you can unify into one process solution. This does not mean that the CMS cannot feed information to an Asset Management System; it means that their purposes are not the same.

Question: A lot of my asset and inventory data is incomplete; should I put off the CMS initiative indefinitely until I get that data addressed?

Answer: Ideally, yes, you should put it off. Realistically, however, try to carve out a portion of the data that is reliable and complete and scope your CMS initiative around that. In parallel, try to clean up more of the data and include that in your next phase of the CMS. Remember that this is a journey, and if you never leave your home, your journey will never begin. So, start with anything you can and go on from there.

Question: I didn't see some processes listed as contributing to or consuming from the CMS. Does that mean they do not play a part in it?

Answer: No, not at all. We tried to provide a wide breadth of information on what data and processes will contribute to the construction of the CMS, as well as those that will consume its contents. We could not identify all processes, nor provide in-depth details about them. We simply wanted to jump-start your thoughts so that you can determine for yourself what you need to include and how you will consume it.

Summary

Leveraging the CMS is more of an exercise in navigating an immense amount of data and identifying only those pieces that are actionable for you. They may have little meaning to others, but to you, the specifics of each element and its interrelationship with other elements are what defines value for you. Think about how the Internet is structured, and how everyone is so overloaded with information that many times you miss out on the important pieces because of the sheer volume of data that means nothing to you. To truly leverage the CMS, you need to sift through this overwhelming amount of data. Similar conceptual efforts are active across the Internet from technology startups, some of which are only in the alpha stage of their lifecycle. Companies such as Wink,[3] Metaweb,[4] and Kayanta[5] are all trying to provide mechanisms of aggregating the volumes of data available on the Internet, piecing together only those that are relevant to the user and presenting the result in a simple and easily consumed format. The Kayanta web site seems to sum it up well, and although it is referring to its efforts to deliver technology that will revolutionize how people consume data from the web, the philosophy it has used to address this overload of data holds true for those trying to leverage the CMS as well.

The Kayanta founder goes on to say, "We're inspired by the plethora of opportunities offered through the Internet but bewildered by the amount of personal effort required to extract even the modest benefit. We admit that the Internet makes most tasks more efficient, resulting in more time for social activities. However, the amount of time spent online to achieve any efficiencies comes at the expense of time spent with family and friends."[6] We, as technologists, need to provide more sophisticated tools that enable our end users to get what they need, act on it, and get on with the next action. Every minute they spend looking for the data that is necessary for decision making is a minute not spent on delivering value to the consumer.

---

3. http://wink.com
4. http://www.metaweb.com
5. http://www.kayanta.com/index.html
6. http://www.kayanta.com/corporate/about.html

CHAPTER 10

Enjoy the Fruits of Success

Establishing a comprehensive Configuration Management System (CMS) requires a long and difficult journey, but one with enormous benefits when you get it right. Along the way, you will enjoy many victories—some miniscule, some huge. The victories will vary from company to company, but they might be as simple as no longer needing a spreadsheet to track server inventory or as complex as getting the OS patch levels on all your computing systems under the Change and Configuration Management process controls. You must savor these wins and reward those who contribute to the success. Celebrate with a free pizza for lunch or cash rewards for the innovators; even a sincere pat on the back goes a long way. The people who make the CMS a reality are among the new generation of IT heroes. They deserve the recognition and the compensation for their contributions.

You also want to proclaim your success to your internal stakeholders (for example, management, IT staff, and business leaders) and to the greater industry community. Our profession needs to know when and how our fellow CMS innovators are making progress toward the dream of the trustworthy information source on which all process execution depends.

Measuring Success

We covered metrics before, so there is no need to go into detail here. In the interest of demonstrating and enjoying your successes, however, you should use your metrics as the guide to defining what success is in the first place. We can work hard and not achieve anything meaningful, or we can work toward improving the metrics we established. We want to measure results, not activity.

Success Criteria

The key performance metrics include those listed in Tables 10.1 and 10.2. These are among the success criteria you will follow. There will be others as well, and these are merely examples and a subset of the metrics you should be watching. These are the same tables from Chapter 8, "Continual Improvement for the CMS," except that we have added one row to each of the tables. These rows address data accuracy and total cost of ownership. These are more business-oriented metrics, whereas the others are technical. There are other business-oriented metrics that you may come up with on your own as well. As you move forward, you should establish quarterly goals for each metric. Maybe you plan to add two more Management Data Repositories (MDR) to the CMS in the next quarter. This ties back to the third metric in Table 10.1. If this is indeed your plan, commit to it by making it a goal for the quarter. If you add the two MDRs, you are successful at achieving your goal for that one metric.

TABLE 10.1   CMS Metrics

Metric	Goal	What to Expect
Configuration items (CI) under management control	No hard value, but it will start large and become huge as the CMS matures.	The number of CIs will prove to be an efficiency metric because you use this raw value to calculate others, such as CIs per IT administrator and cost per CI. Discovery tools cause this value to explode because it captures the complexity with more accuracy. If you think you have 500 servers and discovery tells you there are 800, 800 is the real number you will use.
Percent of CIs populated automatically	As high as possible.	Without discovery, this number will be low. Even Change Management alone cannot ensure a high degree of CI accuracy. You need to augment it with discovery. Seek a rising trend rather than some fixed value as your goal because the ideal of 100% is impossible.
Number of Management Data Repositories (MDR)	The number will start low, but not at one, because many of these exist and just need to be located.	Build an ideal portfolio of MDRs when defining the CMS architecture. The usual suspects (servers, network, and so on) are included, but geography and business unit structure might dictate other divisions. The number of MDRs in your architecture should be the goal, so drive toward filling the voids in this architecture. Note that the architecture must remain flexible to changing needs, and thus the MDR portfolio will also be flexible.

Metric	Goal	What to Expect
Number of federated abstractions for applications and services	Start low and seek rapid increase. The number will then level off as the CMS matures.	You cannot achieve a high value at the onset of your CMS. After you deploy application discovery and dependency mapping tools, you will have the abstractions, but federating to the lower-level MDRs cannot occur easily until your vendors adopt and implement standards—hopefully the CMDB Federation Working Group (CMDBf).
Data accuracy	Accuracy as high as possible, with anomalies as low as possible.	Initially you should expect a high value of anomalies as you work out the kinks in your processes and validate the data in your MDRs. As time progresses and your Change Management controls over the MDRs become more mature, you should see significant drops in your anomalies and higher accuracy for the given MDR. This pattern will repeat itself for new MDRs that are introduced to the CMS.

TABLE **10.2**   CMS Effect on Operational Metrics

Metric	The CMS Role	Expected Results
MTTR (Mean Time To Resolution)	Provide accurate information that was previously missing, incomplete, or inaccurate.	Because MTTR is heavily influenced by prolonged root-cause identification, accurate information will guide toward faster root-cause and therefore will reduce MTTR, maybe dramatically.
Change-related incidents (percent of total incidents)	Provide accurate information to guide configuration changes accurately.	Approximately 80% of all service-impacting incidents are the result of some sort of faulty change.[1] With the right information, most of these changes can be either avoided or executed with much better accuracy.

(continues)

---

1. It is widely known among experienced operations professionals that a high number of incidents are caused by faulty configuration changes. The precise percentage is the subject of dispute, but most research suggests that the typical IT organization experiences between 70% and 90% of incidents resulting from these changes. We use the 80% value as the generally agreed-upon figure; however, regardless of which number you use within the given range, it is unacceptably high.

TABLE 10.2   CMS Effect on Operational Metrics (continued)

Metric	The CMS Role	Expected Results
First-call incident resolution (percent of total incidents)	Provide accurate information to the Service Desk.	The Service Desk is better able to resolve incoming incidents when they have the right information. Thus, fewer incidents need to be escalated to higher-level (and more expensive) staff. Also, automation technologies that assist the Service Desk can be enhanced or developed.
Change Management execution time	Provide accurate information to accelerate change assessments and approvals.	Quicker change execution is extremely helpful to service adaptation. This is becoming ever more critical as technologies and service get more dynamic. The CMS can speed these changes, since decision makers (and automation tools) can act with better insight.
Asset utilization	Provide accurate information on all assets in place.	The goal of most asset management initiatives is to optimize asset utilization. You cannot reach this goal without knowing the assets in place. Such information is seldom known with good accuracy, but a good CMS should make it obvious.
Total Cost of Ownership (TCO)	Provide accurate information on asset utilization of the services delivered.	Calculating TCO for a service requires you to aggregate a lot of granular data that is typically spread out across the environment. The CMS can greatly reduce the effort to identify this data, as well as provide the bounds for your TCO calculation by maintaining an accurate inventory, failure rate, and maintenance history of all the components in the service.

If you try to examine each metric individually, it will be difficult to understand the full impact of the CMS. You should develop a means to arrive at a single metric that is a composite of your others. Aggregate your various goals into this overall quality metric. A good tool to do this is a balanced scorecard. Reporting tools can be tailored to collect metrics and present the balanced scorecard results, but you can even do these in a simple spreadsheet. Table 10.3 shows a simple balanced scorecard to illustrate how the balanced scorecard works.

For those unfamiliar with reading or working with a balanced scorecard, it can be confusing at first, so we have tried to break it down for you a little bit below. For those familiar with balanced scorecards, you should go directly to Table 10.3. The words may change from scorecard to scorecard, but the fundamental structure should be similar. Table 10.3 has three main objectives: CMS Direct Goals, Derivative Use-Case Goals, and Developmental Goals. Each objective has a weight associated with it, 50%, 40%, and 10% in our example, and then each objective splits that weighted percentage among its specific criteria. For example, "Reduce change-related incidents" will account for 60% of the 40% of its parent objective, which means it actually accounts for 24% (60% × 40%) of the overall scorecard. Since the result in our example was that they achieved one unit more than the goal of 7, they reached 114% (8 / 7 × 100%). The Derivative Use-Case Goals objective had one of its goals underperform (80%) and the other overperform (114%), so the net result of the Derivative Use-Case Goals objective when the individual weighting is factored in is 101% (80% × 40% + 114% × 60%). We hope that this clarified the numbers behind the scorecard more than it confused you. If you are still not comfortable with them, do a search on balanced scorecards, and there will be no shortage of information available.

TABLE 10.3   A Simple Balanced Scorecard for CMS Success Measurement

Second Quarter CMS Objectives	Goal	Weight	Result	Score
CMS Direct Goals		50%		105%
Add more MDRs for network and VMs.	2	50%	2	100%
Increase % of CIs populated automatically.	44%	50%	48%	109%
		100%		
Derivative Use-Case Goals		40%		101%
Reduce MTTR (percent).	5	40%	4	80%
Reduce change-related incidents (percent).	7	60%	8	114%
		100%		
Developmental Goals		10%		75%
Achieve ITIL v3 Foundations Certification (number of staff).	4	100%	3	75%
		100%		
		100%		
			Overall Success	100%

The individual criteria are aggregated according to the weights. It is usually best to set it up with a two-tier aggregation, as shown in Table 10.3. We show three top-level criteria with 50%, 40%, and 10%, respectively, adding up to the necessary 100%. Each of these is then broken down into measurable sub-criteria, also totaling 100% within each top-level criterion.

We set the objectives (for example, 44% as the goal for the percent of automatically populated CIs), and then measure the actual results (for example, 48% for the same metric). The weights impose the right influence on each metric. As a result, the certifications metric missed the mark, but we can still celebrate success because the other metrics overwhelmed the loss. You win some and you lose some, but you have to keep your eye on the big picture.

With a balanced scorecard, keep your metrics to a minimum. Make them relevant, but a high number of metrics dilutes the influence of each metric. If you have 10 metrics and divide them equally for the 100% weight, each is only 10%. At only 10% influence, a terrible or wonderful achievement at execution doesn't make much of a difference overall. Our experience is that each group of metrics (top-level and each subcriteria set) should be no more than five entries.

In Table 10.4, we show a more complex balanced scorecard where we have added two additional top-level criteria. We show the five top-level criteria with 35%, 30%, 10%, 15%, and 10%, respectively, adding up to the necessary 100% as before in the simple balanced scorecard. Also, as in the simple scorecard in Table 10.3, each of the top levels is broken down into measurable subcriteria, also totaling 100% within each top-level criterion.

TABLE 10.4   A More Complex Balanced Scorecard for CMS Success Measurement

Second Quarter CMS Objectives	Goal	Weight	Result	Score
CMS Direct Goals		35%		105%
Add more MDRs for network and VMs.	2	50%	2	100%
Increase % of CIs populated automatically.	44%	50%	48%	109%
		100%		
Derivative Use-Case Goals		30%		101%
Reduce MTTR (percent).	5	40%	4	80%
Reduce change-related incidents (percent).	7	60%	8	114%
		100%		
Developmental Goals		10%		75%
Achieve ITIL v3 Foundations Certification (number of staff).	4	100%	3	75%
		100%		
Total Cost of Ownership		15%		112%
Maintenance costs related to HW equipment.	$50k	50%	$40k	125%
Maintenance costs related to SW development.	$25k	50%	$25k	100%
		100%		

Second Quarter CMS Objectives	Goal	Weight	Result	Score
Data Accuracy		10%		115%
Number of data anomalies detected below SLA.	3	70%	3	100%
Number of incidents below SLA-related data inaccuracy.	2	30%	3	150%
		100%		
		100%		
			Overall Success	103%

Reward Positive Behavior with MBOs Tied to Success Criteria

One of the problems with IT is that the incentives are not aligned with the actual needs and hence do not foster disciplined operations. We reward heroics, which naturally encourages situations where heroics are needed. If we change the rewards, we change the incentives to achieve the right outcome.

Sometimes we reward individuals for their heroics even though they may have been the cause of the need for the heroics. For example, Tom, a midlevel programmer, goes into the office on the weekend and works 12 hours to finish developing the last piece of functionality that is required before the system is turned over for integration testing first thing on Monday morning. Rewarding Tom would seem appropriate, but then you are informed that the reason Tom had to go in to the office over the weekend was because he had chosen to participate in a voluntary focus group on Wednesday and Thursday and was therefore behind on delivering his scheduled units of code to the rest of the team on Friday morning. Because of Tom's decision to participate in the focus group and thereby delay his deliverable, three members of his development team had to go in to the office on Sunday after Tom completed his deliverable to ensure their functional units worked properly with his. Should Tom be rewarded for working over the weekend? Who should be penalized if the team is not able to turn over the code for integration testing on Monday morning? If you remember from Chapter 9, "Leveraging the CMS," we used the example of the pharmaceutical sales professional who does not meet his doctor call quota but delivers 104% of sales target. You need to make sure that the behavior you are rewarding is delivering the results you need and want. In the example in this section, you may have decided to reward the three individuals and not Tom had the deliverable been met on Monday morning because they were the ones who showed heroic efforts. Tom's "heroic" effort was for self-preservation and a self-inflicted requirement. As with this example or the one in Chapter 9, you need to be sure that your human resources department is involved to ensure fairness and clear criteria for rewards and/or penalties.

The metrics that gauge success should be the same metrics tied to personal rewards. Objectives must be improvements to the quality metrics. In the Management by Objective (MBO) process, you set measurable goals to be achieved. If you meet your goals, you receive a bonus payout. If you miss the goals, you get no extra bonus. Many of us now have some portion of our income tied to such MBO structure.

In the CMS, the MBOs should reflect the level of success with preset CMS goals. For instance, if you plan to deploy a new discovery tool for the network, you might want to set this as an MBO goal for the coming quarter. If at the end of the quarter, you have successfully installed the discovery tool and have it reflecting a predetermined portion of the network, you receive 100% of the MBO payout for the quarter. Maybe you exceeded this and have complete coverage of the network, plus you actually have implemented the first use case for the network CMS data. Then you can receive 150% of your MBO payout, a bonus on the bonus, if you will. If you deploy the tool but fail to cover enough of the network, you might receive 50% of the MBO payout. This is pay for performance and is a great incentive to pursue the right objectives.

By establishing criteria that is measurable and then tying actual performance to the goals, you have a self-enforcing mechanism to encourage positive performance of team members. This is the correct way to reward the high performers. You will still need people capable of the heroics, and you should indeed reward those capable of such deeds, but do not link heroics to the bonus payouts. You want the incentives to encourage activities that result in customer satisfaction. Customers want improved services, not better firefighters.

Evangelizing Your Success

As a successful participant in the CMS movement (or any successful initiative), it is prudent for you to advertise your success and to help build the body of knowledge in the industry. Every success that is communicated effectively is another proof point that the CMS is not only valuable, but possible. With some of the industry misinformation about the Configuration Management Database (CMDB) threatening the overall CMS movement, we need to show the world that there is a path that leads to success.

You have two audiences for your CMS information: internal parties and the external industry community. There are good reasons for you to actively engage both audiences. Internally, you want to gain support and enthusiasm for the effort. People ranging from senior management and business users to IT technical staff need to know the benefits of your work and your strategy. You will either fail or struggle greatly if you are a loner with the CMS.

Externally, you hope to influence the direction of the CMS across the industry. This book is such an attempt. A better industry view of the CMS will benefit you as well as others because it helps prove that *your* practice is indeed *best* practice. You are not just following—you are leading! The broader community includes others like yourself who are trying to make actual CMS progress and those who are looking to us all as the global force to help them benefit from the CMS. This latter group includes vendors who want to offer technology solutions that will either provide or consume some part of the CMS. It also includes IT staff and even some business users who seek better information to drive their own execution to more success.

In either audience, there will be differing needs and benefits across the individual parties. One size does not fill all. Each party or related group of parties needs its own customized view of the content to suit its interests. All the parties are plugging into the exact same CMS, but their respective interests are reflected in the different views of the CMS.

Think of your communications as your personal or organizational marketing venture because this is precisely what it is. You are hoping to send a message that resonates with your audience, and the goal is to have them accept your strategy and knowledge. This is Marketing 101.

An Individual Victory in Isolation Is a Global Failure

You must promote your wins to engage the stakeholders to fortify their belief in the cause—silence is not going to work. We certainly do not condone narcissism, but if you achieve a milestone and the team recognizes that it is a win, you must announce this triumph to everyone. If people hear nothing, they will assume the whole mission is floundering. You must remember that ITIL and the CMS are all about services, which are ultimately the delivery of efficient and cost-effective business services. Your wins are also your stakeholders' wins. Celebrate the milestones jointly. This will breed more unity and further the CMS's cause.

A winner in the wilderness is a loser! Be proud. Be heard. Be a winner!

Participate in the itSMF

The IT Service Management Forum (itSMF) is a tremendous force in the evolution of the CMS. The British government still owns the copyright to ITIL, but the real work to develop ITIL v3, and its continued development and refinement, was all performed by people within the itSMF. The authors of the ITIL books and both of us are active itSMF members, not employees of the U.K. government. Individual contributors from around the world are the creators of ITIL, and the itSMF is the political body that governs how these individuals contribute to the good of all.

The itSMF is organized in its own federated structure. There is itSMF International, which is naturally the global entity. This body sets the general direction, overall policy, and common themes for the world. Feeding these efforts are several national chapters. As of the end of 2008, 52 national chapters are formally approved and active, with more in the works. Some of these chapters are further federated, with local interest groups (LIG) representing geographic regions within the country and special interest groups (SIG) focused on specific topics. The U.S. chapter, for example, has a LIG structure, and the U.K. chapter has both.

This structure enables good ideas to be formed locally, and if they are worth broader adoption, they can percolate up to the top and therefore be disseminated globally through the same structure. As former U.S. congressional House Speaker Thomas (Tip) O'Neill famously stated, "All politics is local." The big developments in the itSMF start locally. This is not to say that the LIGs are politically motivated; it just means that the grass roots efforts of the LIGs are essential to the overall growth of itSMF.

If you want to learn from your peers, the itSMF meetings, conferences, and other forums are some of the most valuable events in which you can participate. Nothing beats peer-to-peer discussions when it comes to sharing ideas, case studies, and the basic "this is how *we* solved that problem" sorts of answers to actual challenges.

Likewise, the itSMF is a wonderful platform for proclaiming your success and earning widespread industry recognition. Offer to present at a LIG event or a national event. Volunteer to lead a SIG or more informal discussion groups regarding the CMS. Leadership in the itSMF gets recognized, and this builds your credibility as a CMS innovator. Such recognition also pays dividends back at the office. Good employers appreciate when their people are recognized industry leaders.

Social Media as a Promotional Tool

The options available for you to promote your success are more numerous than ever. Certainly, you should employ traditional means such as meetings, email, newsletters, and conference presentations, but social media is also proving to be a powerful mechanism for information dispersal and also for collaborative development and interactive discussion. These various technologies and their impact on society are what we now know as the Web 2.0 phenomenon.[2] They are extensions to the traditional web that enable broad collaboration instead of the one-way nature of the more mature web modes. Common tools include blogs, Wikipedia, YouTube, and Flickr.

Note that there are both public (for instance, Wikipedia) and private venues (for instance, local wikis) for social media. You will likely want to leverage both, but be careful with the public outlets, as you will need to observe your company's intellectual property and privacy policies. If you think content is questionable, it is always a good idea to have your management or legal department review it before you post it. One of the attractive elements of social media is the minimized need for such review, but it's better to be safe than sorry (and maybe unemployed!).

Here are a few of the major social media outlets and technologies that you can use:

- **Web sites:** Web sites are not generally considered to be Web 2.0 developments, because they existed from the beginnings of the web (*Web 1.0* is not accepted as a valid term, although web sites would be considered as Web 1.0). There will be multiple web sites associated with your CMS, including the CMS tool interfaces and the main site you develop for communication to your various stakeholders. This main site should be a portal of sorts to aggregate the many informational bits of interest to the individuals accessing the site. Each person's view should be tailored to her particular desires and needs. An aggregation site like this would probably employ more advanced web technologies such as AJAX, RSS feeds, JavaScript, and .NET.[3]

---

2. Tim O'Reilly, of O'Reilly publishing fame, is usually credited with the birth of the term Web 2.0. The article "What Is Web 2.0" summarizes the early brainstorming sessions where Web 2.0 had its genesis: http://www.oreillynet.com/pub/a/oreilly/tim/news/2005/09/30/what-is-web-20.html.

3. AJAX is an acronym for Asynchronous JavaScript And XML. Many good information sources exist on the web, including a good tutorial at http://www.w3schools.com/Ajax/Default.Asp. RSS stands for Real Simple Syndication. The specification for RSS is at http://www.rssboard.org/rss-specification. JavaScript is a scripting language for developing client-side portions of web applications. It is based on the Java programming language and developed by Sun Microsystems and Netscape Communications (now under the AOL brand). A good JavaScript tutorial is at http://www.w3schools.com/js/default.asp. The .NET Framework is Microsoft's web software platform. You can learn all about .NET at Microsoft's web site: http://www.microsoft.com/NET.

- **Blogs:** Blogs enable you and others to write articles and other statements about the CMS and your progress. Others can then comment on the articles, triggering a dialogue about the specific topic. Think of it as a living, interactive electronic magazine tailored to your CMS effort. Blogs are useful for capturing information, both formal (for instance, an article to announce big improvements) and informal (for instance, you can post a hypothesis or passing thought). The beauty of the blog is its simplicity. It is easy to post something, and it is easy to read and comment. You need to remember that blogs require constant attention and activity to be worthwhile. There is a certain flow that needs to be maintained; otherwise, it will become stale and readers will lose interest. We established a CMDB Imperative blog at http://blog.cmdbimperative.com/, so you can begin your blogging activity right now!

- **Wikis:** A *wiki* is a collaborative knowledge base—in this case, a knowledge base about the CMS that is built and continually refined by the various parties involved with the CMS. The most notable example is Wikipedia, the online encyclopedia written by countless people all over the world. The credibility of the content is strengthened by the fact that the many contributors form a self-enforcing, fact-checking system. In his fantastic book *The Wisdom of Crowds*,[4] James Surowiecki explains the social mechanisms of how this self-enforcement works—and it does! One word of caution is to remember that a wiki can be edited by people who potentially don't really know the material, which could lead to the confusion of others. You need to moderate any information to ensure its validity and mitigate the risk.

- **Podcasts:** A *podcast* is a simple audio recording in MP3 or some other common digital audio format. They are handy for delivering information in the spoken word, and they can be loaded into an iPod (thus the name *pod*cast) or other digital audio player. The convenience of listening to a podcast while driving in your car or on a flight provides another opportunity to present information about your CMS to those who can benefit from it.

  A podcast should be brief (less than 10 minutes is ideal) and to the point (maintain focus on the topic—don't meander through other points). It is better for a podcast to stick to a specific topic, as those

---

4. Information about the book *The Wisdom of Crowds* and the author are available at http://www.wisdomofcrowds.com.

who consume the information can more effectively digest what you want to convey to them. You should use your web presence to provide organized access to the podcasts.

- **Videocasting:** Most people now think of YouTube when they think of Internet-based videocasting, and for good reason. YouTube has revolutionized how we can use video as a means to educate and entertain using the Internet. It is not the only means, but it set the standard with its ease of viewing and its ease of posting videos for others to view. A picture is worth a thousand words, as the saying goes, so video is an effective medium to educate others about your CMS developments.

  Video recordings have now also become popular as so-called *vodcasts*, or video podcasts. Similar to audio podcasts, vodcasts can be downloaded on demand and then viewed on video-enabled players, such as the newer iPods. Obviously storage of video and network bandwidth could become an issue so be careful with that and also make sure it doesn't become a soapbox for your local talking heads. They can use podcasts if they feel the need to publish the message on regular periods.

- **Social networking sites:** Sites such as Facebook and MySpace changed how people connect, exchange ideas, and even entertain one another. Usually associated with young cyber-socialites in their teens and twenties, both are now encroaching into the business community, a domain that has been dominated by the business-oriented site LinkedIn. We recommend using LinkedIn, although others may also prove to be useful. Members linked into common communities can exchange ideas and ask questions of one another. They are valuable for collaborative learning about the CMS.

- **Trade publications, magazines, and newsletters:** Although these are not typically considered a social media component, items such as "The Forum" (itSMF e-newsletter) and other newsletter styles of communication can also prove to be beneficial in socializing and enhancing your knowledge. Some print publications/trade magazines, such as *Network World*, *InformationWeek*, *Computerworld*, and *CIO Magazine*, are viewed widely by industry experts for information and hence can also be used as part of your promotional efforts.

- **Webinars and web meetings:** A great way of conducting online meetings with broad participation is to use the various webinar platforms such as Cisco's WebEx and Microsoft's Live Meeting. We are all familiar with the traditional audio conference call. A web meeting adds content enhancements like video and screen-sharing. They truly are great for holding broadly distributed meetings at low cost. This means meetings can be held frequently.

Any mechanism that helps broadcast the lessons and the benefits of the CMS is valuable. Use your imagination to expand upon the traditional modes. There is nothing wrong with these traditional modes, but we now have other ways to augment them. This is the impact of social media on every aspect of life, from the way YouTube changes entertainment, to how Wikipedia changed knowledge collection and distribution, to how LinkedIn helps build and leverage professional networks. Each of these is not necessarily a new social element (for instance, professional networks have always existed), but they are definitely profound new tools that accelerate the social elements with the speed and broad participation that are characteristic of the Web 2.0 movement.

A trait common to nearly all of these Web 2.0 tools is the inclusion of a potentially widespread community. In this new world, you might create the original content, but feedback and enrichment from others refines the content. The Web 2.0 phenomenon opens great new avenues for you to contribute to the CMS movement. If one person tells the world the right story about the CMS, few may take heed. If two decide to write a book on the topic, hopefully more will follow. If thousands around the world form a collective view that is well vetted by all, there is inherent credibility to the message. This is the future of all knowledge. This is how we overcome misinformation and provide an accurate knowledge base to benefit all. We will all play a role in forming this new knowledge.

You, the CMS Teacher

As you build experience with the CMS, it is good to share the lessons you learned along the way. Indeed, those with the wisdom carry some responsibility to "spread the word" about the CMS. This is precisely the motive behind this book. We gained a wealth of experience through our own victories and failures, as well as those of countless others with whom we worked over the years. We feel an obligation to help others by transcribing our experience into this book. As much as we would like to dream that two people and a book can transform the world, it will obviously take many more people to form an intellectual army to combat the rampant misinformation swirling about. To truly turn the CMDB craze into a CMS culture based on practical processes and technologies, it requires many people around the world.

As the intellectual soldiers in the CMS army, you can help the cause! Teach others in your enterprise about the CMS and the disciplined process execution the CMS enables. Teach others in the global community through itSMF participation, blogs, magazine byline articles, and maybe even your *own* book. Everything you do to help plant the seeds of knowledge will be cultivated into worldwide momentum that will yield the right ideas, the right execution, and the right benefits. The success of the CMS movement rests on the shoulders of us all!

Frequently Asked Questions

Question: What should I do if my metrics tell me I am failing, not succeeding?

Answer: Because the metrics are quality indicators, they will indicate what you need to do to bring performance under control. There may be other factors you need to address, so you can tweak the metrics in the right direction. Investigate what additional steps you need to take. Maybe you are going in the right direction, but not as well as you planned. In this case, you probably need to reset your objectives to be more realistic. You should not rush the CMS. It takes a methodical and careful approach, not an aggressive, audacious assault.

Question: I'm a modest guy/gal. I don't want to boast, but I would like others to know what I've done. How do I do this and not come across as a braggart?

Answer: Humility is a wonderful virtue, so bravo to you! There is nothing wrong with telling the world what you've accomplished. You can announce your victory without exalting yourself, and besides, you will unlikely succeed on your own. When you give credit to those who contributed to your success, you are humbling yourself. You should tell the world about what you've learned. You are helping others. Also, when you succeed with humility, it is a moving story and an example to all! A servant leader is more highly respected than an egotistical leader.

Question: How can I get involved in the itSMF?

Answer: Visit the itSMF International web site at http://www.itsmfi.org
            and search for your national chapter under the Chapters tab.
            Search for your country and click on its link. This leads you to
            your chapter's main web site, where you can get more informa-
            tion. Your chapter may have local interest groups. Search for the
            LIG in your area. When in doubt, contact somebody listed on the
            itSMF site of your choice, and this person will be delighted to
            help you.

            If there is not a chapter or LIG to serve your area, the response
            is rather simple.... Form your own chapter or LIG!

Summary

Success is a reason to celebrate! Bask in the glory and share the glory with
members of the CMS team. You need to establish and measure the appropriate metrics to know when you have truly attained success. It cannot be sub-
jective. Only hard metrics can objectively indicate true success. When you are
successful, announce it! Assure senior managers that the investment is proving its promised value. Help others learn from your victories—and your mistakes. Help the entire CMS movement evolve, and everyone will benefit.

   We hope this book is just the beginning of a major shift in the CMDB discussion. We must all alter the global thinking about CMDB into the more
mature, sophisticated, and realistic CMS. The CMS is a major innovation that
will prove to be a catalyst for profound improvement in service management.
This is an exciting time to be involved with such a transformative movement.
Savor your role in this transition, for you will look back on your work with
great satisfaction and pride!

Glossary

abstraction model

A software model built using object-oriented software that is built from lower-level elements and metadata. Abstraction models represent such high-level entities as applications and business services.

active discovery

A mode of discovery that queries managed elements to obtain the desired data for a CI within an MDR.

ADM (Application Dependency Mapping)

Discovery technology that captures application elements and maps the relationships that link these elements.

agent

Instrumentation that is installed on a managed element so management tools can obtain data from the managed element. An agent is usually instrumentation that is additional third-party aftermarket code (for example, server performance agent), as opposed to instrumentation that is embedded in the standard configuration (for example, SNMP agent on a router).

agentless

A model for management software that does not require aftermarket agents. Agentless management leverages the already-embedded instrumentation.

balanced scorecard

A mechanism to calculate aggregate metrics based on a combination of multiple metrics that are factored in using weights that tailor the influence of the underlying metrics.

BMI (Business Modeling & Integration Domain Task Force)

The standards body formed in 2005 when the BPMI and OMG organizations merged their Business Process Management initiatives to develop business process management standards. BMI is now operating under the auspices of the OMG. See http://bmi.omg.org.

BPEL (Business Process Execution Language)

A language used to construct business process models that can be executed by business process management software. A BPEL model is not just structural (that is, how tasks relate in the business process), but is also behavioral (that is, how information flows through the business process and how it is transformed throughout this flow). OASIS is the standards body responsible for BPEL.

BPM (Business Process Management)

A category of software technologies used to define, execute, and monitor business processes.

BPMI (Business Process Management Initiative)

BPMI is the precursor to the BMI effort that is continuing to evolve the BPMI's early business process management standards. See http://www.bpmi.org.

BPMN (Business Process Modeling Notation)

A standardized graphical notation for modeling business processes. BPMN was developed by BPMI and is now continuing with BMI.

BSM (Business Service Management)

BSM is a perspective of managing IT services with respect to business requirements. In many respects, it is ITIL with more of a business focus. ITIL v3 has built significant new BSM-like relevance into ITIL, so the two are now nearly synonymous. BSM is also sometimes associated with a business-centric view of monitoring tools, but this interpretation is too restrictive. True BSM is much more, as in the previous description.

CCM (Change and Configuration Management)

A category of tools that combine the ITIL functions of Configuration Management (how something is configured) and Change Management (how this configuration is changed, preferably along with some process workflow automation).

CI (Configuration Item)

The software model related to an instance of a managed element. A CI should represent the managed element in the CMS. Multiple instances of otherwise identical managed elements are each independent CIs.

CIM (Common Information Model)

A standards-based object-oriented software model for representing a wide variety of infrastructure, applications, and services. The DMTF is the standards body responsible for CIM.

citizen CMDB

A term sometimes used to describe a CMDB that participates in a two-tier CMDB hierarchy with a Core CMDB. It refers to the lower-level CMDBs in the hierarchy. It is equivalent to what we (and CMDBf) call an MDR. A Citizen CMDB does not quite fit the modular hierarchy needed to fulfill the specifications in CMDBf and ITIL v3.

CMDB (Configuration Management Database)

The trusted source of information that drives all IT decisions. See Chapter 2, "What Is a CMDB?" This chapter describes the CMDB and why it must evolve to become the CMS. Most of the remainder of the book expands on the CMS.

CMDBf

CMDBf refers to both the CMDB Federation standard and the CMDB Federation Working Group that developed the standard. Responsibility for the standard was handed over to the DMTF in November 2007.

CMMI (Capability Maturity Model® Integration)

A process improvement approach developed and supported by the Software Engineering Institute at Carnegie-Mellon University. Most commonly applied to software development, CMMI has been adapted to operations in conjunction with ITIL.

CMS (Configuration Management System)

An improved distributed model for the CMDB introduced in ITIL v3. A CMS implies federation of the many MDRs rather than just the restrictive monolithic model historically used by a CMDB.

consumer tool

Any software tool that consumes (uses) data or information from the CMS. Most of them are used to automate process execution using the CMS as their trusted information source, whereas others can be extensions to the CMS itself (for example, CMS verification functions).

control chart

A graph that tracks a quality metric over time. The control chart is usually a line graph, but can also be a bar chart, and it will indicate control limits that specify the range of acceptable quality. When the metric strays outside these limits, measures must be taken to correct the measured process to bring the metric back within the control range.

copy integration

A form of data integration to a CMDB, where an external data set is imported into the CMDB, resulting in two copies of the data set.

CORBA (Common Object Request Broker Architecture)

An OMG standard for enabling distributed software components to communicate and exchange data. Although still the basis for many legacy systems, CORBA has been largely replaced by XML.

core CMDB

A term sometimes used to describe a CMDB that participates in a two-tier CMDB hierarchy with Citizen CMDBs. It refers to the higher-level CMDB in the hierarchy. It is equivalent to what we (and CMDBf) call a Federating CMDB. A Core CMDB does not quite fit the modular hierarchy needed to fulfill the specifications in CMDBf and ITIL v3.

COSMOS (Community-driven Systems Management in Open Source)

A project within the Eclipse Foundation that provides a set of open-source, standards-based software components for system management.

DCI (Data Consumer Interface)

Defined within the CMDBf specification, it is the software interface to an MDR that enables data consumers to access data within the MDR. These consumers can be other MDRs (Federating CMDBs) or consumer tools that use the data.

discovery

The means by which raw data is collected for the CMS. Discovery tools automate this function to ensure that the data accurately reflects reality. A discovery tool usually acts as an MDR in the CMS because it stores the collected data locally.

DML (Definitive Media Library)

A collection of CIs that is deemed to be the definitive authorized configuration set that is viewed as the master copy of the CIs. The contents have been thoroughly tested and validated. The DML is protected more stringently to preserve the "gold standard" it contains. Many associate the DML to software configurations only, but it should be used generically* for any configurations worth such rigorous controls. A software-only version is the DSL.

DMTF (Distributed Management Task Force)
One of the major official bodies involved in the development of web standards. The notable CMS standards governed by the DMTF are CIM, WBEM, and now CMDBf.

DPI (Data Provider Interface)
Defined within the CMDBf specification, it is the software interface to an MDR that enables data providers to provide data to the MDR. These providers can be other MDRs (making this MDR the Federating CMDB) or provider tools (for example, discovery tools) that supply the data.

DSL (Definitive Software Library)
A DML subset that is specific to software configurations.

Eclipse Foundation
A nonprofit open source community that provides software development platforms and toolkits. Software developed within the Eclipse environment is encouraged to be open source, but this is not required.

event-triggered notification
A mechanism for data transmission between a data consumer and a data provider. Instead of the consumer querying the data provider, the provider delivers the data upon the occurrence of a relevant event local to the provider (for example, the local data has changed).

federated CMDB
A CMDB that uses federation as its structural data management architecture. This is more accurately known as a CMS.

federating CMDB
In the CMDBf hierarchy of related MDRs, the Federating CMDB is the upper level, the consumer of the data from provider MDRs below it.

federation
A model for data distribution that keeps data distributed rather than collecting it into a single point. Its name implies a distribution model similar to many governments, where local control and management is allowed (encouraged, actually) and a strong central point where the federated entities are

connected for a higher purpose. Federation in the CMS will be many levels deep in its hierarchy, with any branch of the hierarchy possibly reflecting its own federated identity.

feedback

A mechanism for feeding information from one phase of a process to an earlier phase. Feedback is used to control the behavior of the process to maintain quality of the process's results.

flexi-sourcing

A sourcing model that includes extensive flexibility in the geographical, organizational, and technological relationships of the parties involved in a process. Talent and task execution can be internal to the IT organization, anywhere in the world, internal, external, paid employees, unpaid community participants, or even performed by automation. The scope can be broad (for example, outsourcing the entire IT organization to EDS) or focused as tightly as needed (for example, SaaS for the Service Desk).

integration

The means to exchange data between software components. Integration is easy when components adhere to standard interface specifications and data definitions, but requires adapter software when the components do not match.

inventory

A collection of CIs, usually representing physical entities such as equipment and software licenses. Few, if any, relationships are reflected between the CIs.

ITIL

A collection of best practices for IT operational processes. Originally called the IT Infrastructure Library (now a defunct representation of the four letters), ITIL is officially owned by the UK government's Office of Government Commerce (OGC), which developed ITIL and first released it in 1989. It has become wildly popular as a set of guiding principles for IT discipline.

ITIL v3

The newest version of ITIL, ITIL v3 is a significant improvement upon earlier versions, adding more comprehensive guidance around service strategy, service design, service transition, service operation, and continuous service improvement. Much better business focus and service lifecycle philosophy characterize ITIL v3, and it introduces the CMS, a huge advancement over the historical notion of a CMDB.

ITSM (IT Service Management)

A philosophy for managing IT services that is based upon ITIL methodologies.

itSMF (IT Service Management Forum)

The international organization of ITSM practitioners focused on expanding awareness, adoption, and refinement of ITSM and ITIL.

JMX (Java Management eXtensions)

A standardized software interface for Java-based applications that allows management tools to interact with the application to collect data about its structure and behavior. Like all Java standards, JMX is the responsibility of Sun Microsystems, not a formal standards body.

KPI (Key Performance Indicator)

Metrics that convey the higher-level performance of a process. The KPIs are collected, measured, and used to drive decisions about the quality of the process.

managed element

An actual physical or logical device (for example, server, virtual machine, network switch, storage array) that is the target for management technologies.

maturity model

An assessment model based upon progressive stages of sophistication with regard to a process. Lower stages characterize less sophistication (maturity), and higher stages indicate higher enlightenment and implementation of the ideal process. Most maturity models now define five distinct phases of maturity, an enumeration popularized in CMM.

MBO (Management by Objective)

A human resource management tool used to guide work performance based upon measurable objectives. Incentives and penalties are tied to the attainment of the objectives, resulting in a self-regulating force for high-quality organizational performance.

MDR (Management Data Repository)

A basic collection of CIs and relationships that forms a self-contained entity in the CMS hierarchy. The CIs in an MDR usually share common attributes, but this is not necessarily required. The most common grouping attribute is the managed technology domain (for example, network, server, storage). MDRs communicate with each other based on the relationships and abstractions relevant to their contents, so they connect in a hierarchy that is bound by many dimensions of relationships.

metadata

Data about data. Metadata expands the context of a data element, qualifying it with more attributes and even enabling remote data linking.

MIB (Management Information Base)

The formal data structure of an SNMP agent. The various data objects in the agent are referenced according to the hierarchical definition of the MIB. It is analogous to the schema in database terms.

monolithic CMDB

The legacy model for the CMDB, it implies a single database that contains all CIs and their attributes. The monolithic model is now regarded as obsolete and unattainable for large complex environments. The federated CMDB is the new model, with the CMS representing the pragmatic future of the CMDB.

MTBF (Mean Time Between Failures)

The average time between failures of a managed element.

MTTR (Mean Time to Resolution)

The average time between the occurrence of an incident and its actual resolution.

negative feedback

Feedback to automatically control the behavior of a system in decreasing manner.

OASIS (Organization for the Advancement of Structure Information Standards)

One of the major official bodies involved in the development of web standards.

OGC (Office of Government Commerce)

A department of State in the United Kingdom. The OGC oversees ITIL.

OID (Object Identifier)

The numerical sequence that indicates an "address" of sorts to a specific data element in an SNMP data tree. The OID is mapped in the MIB for the relevant SNMP.

OMG (Object Management Group)

A standards body responsible for many of the object-oriented standards for everything from software integration to business process management. There is a heavy focus on business systems among the OMG standards.

parallelism

The combination of more than one instance of a programmed instruction and more than one processor executing concurrently.

positive feedback

Feedback that automatically controls the behavior of a system in increasing manner.

punitive outsourcing

Actions that result in punishing in-house IT organizations by contracting out aspects of the IT operation to external professional outsourcing firms.

RCA (Root Cause Analysis)

A problem-solving method by which the true reason for the problem is identified rather than the superficial or obvious symptoms.

RDBMS (Relational Database Management System)

A database management system based on a relational model.

reconciliation

The process of comparing two different objects or pieces of data to determine whether they are equal to each other.

RFC (Request for Change)

A formal document that describes modifications that an individual is proposing to have executed.

RFC (Request for Comments)

A memo issued by the Internet Engineering Task Force (IETF) that describes aspects related to the functioning of the Internet and systems connected to the Internet.

RPC (Remote Procedure Call)

A technology that is used, between computer systems typically, whereby a program initiates a command that is executed on a different computer system.

service broker

A function provided by a distributed software component that "announces" its available software services and then negotiates with other requesting components to provide these services.

service catalog

A listing provided to customers that describes all the functions that an organization can deliver, including the costs, contacts, and vehicle by which the function can be requested.

service chain

The various links or components that, when connected together for a specific function, deliver a complete service.

service desk

A single point of contact on the service provider side that users leverage for incidents, service requests, and other communications between the service provider and user.

service portfolio

All the services that the provider has to offer throughout the full lifecycle.

SME (Subject Matter Expert)

An individual who is considered an authority on a particular topic.

SML (Service Modeling Language)

A language defined by the W3C for expressing complex service and system models and instances of the models.

snapshot

A capture of a subset data in the CMS at a point in time.

SNMP (Simple Network Management Protocol)

A component of the family of Internet protocols used in network management systems to expose the management data.

SOA (Service-Oriented Architecture)

A method of designing and implementing a system so that functional units of the system can be made accessible to other systems. Each functional unit typically correlates to a specific business process.

SOAP (Simple Object Access Protocol)

A standard way to format web services messages. SOAP uses eXtensible Markup Language (XML), Remote Procedure Calls (RPC), and HTTP.

targeted outsourcing

Action taken by organizations to establish contractual agreements with external professional services firms to operate specific portions of the IT organization.

UDDI (Universal Description, Discovery, and Integration)

A common registration specification used by brokers. It is used by web services to mediate the location of and connections to web services. Both public and private UDDI registries are used in web services.

UML (Unified Markup Language)

A modeling language used in software engineering. It uses visual objects such as boxes to help depict the function of a system, including business processes, architecture, data structures, and other programmed functions. The Object Management Group (OMG) maintains the UML specification.

URI (Uniform Resource Identifier)

A series of characters that are used to identify or name a device on a network such as the Internet (for example, http://www.thecmdbimperative.com/index.htm). A URI is sometimes classified as a URL or URN.

URL (Uniform Resource Locator)

A series of characters used to uniquely identify a device. A URL is not persistent.

URN (Uniform Resource Name)

A series of characters used to uniquely name a device. A URN is persistent. One of the most common URNs is the International Standard Book Number (ISBN) used to uniquely name books (for example, ISBN-13: 978-0-13-700837-7).

use case

A defined set of steps that describe the interactions between the initiator of the action who is outside the system and the system(s) that the actions are being taken on. Used to describe how a goal is achieved.

W3C (World Wide Web Consortium)

One of the major official bodies involved in the development of web standards. The notable CMS standards governed by W3C are XML and WSDL.

WBEM (Web-Based Enterprise Management)

A CIM-based initiative for accessing data about infrastructure and applications using web services techniques and technologies. WBEM is the responsibility of the DMTF.

web services

A family of web technologies and methods to enable sophisticated service identification, location, and access across disparate networks. XML is the basis for web services, and additional technologies such as SOAP, UDDI, and WSDL enable the service-oriented data exchange.

WMI (Windows Management Instrumentation)

Microsoft's implementation of the DMTF's WBEM standard. WMI is preinstalled on most modern Microsoft operating systems. It is one of the increasingly popular agentless management technologies.

WSDL (Web Services Description Language)

A W3C standard language for describing and enabling remote access and use of remote services across the network.

WSDM (Web Services Distributed Management)

A collection of OASIS standards for distributed infrastructure and application management. WSDM specifies management *of* web services and management *using* web services. The two distinctions are important, as one defines the purpose of WSDM and one defines the architecture of WSDM itself and the management technologies that leverage it.

XML (eXtensible Markup Language)

XML has become the basis for thousands of official and de facto standards for defining data and information abstractions from this data. A W3C foundation for creating custom markup languages, XML expands upon the ubiquitous HTML that is the basis of the World Wide Web. XML's flexibility lends itself well to model nearly any object you might want to represent in software.

Index

Page numbers followed by *n* indicate information appearing in footnotes.

C

Capability Maturity Model (CMM), 259

capacity management
- as supplemental information in CMS, 274
- user-triggered uses, 287-288

CCM (Configuration and Change Management), 38
- tools, 65-66

Change and Release Management, 66

change management
- integration with virtualization, 238
- maturity of, 141-144
- in processes, 9
- snapshots in, 221-224
- as supplemental information in CMS, 273
- user-triggered uses, 286-287

CIM (Common Information Model), 40*n*, 178-180

CIs (configuration items), 27
- abstraction models and, 43
- application CIs, 32-34
- business process CIs, 35-37
- difficulty of identifying, 18-20
- defined, 17*n*
- document CIs, 39
- explained, 27-28
- human CIs, 37-39
- infrastructure CIs, 30-32
- known error CIs, 34-35
- level of detail needed, 40
- relationships among, 29-30

Citizen CMDB, 52

cloud computing, 32, 212-215

CMDB (configuration management database)
- advantages of federation over, 125
  - accuracy, 127
  - efficiency, 126-127
  - flexibility, 127-128
- asset databases, compared, 23
- Citizen CMDB, 52
- Core CMDB, 52
- databases versus, 89
- federation, 40-42
  - advantages of, 125-129
  - awareness of, 226
  - CMDBf specification, 158n
  - data, location of, 94-95
  - database distribution versus, 130
  - external domains in, 128-129
  - in future of CMS, 226
  - genetics analogy, 43-45
  - integration versus, 105-107
  - metadata, linking data with, 98-105
  - reconciliation and, 45-47
  - theory versus reality, 105
  - web services and, 103-105
- genetics analogy, 43-45
- history of, 26-27
- in ITIL v3, 54
- product classifications, 62-68
- reconciliation, 45-47
- terminology, 21-22, 48
- transition to CMS, 224-225
  - awareness stage, 226-227
  - staffing stage, 227-228
  - technology requirements, 225-226
  - type needed for CMS planning, 76-78

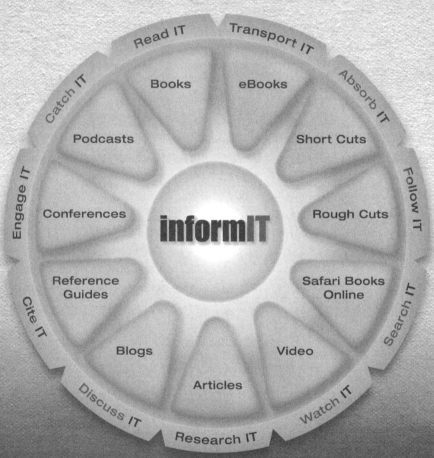

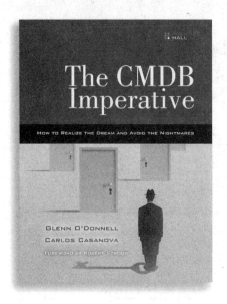

FREE Online Edition

Your purchase of **The CMDB Imperative** includes access to a free online edition for 45 days through the Safari Books Online subscription service. Nearly every Prentice Hall book is available online through Safari Books Online, along with more than 5,000 other technical books and videos from publishers such as Addison-Wesley Professional, Cisco Press, Exam Cram, IBM Press, O'Reilly, Que, and Sams.

SAFARI BOOKS ONLINE allows you to search for a specific answer, cut and paste code, download chapters, and stay current with emerging technologies.

Activate your FREE Online Edition at
www.informit.com/safarifree

> **STEP 1:** Enter the coupon code: JHULPWA.

> **STEP 2:** New Safari users, complete the brief registration form.
> Safari subscribers, just log in.

If you have difficulty registering on Safari or accessing the online edition,
please e-mail customer-service@safaribooksonline.com